Ghetto Medic
A Father in the 'Hood

A biographical memoir
by Rachel Hennick

GHETTO MEDIC: A FATHER IN THE 'HOOD

Disclaimer: In a few cases, names of characters have been changed
with respect for their loved ones and reputations.

Editor: Clarinda Harriss
Graphic design: Ace Kieffer
Cover art: © 2012 Mark Cottman

BrickHouse Books, Inc. 2012
306 Suffolk Road
Baltimore, MD 21218

Distributor: Itasca Books, Inc.

ISBN: 978-1-938144-02-8

Printed in the United States of America

For my father Bill, whose anecdotes are one-of-a-kind: I will forever cherish our shared journey to the recesses of his mind.

For my mother Eunice: I am grateful for her continued prayers and insight on Dad's mind, which she says he's lost.

EXIT
ROYAL
ROYAL
NOW SHOWING
NORTH AV.
PENNSYLVA
SPHINX CLUB
LIQUORS
BALTO FIRE DEPT 52
52
52
COTTMAN

Years ago, Bill heard the following lyric performed by the Morgan State University Gospel Choir conducted by the late, great Nathan Carter. To him, this says it all:
If I can help somebody, then my living shall not be in vain.
—Alma Bazel Androzzo

Only sometimes (an excerpt from "Local Flora")
. . . a white late-summer dime of sun
dribbles a stream
of powdery light through the junk and murk, you see
some pale translucent
jelly waft like Loe Fuller's blooming silks, writhe
like ghosts of smoke
over Sonny Stitt's and Sonny Rollins' steaming saxes
in the whiskey-brown
velvet deeps of the Red Fox Club, circa 1960,
down there
next to the Tijuana Lounge on Fulton Avenue.
—Clarinda Harriss

Table of Contents

A Word From the Artist

Rachel asked me to create a painting to capture Bill's life from childhood through Baltimore city firefighter to paramedic. I met Bill for the first time on St. Paul Street in Baltimore; we planned to talk about his life over a meal. We never had that first meal, but our conversation that day became much food for thought.

Ghetto Medic is a great American story. It's not about race. It's about humanity. For Bill to overcome tremendous physical obstacles and dedicate his life to the service of others at the risk of his own life is a humbling miracle within itself. He understands that selflessness is the glue that will give hope to people in the poorest communities. To this day he is still a fighter for the rights of firefighters and rescue workers with the passion of his words.

I grew up in Baltimore, the city of my and Bill's birth. During the '68 riots, I witnessed as a child, firsthand, the devastation, the confusion, the frustration, anger and hopelessness. In the middle of all that, it was comforting to know that Bill and other firefighters and rescue workers were out there somewhere helping, trying to make a difference.

Mark Cottman
Artist and Poet

About the Mark Cottman Gallery
The Mark Cottman Gallery is located in Historic Federal Hill, Baltimore, Maryland, and features exclusively the art of Mark Cottman. His artwork expresses passion and humor, captures the imagination and inspires the viewer to appreciate Cottman's vision.
1014 S. Charles Street
Baltimore, MD 21230
markcottmangallery.com

Prologue

This book centers on two interlocking stories, both of them forged in flames. One story starts in 1945 with a fire that burned a little boy almost to death, permanently scarring him from head to foot and altering his life, as well as the lives around him, forever. The other story rises out of the blazes that forever altered the city of Baltimore during the 1968 riots following the assassination of Dr. Martin Luther King.

I am that little boy's daughter. His name is Bill. Whenever possible, I use Bill's own words, his intense and pithy observations, to tell the story of his battle against fire, which he identifies as "the enemy."

Bill's story is set against the history of Baltimore, once known for its rich black heritage as the home of jazz legends such as Billie Holiday and Cab Calloway. He embarks on a spiritual journey as he risks his own life in caring for the poorest of the poor in a city with one of the world's highest crime rates. The story of how Baltimore fell into poverty and crime, an essential backdrop for my dad's story, is in many ways the story of America as a whole. Some say that America was torn into two halves by the War Between the States and has become whole again. But that is too simple. In fact, it was fractured from the start and was shattered during the Civil War. The pieces are still being put together. If you were to ask Baltimoreans today whether their state, Maryland, is northern or southern, many of them would not know. And if you made an assumption either way you might offend someone. The interests of the nation's individuals were never divided by a neat black line. Some southern states were free, and a few northern states condoned slavery.

English surveyors Charles Mason and Jeremiah Dixon were once hired to draw a border to settle a dispute between the early landowners of Pennsylvania and Maryland, the Penn Family and the Calvert Family. The boundary simply distinguishes the territory of the two states; a transnational divide does not exist. However, Americans often refer to the territory below the Mason-Dixon Line as southern and the land above it as northern, as if to simplify the complexities of the Civil War. To portray the nation as having been split perhaps makes its history easier to explain, as if the problems could be mended by erasing the line. Even prior to the Civil War, Baltimore had the greatest number of free blacks in the nation, more than 25,000, and the city is believed to have had Underground Railroad sites. Many residents both white and black helped fugitive slaves to reach freedom over the Mason-Dixon Line. Despite this, Maryland was a slave state.

Baltimore has many nicknames. It has been called "The City of Firsts" for its vast historical contributions. It is where, in 1743, America's first professional sports organization, the Maryland Jockey Club, was founded; the Baltimore & Ohio Railroad in 1830 became the nation's first public rail system; and Eubie Blake wrote Broadway's first black musical, "Shuffle Along," in 1921. Still other firsts are tragic.

The first bloodshed in the American Civil War occurred in Baltimore. Although Maryland is a border state extending both into the north and south, most residents were originally southern sympathizers because of strong ties with Confederate Virginia. The state's economic interests were divided. Wheat, the predominant crop in northern Maryland, was not as dependent on slave labor as the tobacco plantations in the state's south. Twenty minutes outside of Baltimore, a few stately mansions still remain nestled in the valley on green pastures, evocative of the days when slaves toiled the land.

On April 19, 1861, one week after the war began, Confederates fired upon South Carolina's Fort Sumter, controlled by Unionists. On President Abraham Lincoln's orders, members of the Sixth Massachusetts Volunteer Militia Regiment were en route to Washington, DC, as part of the journey south to repress the insurrection when a pack of Baltimore's southern sympathizers tried to prevent the Union troops from catching the train. The rebels blocked carriages, threw stones and cursed the troops. The soldiers opened fire, and in the ensuing mêlée four soldiers and a dozen rioters were killed. After the attack, Lincoln believed it was critical to capture Maryland as a buffer that would make Washington, DC, inaccessible to the Confederates. The Union army infiltrated the city and occupied Baltimore. Maryland never broke away from the Union, and, in 1865, the north won the American Civil

War. Over 50,000 Marylanders had sided with the Union, while 22,000 fought for the Confederacy.

Could Baltimore's divided interests explain why a peculiar tension wafts in the air of the city even today? What is this tension? Is it the forlorn look of lone mothers dragging their runny-nosed children through the streets after midnight? Is it the tone of desperation in the junkie's voice when he asks, "Can you help me out, man?" Is it the perpetual screech of sirens, signaling that someone, somewhere in this old port town, is in pain? And why is it that such a disproportionate number of Baltimore's poorest are black?

When the war ended, former slaves were drawn to Maryland and settled in Baltimore's northwest, making it America's most heavily populated black district. Upon graduation from the City of Baltimore Fire Department School in the autumn of 1965, a hundred years after the Civil War, my father was assigned to E-52, one of the top ten Baltimore companies, on the fringe of this area.

Around the same time that Dad launched his new career, Whitney Young, President of the National Urban League, standing before more than 250,000 people at the March on Washington, stated that the impact of discrimination in America had been just as devastating as it had been in Europe in the aftermath of World War II. He suggested that America invest in its ghettoes as it had in war-torn cities abroad, arguing that the support would boost the nation's economy and strengthen the country for all of its citizens. Perhaps if America had heeded Young's call to adopt a Marshall Plan and respond to the needs of its impoverished people, the country would be in better condition today.

Baltimore's discord is evidenced in its clash of worlds: genteel and industrial, stately and undignified, subdued and lurid, disciplined and feral, ostentatious and ordinary. This is where Francis Scott Key wrote America's national anthem, "The Star-Spangled Banner." This is Baltimore: "America in Miniature." This is the city that burned in 1968. This is where my father burned in 1945. This is where he has dedicated his life.

God Bless the Child

Dad has a faint scar behind his right ear where the skin folds. Without looking closely you won't notice it, and most people who know him don't know what happened to him when he was a little boy. We rarely discussed it over the years, but I could always sense that, for my father, the real scars were massive. When I was young and living "at home," I only saw him wear shorts once, when he dashed to the bathroom from the bedroom. That's when I caught a glimpse of the wound he'd told me about, the one behind his left knee: the one about the size of a bullet and almost black. To this day, I have never seen the scars that I know cover most of the rest of his body.

His childhood tragedy occurred in 1945, just days before the world's first atomic bomb was dropped on Hiroshima. My father was in a war too, but it was a different kind of war.

Bill, Billy, Daddy, Dad, my father.

The paper plane soars to phenomenal heights, descends in a smooth spiral, then drifts and vanishes out of sight. Billy is leaning over the iron fence, as transfixed and wide-eyed as any four-year-old boy would be. His neighborhood pal, Wishy, seven years his elder, has instructed Billy on the proper assembly of paper airplanes. Together they test their handiwork across the street from Billy's Baltimore City home. This is the perfect spot. A stone wall about three feet high, trimmed with a short iron fence, lines 26th Street and overlooks the railroad tracks sixty feet below. The distance allows for extended flying time. They assemble their planes with diligence, then stand up on the wall and launch them over the fence, watching them sail one at a time into the wide open space. Their excitement increases whenever the wind currents generated by a passing train direct the aircraft skyward for a longer flight.

The hot breath of another relentless July day in Baltimore drains Billy. Yawning, he unbuttons the sleeveless top of his blue seersucker suit. He wants nothing more than to be rid of his shirt and heavy brown shoes, to be free to play, dressed only in shorts. But his mother will not approve. She won't say a word; she will only haunt him with her dreaded "white-nosed" look, produced by squinting her eyes, pursing her lips and punctuating her tense, red face with a blanched center point.

The last of their squadron glides to a seamless landing, and they stand gazing in silence.

"Want to see my father's flower shop?" Wishy asks.

"Sure."

Wishy tosses an unfinished paper glider to the ground. "Come on."

They walk to the red brick building just at the end of the block on the corner of Charles and 26th Streets. The enchanting shop has candy-blue shutters and reminds Billy of the story of Hansel and Gretel. They enter the front door and explore the display room. Imagining himself in a jungle alone with wild beasts lurking in the trees, Billy brushes the plants with light strokes.

"Billy, come here." Wishy waves to him, beckons him to the storage room in the back. Billy scans the shelves packed with baskets, rolls of ribbon and colored paper. The gray steel toolbox on the bottom shelf catches his attention. He can hardly wait until he is big enough to hold the heavy tools in his hands. To hammer nails, to twist screws, to saw wood.

Later, my father couldn't recall exactly what happened after that. "We were kids. Wishy was innocent."

Wishy pulls a box of matches from his pocket. "Want to see something swell?"

"Won't we get in trouble?" Billy twists his mouth into a wad of skepticism.

"Nah. My dad's gone to lunch. He won't be back for an hour. Where's your dad?"

"He's fighting germs in the war," Billy says.

"You mean the Germans." Wishy rattles the box of matches. "Let's pretend we're fighting the Nazis." Grabbing a bottle of antifreeze from a shelf, Wishy dumps the liquid into a metal pail, spilling some liquid onto the carpet. "We'll blow 'em up and then we'll run. Okay?"

Before Billy can answer, Wishy strikes a match and tosses it into the container. There is a thunderous flash. Accidentally he knocks the bucket over. The door blows shut. Billy sees Wishy's startled expression melt into terror behind a veil of fire before he leaps out of a window, leaving Billy to be devoured.

Trapped and on fire, Billy is helpless. He tries to sweep the ravenous flames from his arms and legs but vicious stings rage hornet-like across his body until he feels nothing. Not even the ghastly howl escaping from his throat.

We've Gotta Get Out of this Place

"Working hard, or hardly working, Bill?"

Dad called his job as a control clerk with the Social Security Administration "a fate worse than death." Usually he smiled as though it was the first time he'd ever been asked the question. But it wasn't. Every single weekday for over three years, my father, twenty-four years old, had been coming to the Division of Disability Operations (DDO), and every day half a dozen colleagues asked him the same question. He just hummed a grim note and continued to shuffle the papers in front of him. A dim fluorescent light, which should have been replaced long ago, blinked above Dad's desk. My father found the monotony of the job, and the predictability of his co-workers, torturous.

The walls, cabinets, desks and football-field-size floor of the Social Security building were all painted government gray. There, Dad did not even know what the weather was, because in his area there were no windows. He longed for daylight but could not even see beyond the walls of his own cubicle.

Once, a woman who worked next to my father began sneezing loudly for minutes at a time, apparently to get attention from her co-workers. A few weeks later she started jogging in circles around her desk while talking to herself until two armed security guards escorted her out of the building. Dad never saw her again.

At times, prostitutes loitered in the halls and stairwells. Dad's supervisor would say that he was taking a few hours off to go golfing, but everyone knew that he was splitting with Maggie the hooker to the motel at the end of the block.

My father's brown hair was neatly combed and parted on the right side. Like the Ken doll's, his hair never moved. He was, and still is, an attractive man with wholesome good looks which seem to reflect his moral well-being. At his job he would complete forms, staple forms, file forms. He imagined an endless future of identical days if he did not escape. At 10:00

a.m., a bell would ring. My father would drag himself to the staff room and drop a dime into the slot. "The vending machine would crap out coffee that tasted like oil." He'd gulp the steaming black brew thinking he would rather be in the Amazon Jungle drinking snake's blood. Maybe he should have been a missionary after all.

A few years before, after graduating from high school, Dad did a brief stint at Prairie Bible College. At his local Christian youth group, he was inspired by Ingrid Stippa, a missionary from Borneo, to attend the college where she herself had trained. The college broke up the monotony of a great expanse of the western prairie land in a remote area of Alberta, Canada, ninety miles north of Calgary. Close by was Three Hills, a town inhabited at the time by fewer than a thousand people. Dad, desperate to do something significant with his young life, said, "That's for me," bade farewell to the familiar, then packed his belongings into his trusty 1951 Ford Sedan with its recapped tires and its "Earl 'I'll paint any car for $19.95' Scheib" Tropic Turquoise paint job. He headed west. Two days later, Dad and his good friend Wayne, a "professional student" who wanted to give Prairie a try too, arrived at the Prairie campus.

As they drove along the dirt of a main street still accented by hitching posts, my father was reminded of the westerns he saw every Saturday at his local movie theater. He was overcome by an eerie feeling. "I was tempted to vamoose out of town by sunset rather than face the prospect of a gunfight."

Wayne and Dad stopped in at the local watering hole and, over coffee, they contemplated an immediate retreat back to Baltimore. But, being young, adventurous and curious, not to mention fearful that the 1951 Ford would not survive a return trip, Dad and his pardner moseyed over to the compound and enrolled.

At Prairie, the wooden buildings were Spartan: army barrack–chic. The men's and women's dormitories and an auditorium were plunked down on a 2,000 acre farm. Indoor plumbing had only recently been installed. The "heavenly" environment was devoid of such distractions as television and radio. Record albums deemed unacceptable by the Dean of Men could not be played in the dormitories' music room. The Dean even banned the Blackwood Brothers of Gospel Music, a famous quartet, on the grounds that one of the Brothers was the bass vocalist for Elvis's group. However, he did put a stamp of approval on Mantovani's "Moon River."

The days were jam-packed with classes followed by long study hours in the dorm. The school president, Dr. L.E. Maxwell, strutted the campus with chest out and head back. Beloved by all, Maxwell was a lion when addressing the student body. He testified that each person had a purpose in life and encouraged the students to embrace their assigned mission from God. Maxwell stressed perseverance, tenacity and faith. Many students would eventually become missionaries throughout the world, and these attributes, he promised, would empower them to overcome adversity and to embrace the arduous tasks that lay ahead.

After one of Maxwell's sermons, my father managed to slip away for an evening stroll. He loved the rugged beauty of the foothills of the Canadian Rockies—the snow-covered trees, the wild horses and bears. This was a whole new world for a city slicker. The Aurora Borealis shimmered brightly in the unbroken night sky. Spellbound under the bright light of a full November moon, my father searched his soul and came to the conclusion that he was not cut out to be a missionary. He returned home to resume his search for a meaningful life's work.

"You give me a liquid bowel!" my father heard Stanley shout from the office down the hall. Stan and the boss were at it again. A bearded Jewish man with the body of an athlete, Stan was my father's only reprieve from the tedium. The boss had just reprimanded Stan for exceeding his lunch break by five minutes. Stan charged out of the boss's office.

Soon he called Dad over to his desk. Stan had wanted to be a firefighter ever since he was a kid. He loved everything about fire. The way it smells, the way it moves. The danger. He kept the radio on all day. He even kept a coat, boots and helmet in his trunk so that, if a second alarm came in, he could take leave from work and head to the scene to see if the men needed help. He'd hang out at a local station hoping to go on runs. He helped feed the line, pack the hose, clean up. Now, with Dad beside him, Stan turned on the fire radio and rolled the dial to low volume.

They heard something like "Silent Alarm Engine 25, Truck 4 respond to Gold and Brunt Street for smoke in the area . . ." and then crackling static at the end of the message. Dad loved the sound of the radio noise, the urgency of the reports called over the channel. They turned the volume up a little more and together listened to the fire radio.

"Engine 25, Engine 25, Strike out the box." My father became mesmerized by the voices of the firefighters in action. If his thoughts flickered to his own near-death by fire, he didn't tell me so. What he thought about, he says, was a tragic event which had occurred just before he went away to Bible College, and one which often haunted him as he worked his way from A to Z in the dismal office space.

It was a bleak December day in Baltimore, cold and overcast with trees devoid of leaves. As he walked toward the church that morning, Dad saw a trail of red human footprints imprinted in the one-inch blanket of snow. For a second he thought that the scenario had been staged by one of the members of his youth group as part of a lesson. Then he saw the somber expressions on the faces of his friends who huddled nearby and realized that the bloody prints of bare feet which went to the main door of the church and then to the right, stopping at the side door, had been made by someone in desperate need of help.

My father asked a man standing next to him what had happened. The man pointed to a burned-out building, not more than half a block from the church, and said that the footprints were those of his neighbor, a heavy drinker. A fire had erupted on the second floor of the victim's house. Jumping out of the window to escape, cutting his feet in the process, the man had staggered to the church in search of aid. But the church was closed.

Northminster Presbyterian Church stood on the corner of St. Paul Street and North Avenue, a beautiful Gothic building with large stained glass windows and a big pipe organ inside. It was under threat of being shut down, and the congregation was fighting to keep it open. At this time the church was unlocked only on Sundays for the youths and the visiting pastors who met at the church manse to study devotions, read scriptures and pray.

Dad pictured how the man must have made his way home the night before, walking against the brutal December winds. Dad imagined him climbing shaky steps to his dreary two-room apartment on the second floor of the three-story row house, fumbling with a worn key for the right spot in the lock, and opening the door to the darkness which always greeted him.

Clutter, filth and vermin lurked in the shadows. My father imagined the man lighting the candle on the nightstand beside the bed, his only light source, and then reaching for his sole companion. He grabbed the bottle and pressed it to his lips to chase away his loneliness, his mind long ago surrendered to alcohol and his body wasted by accompanying disease. Growing tired as he savored the last drops, he dozed off into a restless sleep punctuated by nightmare. Dad saw the inebriate swinging his arms and inadvertently striking the candle, the fire catching hold and ravaging the filthy mattress. The man would have awakened to an even greater horror, grimacing in pain as the flames lapped at his body, scorching his skin. Panicked, he must have leapt from his bed, pushed his way through the web of heat, then plunged through a window, escaping to the rear porch roof.

Dad pictured him relishing the soothing relief of the cold air and the light dusting of snow on his burnt skin as he sat motionless on the rotting roof for a moment. Hoping to take refuge at the stone church on the corner, he summoned his remaining strength to jump to the concrete yard below.

Limping, struggling, leaving behind a bloody trail, he made his way to the front entrance to pound with both fists. A yellow neon sign blinked "COME" above the door. Unable to open that door, he must have limped to the side door, where his worst fears were realized. The fortress of faith was locked.

In the morning light that Sunday, my father stood silently observing the tracks in the snow. The body found slumped against the door had already been carried away. At that moment my father began to think about his relationships to both God and mankind, about the purpose of his own life.

As he sat there listening to the radio, not only did he become aware that Stanley was enamored with fire, the thing Bill feared most, but he also realized he shared Stanley's obsession with fire. Lured by the action broadcast from the radio, they both sat together in silence.

As he listened intently, he made a decision. He knew that he wanted to be a part of the action. He didn't want to be an outsider looking in, but a full-time insider in a new and exciting career. He wanted to be a firefighter. When Bill told people at DDO he was leaving, they said, "Nobody leaves after just three years." But later my father would say, "I did—and I never looked back."

Eventually the church was demolished. Today it's a KFC. Some things my dad couldn't save.

Papa's Got a Brand New Bag

The black-and-white headshot of Bill Hennick in his fire department dress uniform, taken in a photo booth when he was twenty-five years old, depicts a fearless man. My father doesn't show his teeth when he smiles. Instead, he wears a semi-smirk as though lost inside a private joke with himself. He has subtle gray circles beneath his deep-set blue eyes. They are not necessarily from weariness; they're a genetic trait, giving him a stern expression that worsens when he's tired. In the picture, the brim of his cap casts a shadow beneath his brow. The fact is, conformity and authoritarianism are two things that my father despises. And although he never admits it, he was and is more of a pacifist than a militarist. In the photo, however, he appears at once courageous and naïve: a dashing young soldier eager in his conviction to serve God and his country.

The two-story red brick station, Engine 52 or E-52, stood at 3235 Woodbrook Avenue. (Firefighters refer to the actual firehouses as "engines" or "trucks.") E-52 was erected in about 1920 and had floor space for one pumper. The men slept in an upstairs bunkroom sandwiched between the officer's room and a locker room with a two-sink, two-toilet bathroom. There was also a kitchen. Three fire poles allowed quick access to the first floor. A hose tower, where the firefighters routinely hung the cotton-jacketed lines out to dry, adjoined the building.

Sometimes E-52 was beyond uncomfortable. The roof over the bunkroom area was black tar, so the heat of summer radiating into it would last late into the night as the men tried to rest with no air conditioning. There were no screens on the windows. Dad used to say, "The mosquitoes were treated to a human buffet."

Some of the firehouses were decrepit, drafty buildings that dated back to the beginning of the century, with stalls decorated with horseshoes extending from the kitchen. One firehouse even had an inoperative horse hospital with double doors attached to the two-story station. There were still dents in the ceiling where the harnesses had hung.

At the time, the Baltimore City Fire Department comprised ten battalions including fifty-eight fire companies with two fireboats, thirty ladder truck companies, four hose companies, two chemical units and fourteen ambulances. A captain ran each company, either engine or truck. Men were assigned to the company and broken up into three squads, supervised by the captain or one of two lieutenants. The department served more than 900,000 people and went out on nearly 140,000 runs per year.

"E-52 was one of the ten busiest companies in Baltimore, and this was a dream crew to work with." Dad referred to the men he worked with as his "other family."

"The captain of E-52, Paul, was an imposing, heavyset guy. He wore an impeccable blue uniform and carried an executive-style leather briefcase to work," Dad told me. He privately called him Foghorn Leghorn because he looked and acted like the big chicken in the Looney Tunes' cartoons, but "Tall Paul" envisioned himself as a great lover and would share his supposed expertise with his subordinates. His exploits were global: they involved beautiful women throughout the world. "One time I met this girl in Sweden . . ." he'd begin. Or Berlin, or the French Riviera, or Bali. His infamous briefcase was rumored throughout the battalion to have contained a priceless collection of paperback porn classics. Everybody endured his tales in the hope of getting hold of his briefcase. Although my father never questioned his captain on this subject, all the men knew he got his stories from the books he carted around.

When lounging around the firehouse lost in his reveries, Tall Paul was pleasant, calm, cordial. But as soon as a fire call came across the watch desk, he became possessed. His face contorted and his eyes widened behind his dark-rimmed glasses.

After settling his large frame into the front seat of the Old Mack, he would shout, "Let's go" to Smitty, their venerable pump operator. He would give a rope clenched in his right hand a series of rapid yanks, sounding a large brass bell as they raced through the streets. Increasing the frequency of the strikes as they approached the intersection, the captain would glare at motorists and shout curses while waving his free arm as if to say, "Get the hell out of the way!"

Each of the Battalion Chiefs had a red-car driver who did nothing but chauffeur the chief. According to my father, it was a "gravy job." Gil Thompson was the red-car driver on my father's shift. His job was to drive Chief Shamberger of the Fourth Battalion. For him, home base was the firehouse on McCullough and McMechen Streets, about two miles from E-52. A complicated bureaucracy reigned within. If the men of E-52 or some other firehouse needed the electric floor buffer, they had to call the chief's driver and request that he deliver it to their firehouse. They had to ring him whenever the toilets at any of their firehouses stopped up. On the phone they'd say, "We have an emergency. Bring the battalion plunger." Gil would drive the red car round and present them with the Holy Grail of plungers. It had a solid brass neck with scroll engraving and scripting and a handle that you pumped up and down. After they unstopped the toilet, Gil would reverently transport the plunger back to the chief's quarters.

"We were the envy of a strange breed of people known as fire buffs," Dad said. Buffs, sometimes called "House Cats," are knowledgeable about firefighting and are dedicated to their passion. Many are professional or business men, all with a burning interest in fire department activities. Fire buffs, then and now, are devoted to the pursuit of all things related to the fire department. They love firehouses, fire engines and trucks, fire equipment, fire department protocol, firefighters, and, of course, fires. The buffs relish spending time with firefighters and often respond with the fire crew on actual runs.

Who could ever forget Captain Wheels? This buff was in his late thirties. His face was pockmarked. What he did for a living was a mystery. What he did during the day was to frequent the local fire stations. The "Captain" had a red bicycle with a bright red frame, a small siren on the handlebars, and a kitchen fire extinguisher tied behind the seat. Firefighters place a large, wedge shaped wooden chock behind the rear wheel of the truck to prevent it from rolling. Captain Wheels put a large wooden chock behind the rear wheel of his bicycle when he parked it.

He knew the district, though. When the alarm sounded he would rush to his bicycle and, donning his gear, which included a red plastic child's fire helmet, he would lead the charge to the fire scene, screaming like a siren. He pedaled feverishly ahead of the wailing trucks and somehow often arrived before the firefighters did. He would dismount from his fire-cycle and direct pedestrian traffic. The men adopted "Wheels" and treated him like one of the boys.

After a hard day of pedaling, he would be rewarded with a huge plate of firehouse chow; he had a voracious appetite. The firefighters donated turnout gear to him and once held a ceremony in his honor at which they presented him with a brand-new plastic helmet with "Captain Wheels" emblazoned on the front. Wheels beamed.

On my father's first night on the job, he felt the adrenaline rush as he fought two car fires and a house fire. But his real test came later that evening during a four-alarm fire at a chemical company. This would be his day of reckoning. He would confront his adversary head-on for the first time since his boyhood.

They pulled up in front of this old, brick commercial building, spread over an acre, on the corner of Laurens Street and Fulton Avenue. Heavy smoke obscured the top floors. The sign **Peerless Chemical Company** in bold black print hung between the third and fourth stories on the faded red brick surface, discolored by age. The lieutenant and Bill pushed open a wooden door situated on the Fulton Avenue side of the doomed building.

Dad advanced a hose line up the steps to the second floor. At this fire, Lieutenant Oscar Krause allowed him to lead the men up the steps while egging him on from behind. He had confidence in young Bill Hennick and wanted to see how much he could take.

Following orders, Bill struggled up one rickety step at a time, gripping the hose nozzle tightly in his hands. Thick smoke and chunks of falling debris from above drastically hindered the men's mobility as they negotiated their way up the wooden stairs. He was halfway up to the second floor when part of the ceiling collapsed onto his helmet and knocked him down the steps. Regaining his composure, he continued to where the fire beckoned.

Visibility was near zero until they approached the rapidly spreading fire consuming the second and third floors. At last they were positioned to strike at the heart of the blaze. The fire became increasingly intense because the truck company had knocked out all of the windows, allowing it to breathe. The roar of the inferno was punctuated by the sounds of bottles exploding, glass shattering, and wall and ceiling sections collapsing. As they cautiously edged closer to the heart of the roaring flames, my father felt the ever-increasing heat permeating his thin rubber turnout coat. He gradually opened the nozzle and cascaded a pressurized stream of water from the one-and-a-half-inch hose toward the fire. "The fire was my enemy," Dad said later, "and I was determined to win."

Mercifully, some sort of protective wall in his brain allowed only a few jagged remnants of his childhood memory to reach his consciousness. As he stood there surrounded by flames, Dad remembered the sound of the florist shop's door slamming after the explosion and the door being broken down by his savior. He had been told that, in the heart of the blaze which threatened to consume him, a man appeared and scooped him up into his arms, holding him tight against his chest as he fled the building. This Samaritan beat the few remaining flames from my father's nearly lifeless body, put him into a black car nearby, and raced with him to the Union Memorial Hospital a mile away. He cradled little Billy Hennick in his arms as he carried him into the emergency room.

When my grandmother received the call from the hospital her first desperate question was, "Are his eyes hurt?" They were not. But she had no idea of just how badly he *was* hurt.

My father's older sister, Nancy, remembered that, when Billy arrived at the hospital, his little seersucker pants and jacket were burned to tatters and his brown shoes charred. Second- and third-degree burns caused his skin to peel and bleed in places. Oozing bodily fluids had coated his skin, making his flesh appear slippery and red between crispy black patches.

The doctor shook his head in dismay. "He's not going to live. He's not going to live."

Burn wards were torture chambers. My father remembers a twelve-inch rod that was inserted through his left heel with a cord attached on both ends. The cord connected to a pulley above his bed, and a weight placed on the other end kept his leg elevated and straight so it would not be deformed when it healed. The damage behind his left knee necessitated this crude appliance. His little body was bandaged up like a mummy.

My grandmother sat teary-eyed at Dad's bedside every day while he received forty transfusions of blood donated by relatives and friends. Even his sister Nancy, who fainted at the sight of the needle, was a donor. The congregation in a nearby Presbyterian church—the same Northminster which later was to become the scene of the fire-related death which was to haunt Bill in his adulthood—dedicated entire evenings to praying for Billy's survival.

The burns on Dad's face, three as big as quarters, eventually healed. Nancy recalled that the nurses frequently changed his bandages, anaesthetizing him to alleviate the pain while they did so. His tender four-year-old flesh was torn in the process of peeling off the gauze.

My grandmother bore the stress of caring for her burnt son alone; Grandfather was a captain, stationed overseas at the tail end of World War II. He wrote briefly about the incident in his diary:

"August 6, 1945. Letter from Helen today. Little Bill not so good." The atomic bomb, Little Boy, was dropped on Hiroshima the same day, but the diary did not mention it.

"August 29, 1945. Went to hospital. Saw little Bill. Poor little fellow didn't look good at all."

Skin grafting, a new procedure at the time, failed to heal the wound behind my father's left knee. The hole was as wide as a silver dollar and an inch and a half deep. He would have trouble with that knee for the rest of his life. Nevertheless, he continued to improve. Soon he was even participating in illicit wheel-chair races in the hallway with other kids. Knowing that burned skin contracts as it scars, tightening up like rubber and restricting mobility, the physicians encouraged him to play. He remembers tossing a beanbag back and forth with a child whose face had been completely destroyed by a fire.

Smoke had damaged Dad's lungs. The doctors would hold him down and lean on his shoulders so he would not jump, then stick needles in his back to drain the fluid from his chest. Dad still remembers the excruciating pain. "It was like being knifed in the back." He was given heavy doses of penicillin. But in spite of the treatments, he would suffer respiratory problems for the rest of his life: asthma, bronchitis and severe sinus infections.

Dad eagerly anticipated his mother's visits. Every morning he would ride his tricycle to the big window of Union Memorial Hospital and wave to her as she entered the building.

After three months in the hospital, little Billy finally went home to a great celebration, which included a Welcome Home cake complete with candles. He screamed in terror at the sight of the tiny flames. At the age of four he had to crawl until he learned to walk again. He even had to learn to talk again. He remembered sitting on the kitchen floor while my grandmother was cooking. The sound of fish sizzling in the hot pan made him scream and sent him crawling in terror across the linoleum into another room.

My father often thought of the man who lifted him out of the inferno and carried him into the emergency room. The rescuer just happened to be there at the right time and must have heard the screams. My father often said, "If he hadn't, I wouldn't be here today." He mused, "The pain of something like that is so intense, it's unbelievable. Then the body goes into shock and the mind blocks it out."

Later, Dad learned the name of the man who saved his life: John Barron. It was rumored in the neighborhood that he was an alcoholic, but my father was unsure whether or not this was true. At first, he did not even know where the man lived or where he came from. One night, when my grandmother invited Billy's rescuer for supper in gratitude for his heroism, she was disquieted to smell liquor on his breath. Then she saw that his hands and arms were singed with burns, and suddenly his reputation as a drinker didn't matter. He had saved her son's life.

My father remembers that for a long time, whenever he watched people light candles for dinner, ignite sparklers on the Fourth of July, or fire up the coals for a barbecue, he felt rage at what had happened to him. His throat would tighten; he would perspire and tremble inside. He thought constantly of the unhealing wound behind his knee. This permanent sore would often break open, allowing blood to stream down his leg. He had to worry constantly about infection.

When Dad hit puberty, the injury became more than just a worrisome nuisance. As a teenager he was embarrassed to go swimming because of the visible scars, even though they were much worse in his own eyes than in those of others. Thinking ahead to courtship, he feared that the sight of his body would disappoint a woman. When he recalled the flames that had wrecked his childhood, his heart would begin to pound. He despised fire. He hated how the sight of it haunted him, had permanently damaged his body, had burned not only his skin but his psyche, imprinting it with a feeling of weakness, of inferiority.

So, twenty years later, on that night when he stood in the inferno of the Peerless Chemical Company, the phoenix rose. "It was my turn to get even," my father said. Firing the hose, relentlessly attacking the blaze, my father couldn't help but laugh as he watched the flames tremble, then cower and weaken as he beat them one at a time. Spraying them over and over, he watched to his left and to his right for new flames to emerge. The heat was palpable through the heavy smoke as he directed the stream toward the elusive orange glow. In spite of the dryness of his mouth, for the first time in his life my father tasted the sweetness of power.

"Now it's my turn," he silently shouted over and over as he helped his comrades to defeat the hostile army of flames.

And just then millions of bubbles burst into the air like balloons in a grand Hollywood celebration. My father was puzzled for a moment until he realized that the contents of the building were mostly large cardboard boxes of detergent. As the bubbles neared my father's face, in the glow of the embers he could see his reflection in a million fleeting convex mirrors. Had he been able to make out the details of his image, my father would have seen himself smiling.

Little Ole Man (Uptight-Everything's Alright)

As a young, macho firefighter, my father would have been embarrassed to tell his colleagues how he was once rescued by a patient. Much later, when he shared the tale with me, I wanted to tell the world.

My father described the nursing homes of the late sixties as "poorly regulated fire traps." The three- and four-story brick buildings lacked sprinkler systems, safety procedures and skilled employees. They usually "warehoused" twenty-five to thirty forgotten senior citizens. Dad regularly witnessed evidence of abuse, such as the nursing home resident who was nearly beaten to death with a cane by an orderly.

Another time, a worker (with the best of intentions) delivered CPR to an elderly woman whom she thought was unconscious. The resident had merely been asleep. She suffered multiple fractures.

On another occasion, when he was a new firefighter, Dad was detailed to Ambulance 14 on Cross Country Boulevard with his partner Ernie. They found a woman lying under filthy sheets, "all skin and bones." She had a gaping wound on her right forearm clotted over with blood. The staff had ignored her, one eight-hour shift after another. As Bill and Ernie cleaned and bandaged the infection she whispered, "Please get me out of here."

They stabilized the patient and were heading out of the building when Ernie shouted to a few employees milling around on the first floor, "I want everyone who works here to get down here now." Hearing the threat, a few workers scurried off, returning in moments with their colleagues. Ernie paced around the room with long strides and barked drill-sergeant style, "What is wrong with you people? You ought to be ashamed of yourselves." Pointing at the patient in the stretcher, he said, "This is an old wound. You left this lady unattended for days. You mean to tell me you can't run a place better than this? Every one of you should get your head examined." As they took her to the hospital my father, in admiration of Ernie, thought, "I wish I'd had the guts to do it myself."

By a stroke of fate, one case of neglect would ironically save my father's life. On this day, he was detailed on 10 Truck and 8 Engine on Lafayette and Fulton Avenue when he and four colleagues received a report for "odor of smoke." They raced out in a single engine and screeched to a halt in front of a West Baltimore nursing home. The firefighters rushed in to ensure the building had been thoroughly evacuated. The lieutenant ordered my father to search the top level. "I thought I'd prance through the third floor and return down the steps," my father recalled. He ascended the narrow stairway that "seemed like it had been built as an afterthought." As he reached the third floor, the smoke thickened into a dense haze. Dad knew the oxygen in his cylinder was rapidly being used up. He began with twenty-five to thirty minutes of air, but running up the steps and dashing down the hallway cut his supply by two-thirds. He scanned the corridor and found no one in the rooms. Confident that everyone had been led to safety, he was not going to bother to check the final room at the end of the hall on his left—doing so would slash his already sparse air supply in half. He hesitated a moment and reminded himself, "I have a job to do." He sprinted to the open doorway where he did a double take. There, in the lingering fog, he saw the silhouette of a lanky "Humphrey Bogart." A man in a fedora and trench coat sat motionless in a chair with his back to my father. Dad walked over to the man and knelt in front of him. The frail black man continued staring, his eyes apparently fixed on the wall in front of him. He'd either been unseen or forgotten by the staff.

"We have a problem," my father said (when telling me the story he'd always say, "Houston, we have a problem"). "We need to get you out of here. The smoke is getting thicker." The man began coughing; his eyes remained still. To my father he looked like a cat patiently waiting. Dad continued, "We cannot go back the way we came. The smoke is too thick in the stairwell and I'm running out of oxygen." Knowing that stairwells are a natural draft where fire can swoosh up and cut off any possibility of escape, my father feared that they'd be incinerated if they returned the way he came.

Dad began to panic, but the man remained placid.

"Follow me," the blind man beckoned in a way that my father said could only be described as "Christ-like."

The man stood to hunched posture and my father trailed him out of the room, turned left, and together they walked fifteen to twenty feet until reaching a door resembling a janitor's closet. It was, in fact, a stairwell.

Dad imagined a photo of "Humphrey" beaming on the front page of the local newspaper: "80-Pound Blind Man Rescues Young Firefighter from Near-Death Experience." By the time they were safely out in the fresh air and sunlight several more fire companies had arrived. "Humphrey" joined the residents waiting nearby and Dad met up with the other firefighters on the ground. "I don't remember telling anyone about it," Dad said.

Mercy, Mercy, Mercy

To do their job, the firefighters from E-52 could never let their personal lives interfere, and yet the men behind the masks often met challenges more difficult than anything they would ever experience on the fire ground. My father often used stories of his friend Smitty to illustrate resilience in the face of death.

"His name was Maurice B. Smith. He was the driver and pump operator on my shift. He was an iron man, no doubt about that. Smitty nearly became a lieutenant, but it seems some behind-the-scenes monkey business obstructed his promotion. I always felt safe and secure with him behind the wheel of the Old Mack pumper."

Smitty was a rugged Eastern Shore man, craggy like a fisherman who has been out at sea a long time. He always wore an old beat-up blue hat as if he really were going boating.

Smitty had survived the Great Depression in the 1930s—but barely. He grew up in Crisfield, Maryland, a land of farmers and watermen; there, as a kid, he existed on a diet of potatoes and watermelon. Smitty told my father that he once loaded so many watermelons into his family's car—onto the running boards, bumpers and roof—that it got stuck in the field.

Back then, the firefighters at E-52 depended on a 1948 Mack 85 Pumper. They called it a Bulldog Mack because of its bulldog hood ornament. And because they were tough. Already a seventeen-year-old vehicle when Dad started, E-52's Mack had an open cab, which made it antiquated even by the standards of the day. Dad always said E-52, besides not shielding the men from wind, rain or snow, was a mule to drive. However, it was sturdily built and reliable. "We knew this old warhorse would be there for us during difficult times."

If Smitty was absent, others filled in to do the driving. My father drove the Old Mack with considerable apprehension. "During breaks in traffic I'd focus on the tiny silver bulldog perched on the front of the hood, the symbol of one rugged machine. I was proud to drive the old battle wagon." Dad always grinned when he talked about the Old Mack. He said, "Smitty, pump operator and driver extraordinaire of E-52, seemed to have a fatherly love for that vehicle." An Old Mack could pump for long periods of time without mechanical breakdown. Smitty had seen that pumper through its infancy, puberty, and teen years. The two were inseparable. Every Saturday morning Smitty crawled under the framework and meticulously cleaned every visible part. He'd top off the transmission fluid, hydraulic fluid and gear lubricant. "The Old Mack and Smitty were made for each other."

On rare occasions, Smitty would reluctantly discipline the Old Mack by striking specific points beneath the engine with a rubber mallet. Working his magic, he would free a stubborn valve or encourage the essential bits to do their duty.

"With a stern yet gentle parenting style, he lovingly chided the Old Mack. 'Come on Baby, kick in.' I guess you could say that this was an unusual relationship between a Bulldog Mack and a stubborn mule," Dad chuckled.

Smitty expertly drove the open-cab pumper in the searing heat and bitter cold. There was no roof, just a windshield. The door had no seals, and rain would run out of the cracks at the bottom. He had to confront dangerous intersections and unyielding traffic while totally exposed to the elements. The men relied on him to supply the proper pump pressure to the hose lines, and he worked feverishly so they would not become trapped in a life-threatening situation. Driving the Old Mack even in nonemergency situations was not easy. There was no power steering. The clutch pedal was hard to depress, and the driver had to double-clutch through the gears while enduring the noise of sirens, clanging bells and the ranting of the company officer next to him.

At first my father didn't understand some of Smitty's peculiar ways, especially his "penny-pinching." If Dad was having bacon and eggs for breakfast, Smitty cadged the grease from the bacon to give flavor to his one egg. He used fire department lye soap for shaving and threaded a piece of rope through his belt-loops. He maintained his 1953 Chevrolet himself. But Dad later discovered the reason for Smitty's behavior.

One day, at about 5:00 p.m., the phone rang at the watch desk.

Smitty's wife was on the line. She told the officer who answered that their son was behaving strangely. The firehouse phone was off limits for personal calls, and Smitty was so afraid of breaking the rules and losing his job that he requested permission to walk to the gas station on the corner to use the payphone. He returned to the engine ashen-faced. He needed to go home immediately. Anticipating something terrible, Lieutenant Frazier, an aloof intellectual with glasses and dark slicked-back hair, asked Dad to drive Smitty home. My father and Smitty jumped into Dad's car and sped off.

On the way, Smitty told my father how proud he was of his only child. He was in his last years at Johns Hopkins University and was soon to receive a doctorate in nuclear physics after twelve grueling years of higher education. Smitty confided that he and his son painted houses in the summer in order to afford the tuition fees. Dad told me, "It was tough raising a family on firefighter's pay. For some reason, cab driving and serving in the military reserves were just about the only occupations allowed if firefighters moonlighted. But men broke the rules at times from sheer necessity." Now my father realized the reason for Smitty's frugality. His colleague had denied himself everything to pay for his son's education. He felt extreme admiration for this man by the time they arrived at his home.

Smitty's wife was sitting in the living room trembling. Dazed and confused, all she could do was point to the stairway. My father bounded up two steps at a time and arrived at the doorway of the bathroom. Blood and pieces of bone were splattered all over the floor and walls.

Smitty's son had waved goodbye to his dad two hours prior, giving no indication of any problem. He then went to the gun cabinet and took out a twelve-gauge shotgun. Propping himself in the bathtub, he had cushioned his head on a pillow, placed the barrel under his chin and squeezed the trigger. Just before my father arrived, his body had been carried out.

By now Smitty was in the doorway jabbering, "Oh my. Look at this, what's happened? What's going on? Where's my son, where's my wife?" He was in shock. He reached down with a shaking hand and picked up a piece of skull with hair on it. A guy nicknamed Reds, a friend of Smitty's who worked in the Fire Department, showed up. Reds and Dad cleaned up, filling several trashcans with debris. Dad said, "It was a nightmare. I almost had to throw Smitty out. 'Smitty,' I said, 'Why don't you go downstairs? Your wife needs you.' That way we were able to finish."

As Dad remembers it, a neighbor stayed with Smitty's wife. My father rushed Smitty to Union Memorial Hospital, parking hastily in front of the entrance to the emergency room. By keeping eye contact and speaking words of comfort to him, he diverted Smitty's attention from the trail of blood on the floor that led from the doorway and down the hall. The two men reached a small waiting room.

Anguish and concern overwhelmed Smitty as he began to suspect the unthinkable. My father implored him to have a seat and try to relax. Glancing over Smitty's shoulder, he caught the eye of the attending paramedic who had just transported the young man. The paramedic shook his head slowly from side to side, and Dad knew the worst. He placed his hand on Smitty's shoulder as the ER physician approached with the dreadful news.

"The iron man wept."

Not knowing quite what to do, Dad thought of embracing him. Instead, he just patted him on the shoulder.

Smitty cried for a few moments, then, seeming to draw on some tremendous inner strength, composed himself and quietly said, "My wife needs me. I have to be strong for her."

My father came close to tears but didn't cry. At that moment he willed himself to sympathize but not to feel.

He and Smitty never discussed the incident. They came from the old school. Dad said, "You had a job to do, and you did it, that's all. Smitty didn't try to get out of the fire service on a psychological disability. Yet I know that when this happened, his whole world collapsed."

Smitty took leave for a few weeks to care for his wife but then returned to his position at E-52. "I sure was glad to have him back behind the wheel. He and the Old Mack belonged together. I felt privileged to ride on the back step with this great man in the driver's seat."

For days after the suicide, Dad couldn't shake off the memory of the skull fragments splattered across the bathroom. "It replayed in different ways; I couldn't get it out of my mind." Dad remembers sitting in the kitchen looking through the side window that faced a brick wall while his mother was preparing breakfast. The next day she placed a glass of grape juice in front of him. A sip of it tasted like blood.

My grandmother kept a little glass placard hanging next to the front door that read "Only one life shall soon be past, only what's done for Christ will last." The words consoled Dad when he left for work.

Amazing Grace

If Bill heard a fire engine in the middle of the night when he and my mother Eunice were first married, he would get up and get ready to go, whether or not he was actually on duty. Eunice would get ready too, dressing, applying lipstick, stepping into high heels. She did not have to ask where they were going. They would follow an engine around all over Baltimore to watch the fire. My father would analyze it and describe exactly what type of fire it was, what the men were doing, and so on. Then they would drive home and go back to sleep.

"He couldn't get enough of it. Just couldn't get enough of it," she said. What a handsome couple, people would say of my parents. Eunice—slim, with delicate features, her brunette hair long and flowing—seemed oblivious to her beauty. My maternal grandfather, Howard Riggin, came from a long line of Irish fishermen and farmers who had arrived in America in 1667. Two of his ancestors married Algonquin Indian princesses, and as a child I loved the idea that I might be related to Pocahontas. Like Dad's friend Smitty, Pop-Pop Riggin had survived the Great Depression by eating potatoes and watermelon on a farm near the Eastern Shore where he was raised. He moved to Baltimore to work as a boiler technician for Bethlehem Steel and start a family.

After my parents married, she told me, "We lived in a one-bedroom apartment and I was bored and alone most of the time. He didn't want me to work. 'No Hennick has a working wife.'

"I'd say, 'What am I supposed to do, sit in this room and wait for you all day?'

"So I took jobs before you kids were born and later when you were at school." Eunice held secretarial and volunteer jobs; later she worked as an executive assistant for an accounting firm. "My first priority, though, was being home for the family."

Back then, in the honeymoon stage of their marriage, she would burst into tears every time he went off to work, fearing her goodbye kiss would be the last. My father shared the dangers of fire with his young wife. "Sudden explosions can catch you by surprise. You could become surrounded by flames in an instant and without warning."

Basement fires were particularly terrifying; the men had to exercise extreme caution while negotiating the floor above. Entering windowless lower level basements was always a harrowing experience, because the fire and smoke were concentrated in a closed environment. Descending into this hell scared even the most seasoned veteran. Escape routes in such circumstances are limited, and claustrophobia is an additional enemy. A fire could move upward, consuming the stairway. During such fires the men would test each potentially weakened step as they ascended or descended.

Experience became my father's best teacher during those formative years. Not only are most fires fought in complete darkness, but spongy floors, fragile stairways and collapsing ceilings weakened by the extreme heat make locating and extinguishing the flames a real challenge.

"Fire can hide inside interior walls and leap out at you when you least expect it. A small black dot on a wall that rapidly expands into a larger, darker area is a sign that the fire is probably going to suddenly burst into the open. A fire can rekindle, even after apparently being extinguished, and the flame may become stronger than before. Fire needs oxygen to breathe and has an insatiable appetite.

"It's not like it is in the movies," Dad would say. "I didn't talk to my colleagues. You know, when you've got flames belching out at you, you're not going to stop and say stupid things to the other men like 'It's showtime' or 'Geronimo.'"

A major problem was the inadequate turnout gear provided for firefighters in 1965. The long black coats were made of a thin rubber material that became hot to the touch. The helmets were lightweight plastic, fragile, not suited for aggressive firefighting. Decent gloves were nonexistent. Firefighters wore low-grade khaki uniforms, which quickly showed the grime and shrank when washed. "Obviously, a city low-bid item."

The all-service mask was simply a canister containing charcoal filters which hung around the neck. It was not supposed to be used in basements or garages or in any area with less than 14 percent oxygen, but the firefighters had no way of knowing when the oxygen dropped that low. When wearing the full respirator equipment, Dad learned to keep the air mask on even when the blaze was extinguished, fearing the possible release of toxic gases. A metal cylinder containing about twenty to thirty minutes of air, depending on the wearer's rate of breathing, fed through a hose connected to an enclosed face-piece. A warning sounded when five minutes' supply remained.

My father said he and his buddies were too "macho" to give much thought to personal injury or internal damage from smoke and heat; they refused to wear the bulky masks that could protect their lungs from toxins and carcinogens. In a dangerous yet friendly rivalry, firefighters would often forgo putting on protective equipment in order to save a few seconds and thus gain entry to a rapidly spreading fire before another engine company could beat them to the punch. "It seemed gallant and brave," reflected my Dad, "but in the long run it was careless and stupid."

As the Old Mack approached a two-story row home on Woodbrook Avenue, my father didn't see a puff of smoke or a single flame, but the truck lights illuminated a man in his boxer shorts perched on the corner of the roof. He was locked in a crouching position, obviously paralyzed with fear. Dad sprang from the rear step of the engine. In a few seconds he was proceeding down the hallway. To his immediate right was a pair of French doors. He peered through the small panes of glass and locked eyes with an elderly lady. She was expressionless, as if nothing out of the ordinary was happening. (She escaped unharmed).

My father raced along the hallway and headed toward a stairway leading to the second floor. As he turned right to climb the steps, waves of fire were rolling down the stairs, voraciously consuming everything in their path. "Surf's up in hell!"

E-52 arrived first; Truck 10 and Engines 8, 13 and 25 were on their way. My father needed to decide whether to fight the blaze alone or wait for the other men. He had a small, three-quarter-inch booster line (about twice the circumference of a garden hose) slung over his shoulder, definitely not the weapon of choice for such a formidable opponent. He gazed for an instant at the roaring Goliath, then turned and peered around the corner and down the hallway. Through the window of the door he could see Smitty banging on the underbelly of the Old Mack to make the pumps kick in. He hit the right spot and water streamed from his hose line.

A quick decision was imperative. Dad later told me that in most cases it would have been foolhardy to go up alone with nothing but a booster line. "Nobody would believe me if I told them I went up with a garden hose. But I did, and I loved it, because I had that fire all to myself. I relished another opportunity to conquer my enemy."

Overwhelmed with excitement, Dad felt an adrenaline rush akin to a state of euphoria. He was soaring on a natural high. He felt powerful. His senses and concentration were heightened. He climbed the steps one at a time, shielding his face and body by spraying the flames with a protective fog from the nozzle.

As he ascended, my father felt the heat from the floor above. He was halfway up the stairwell focusing on the flames directly above him when a metal and glass skylight crashed on his head, and he collapsed on the stairwell. Dad later learned that the skylight was dislodged by members of Truck 10. They had no idea he was under it when they knocked it out to ventilate the building. He was stunned for a moment, then struggled to his feet and knocked down the fire in front of him and to his right. Gaining ground, Dad began to sense a victory.

As soon as he reached the top step, the fire abated, and another firefighter arrived. After the fire was contained, the two men put out the hot spots, tearing out the ceiling and walls to make sure fire wasn't hiding. Still savoring his experience while removing the smoldering remains of the closed middle bedroom door, my father saw in the dissipating smoke the outline of a partly burned baby crib just inside the doorway. Searching with his hand in the confines of the crib, he found what he thought was a small baby doll. But no, this was a real baby. The infant was unconscious and had small blisters on his head indicating second-degree burns.

Moments later the other firefighters arrived, lining along the steps and down the hallway. Dad handed the infant to the first of his colleagues who passed him from embrace to embrace until he was safely outside.

Knowing that kids hide under beds, in cupboards and in corners, my father opened a closet door, revealing an unconscious nine- or ten-year old boy. Dad hastily removed him and passed him along the human chain. The cold, fresh air outside revived the survivors, and as my father joyously listened to the cries of both children, he couldn't help but think that if he hadn't gone up the stairwell, they would have died.

The fire had destroyed the front room, the hallway and the rear room. The interior was charred to the brick between the houses. The only door shut was that of the middle room where the kids were sleeping. The fire had just begun to eat through the door and had already singed the baby's head. Dad said, "That infant was two seconds away from being killed."

It was then that my father felt his foot squishing inside his right boot. He peeled down the top of the boot, and in the glow of the floodlights brought in by the truck company, he could see that his khaki cotton pants were stained red. Initially, he thought that he must have spilled an open can of red paint down his leg in the scramble. But when he peeled the boot past his knee, blood was spurting in rhythm to the beat of his heart.

Lieutenant Frazier from Engine 25 sat my father down, removed the damaged, blood-filled boot, and tossed it out of the window. The onlookers outside shrieked as the boot landed, spewing crimson spray onto the new fallen snow. Dad himself controlled the bleeding by holding the pressure point above his knee until his leg could be bandaged. A medic took him to Mercy Hospital for evaluation and stitches.

The half-naked man on the roof must have been sleeping in the front room, my father conjectured. He had smelled the smoke, run down the hallway, bypassing the children's bedroom, and leapt out of the rear window. Somehow he managed to grip the ice-covered rainspout and pull himself up to the relative safety of the roof. "Terror must have given him superhuman strength," Dad reflected. "It was his apartment, and he knew the children were in there. I'll never understand why he didn't even attempt to save them. I guess he awoke startled. But he should have tried anything: dropped the baby in the snow or tried to get down the steps. Anything."

Later, it became evident that an arsonist had set a rollaway bed on fire in the hall.

In the early days, whenever Dad spoke to Mom about work, his face would become awash with bliss. She could see that when he discovered those unconscious children in time to save them, my father also found his purpose in life.

What a Day for a Daydream

You'd think that when a man slaves away all year, he'd look forward to that one time when, at least for a week, he can just forget about everything, put it all behind him, and not even think about work. Not my father. For Dad, the family vacation in the mid-1970s was an opportunity to hold us captive in the car for the three-and-a-half-hour trip to Pine Haven, a campground near Ocean City, New Jersey, while he bombarded us with war stories. It would take my mother the same amount of time to pack the car. We were only going camping for five nights, but she would pack just about our entire wardrobes, including all of our church clothes, her finest dinner dresses, stilettos, several pairs of pantyhose and long underwear. She couldn't possibly go without her jewelry, hot rollers, curling iron, makeup mirror and a suitcase filled with toiletries. Also essential were the clothes iron, ruby dishware, china teacups, silverware, four reclining chairs, three electric blankets and a Bible.

After the tent, propane stove and sleeping bags were loaded, we'd discover that there wasn't any room left in the van for us. It would take another hour for my parents to "discuss" what was essential and for my father to secure the camping gear to the roof with bungee cords.

My mother made my brother, Craig, and me change into matching plaid jumpsuits. We were a year apart in age, but she dressed us up like twins, and we both had the same blond bowl haircuts. We'd finally squeeze into the van, pull the doors shut, and brace ourselves to hit the open road.

I suppose some families sang songs during road trips or played a few rounds of "I Spy" to pass the time on long journeys. Not us. When Craig and I were little kids, we'd half-listen to our father's tales about his early days as a firefighter before we were born. We'd hope our mother could successfully steer the conversation in another direction, in vain.

Before we reached the interstate border, before we stopped for gas, before we pulled out of the driveway, before he even turned the keys in the ignition, Dad would flash his semi-smirk and begin. He often began right in the middle, as if he were simply picking up where he'd left off minutes ago.

"Yeah, that Oscar was something. When he stormed in and slammed the door we all suspected he'd probably had a fight with his wife and that it would be a long shift . . . "

In the spirit of vacation Mom would sometimes temper my father's stories. "God willed Daddy to have an Oscar in his life. After all, if he couldn't handle an Oscar how could have he have dealt with a career in the fire department?"

She was trying to teach my brother and me that God has a purpose for every "dirtbag" on the planet. I knew that if Dad didn't like someone, he must have had a good reason. He rarely used the word hate. And although at times he said that he hated Oscar, he didn't. He just hated injustice. All of Dad's stories incorporated a theme of good versus evil, the underdog facing insurmountable odds. My father taught me the meaning of the very word *underdog*.

"I always root for the underdog," Dad often said. Barely out of kindergarten and just learning to read, I must have looked perplexed. "It's like in a horse race," he continued. "If I were a gambling man and the odds were fifty to one, I'd pick the horse least likely to win. The underdog struggles more than anyone else and deserves recognition. There are a lot of people out there like that; they start out with nothing and you've got to root for them. They are always fighting against the powers that be just to survive, and when they succeed they deserve to be rewarded and respected. They persevere and they make it. It's all a matter of believing in yourself: that no matter what obstacles stand in your way, and no matter what people say, you will come out ahead." Then, invariably, he would muse, "Well, I don't look back, I never look back." But he was always looking back.

One of his stories' main characters was a man whom I'll call Lieutenant Oscar Krause. Dad described Krause as being a stocky man, "in good shape," with piercing eyes and a mean expression. "He had that rough blue-collar look."

Krause hailed from all-white Hampden, a neighborhood which, back then, was thought to be strongly racist. He would storm into the station, swagger past Dad and jeer, "How you doin,' Bunky?"

"As the shift officer, Oscar was the boss, period. You didn't talk back to him."

The union had little voice to protect a member. Firefighters had to adhere to strict regulations. The fire department was a semi-military outfit governed by the Book of Rules, the only reading material Krause allowed the men to read during watch desk duty. It was a miniature three-ring loose-leaf notebook; strangely, the title didn't appear anywhere on the black jacket. The Book of Rules stated: "No skylarking in the fire department." Out of the corner of his mouth, Dad said, "I thought I would try not to do any skylarking—if I knew what it was."

At change of shift, the men all had to line up in a row and stand at attention, each clutching a copy of the Book of Rules, their hose straps, their spanners (adjustable wrenches) and their door keys. Krause would sound off these four items and throw a salute. "Hose strap, keys, spanners, Book of Rules." The men would counter with another salute

Dad glanced at my brother and me in the back seat to check if we were paying attention and said, "We better have the hose spanner and strap in the pocket of our turnout coats and the Book of Rules in our lockers, or else. Krause would examine our keys and ask which one was the fire department key. Sometimes he'd make one of us try it in the lock." If the chosen key didn't fit, the firefighter would be reprimanded.

"When we weren't fighting fires, bunk use was strictly prohibited until nine at night. Since we could not lie on the bunks, men would lie under them, or in the locker room on the floor, or the bench. If he saw anybody resting, Krause would bark, 'I've got something for you to do.'"

Household duties were to be completed daily without exception. They included shining brass poles, washing windows, cleaning and polishing floors, scrubbing the walls and kitchen, and maintaining the grounds.

"Krause made us walk through the high-crime areas on our own to make sure the hydrants were intact. This was tough work, particularly in bad weather. We'd be trudging through two feet of snow in subzero temperatures with the wind blowing forty miles an hour. Heck, I was only making a dollar fifty an hour."

Dad thought the procedure was unjust and dangerous, because sending someone out on a hydrant inspection left the station one man short. Eventually, as at other houses, weather permitting, the men had hydrant inspection at times when everybody could go out on the engine together. "Why didn't you tell Krause to do it himself?" I asked as I untwisted the wrapper from the mint my mother gave me to ease my car sickness.

Dad spouted, "Somebody's got to put food on the table."

Craig could create voices like Mel Blanc, the vocal genius behind the Warner Bros. Looney Tunes, and he was as hilarious as my father. He flapped our stuffed penguin Pee-Wee's fins and made him dance. Then he bopped me over the head with Lit Boo the teddy bear and gibbered, "Whaddya tink money grows on trees or somedin?"

I laughed and punched my brother in the arm. Then he shoved Pee-Wee in my mouth. I whacked him in the chest with my doll Fran until my father told us to knock it off.

"He started it."

"No I didn't."

"I don't care who started it, end it now. When you get older, you'll know life's not about fun and games. Okay? You have to work. I go down there and do what I have to. I don't always like what I do, but I do it."

My brother rolled his eyes and folded his bottom lip in his mouth to look like he had buckteeth—a secret code for, "Oh no, here we go again."

Mom always said, "Your father doesn't put periods in his sentences." At times, one of us would start a well-known Dad-story which he would then finish. Sometimes we were bombarded by a rapid succession of vignettes. At other times, they were dealt to us randomly like cards from a deck.

"You kids laugh, but do you think I enjoy dealing with this stuff day after day?" And soon he was smiling again, spilling story after story.

What my father disliked most about Krause was how he, as well as a few of the other white firefighters, treated their black comrades.

Although the Baltimore City Fire Department was founded in 1859, it would be nearly 100 years, after long battles fought by organizations such as the National Association for the Advancement of Colored People, the Urban League and Baltimore's *Afro-American* newspaper, before black men could join the fire service. It would be decades more before they would receive equal compensation and opportunities. Institutionalized racism could still be felt in the attitudes and actions of men like Krause.

Dad told us that, despite being excluded, many black men voluntarily combated blazes and worked on the fire grounds, risking their lives in order to protect people and property. The SHC Fire Buffs Club, founded by Arthur "Smokestack" Hardy in 1949, was America's first black firefighters' club. Named after James M. Smith, Hardy and Elbert C. Carter, the SHC Club helped to dismantle segregation in the Baltimore City Fire Department. The Arthur "Smokestack" Hardy Fire Museum, a collection of black firefighters' memorabilia, included among its artifacts a faded blue playbill from a minstrel show held by the Baltimore City Fire Department in the 1940s.

In the early 1950s, not enough white men were passing the examination to join the fire service and the International Underwriters' Association threatened to increase Baltimore's insurance rates if the city did not recruit more firefighters. In 1953, Mayor Thomas J. D'Alesandro, under the pressure of civil rights organizations, gave black men the opportunity to take the test. Forty-one out of 150 African-Americans passed the test. Out of hundreds of men, black and white, Charles L. Scott, a black man, received the highest score. The first black men were appointed as firefighters in the same year. Members of the SHC Club regularly visited the firehouse. Guy Cephas, a clever and passionate black man, had voluntarily battled some of the same blazes as Dad. It was he who later established a museum in honor of Arthur Smokestack Hardy.

"Smokestack Hardy was a congenial guy who hung out at E-13. He was always supportive of the firefighters. His hairline receded to the middle of his head, so he painted black shoe polish across the front of his scalp to make it look like hair. There was a rumor that he also had a shoe polish moustache.

On a hot day the polish would drip down his forehead. He resembled a black Chef Boy-Ar-Dee." My father laughed his signature laugh, a hearty "uh hee, hee, hee," ending with a loud exhale and an, "Oh, man, that was funny."

"Oh, Mom that reminds me, did you pack the Spaghettios?"

"Yes, but you're not eating junk every day. If I've got to freeze on a broken cot for five nights, we're at least going out to a few decent restaurants." Mom hated camping and despised washing in a public shower. She went along anyway because my father, brother and I loved it. Dad would sing tunes by the Carpenters or the Everly Brothers while he cooked meals on the portable stove. Meanwhile, she would be shivering in the woods wishing she was in a hotel. "Watch the speed limit, Bill, we're not in the fire truck."

Dad eased up on the accelerator and sang along with a few bars of "Johnny B. Goode" playing on the car radio. Then he continued Smokestack's story.

At the age of three, Smokestack witnessed the Great Baltimore Fire of 1904. It blazed for forty-eight hours and required the assistance of twenty-four local and interstate fire departments. More than 140 acres, 15,000 buildings and almost 3,000 businesses were lost, resulting in millions of dollars in damages. While the fire caused only one death, 35,000 people were left without jobs. Within two years, however, Baltimore had come back to life. People had worked frantically to rebuild the city.

The Great Baltimore Fire kindled Smokestack's passion for firefighting. As a child, he began following horse-drawn fire wagons. And although he wanted nothing more than to join the fire department, this was forbidden. It wasn't until 1952 that Smokestack, along with five other black men, was at last permitted to support the paid companies as a volunteer with the integrated Baltimore City Firefighter's Auxiliary. Regularly attired in a blue dress uniform, Smokestack Hardy, the photographer, historian and civil rights activist, became a legend amongst firefighters nationwide. He died in 1995 at the age of ninety-four. Today, the firehouse at 405 McMechen Street is named after him.

They could have named the school after Smokestack Hardy, but of course, because he was black, that would have been unthinkable back then. Sometimes my father dreamed that they could have named the fire school after his ancestor, John Hennick, one of the first fire Chief Engineers of Baltimore. After all, he is in a book of Baltimore's firefighting history, *Unheralded Heroes*. John Hennick was a hands-on person. He didn't just sit back in the office. A big piece of glass went through his shoulder on the fire ground, ultimately leading to his death. My father always smirked and said "My ancestor and I have a shared mentality. We even look similar. You had to be crazy; dozens of crazy people worked in that job." Dad admired John Hennick's leadership because he got in there with his men and unhesitatingly put himself in jeopardy.

Hard as I tried, I could not mentally connect historical events to my hometown and my father's occupation until I was much older. But I knew that my Daddy had helped to keep the entire city of Baltimore from becoming nothing but a pile of ashes. And, even as a child, I knew he was fighting more than fires.

When my father began his career, at the height of the Civil Rights Movement, the department was segregated. Promotions for blacks were scarce; they had finally been allowed to join the Union Local 734 only a few years prior, in 1961. Blacks were still expected to use separate toilets, showers, dishes and sinks. The last person to cover watch desk was required to make coffee. If he happened to be black, he was not permitted to use the firehouse cups to drink the coffee he himself had made. White firefighters considered those cups theirs exclusively. Whites talked among themselves, ignoring the black men. Outside the firehouse, some whites actually wouldn't allow black firefighters into their burning homes.

"You kids awake?"

After exhausting car games such as hangman and magnetic checkers, Craig and I would doze off on long trips. "Yeah," we groaned. No more than an hour into the journey, we were bored.

"Most of the black men I worked with were good firefighters, hard workers..."

He explained that there were three rotating shifts: the A Shift worked four ten-hour days in a row before having seventy-two hours off, the B Shift worked four fourteen-hour nights and was then off for forty-eight hours, and the C shift had time off. Two men out of six on his B Shift were black; they were both seasoned veterans who offered Dad their guidance and good common sense. They were instrumental in teaching him how to confront difficult circumstances. These men belonged to a black social club called the Vulcan Blazers. At the time, most blacks didn't mention that they were members of the club. Randolph Handy, who they called Randy Handy, was among the first members. Dad tapped the steering wheel with his thumbs as he spoke. "Randy was thirty-nine years old and extremely sensitive to things any white person said, so I found myself being extra careful not to offend him."

Randy didn't smile much, Dad told us. "He was reserved and hard to get close to. Yet when he laughed it was contagious. Beneath his suspicious exterior, he had a hidden treasure trove of joy."

Randy's trademark "Ho, ho, ho" signaled that he was in a good mood and approachable. If he grunted, Dad tried not to engage in long conversation. "As he began to realize I appreciated him as my co-worker, without malice or prejudice, we became friends. Randy eventually felt comfortable in my presence and shared his experience and wisdom with me. I needed that. Everything was new to me.

"People would misguide firefighters just to see our reaction. I didn't know this, but Randy did. If someone says, 'My dog is trapped in there,' your first impulse is to run into the burning building to rescue their pet. Randy told me once that he almost got killed trying to save a dog that wasn't there. After years of experience, Randy could discern whether people were telling the truth.

"Some people just liked to see the action even if they put your life in jeopardy. Others would overreact. Sometimes in the pandemonium and shock they just didn't know what was going on." Randy could identify the liars and taught my father to exercise discretion as well.

Dad glanced into the rearview mirror and continued, "Randy knew the streets. Just before approaching a pothole, he would tell me to hold onto the railing. The Macks weren't a smooth ride, and if you hit a pothole you could get thrown off. 'Bend your knees like shock absorbers,' Randy would instruct me. 'Keep your helmet on tight. If you lose it they'll put you on report.'" When the trucks were eventually fitted out with straps to hold the firefighters on, Randy would caution my father to make sure his buckle was tight so he wouldn't fall off of the back of the pumper. Dad hated those flimsy nylon straps. He felt they gave a false sense of security. The men hooked them into the overhead railing and wrapped them below their armpits.

"If you bounced off you could be dragged to death. Every once in a while that actually happened."

I knew Dad was referring to Maurice Blow and Tom Brand, the men at Engine 25 on McCullough and Gold Street who "lived for firefighting." Mo was black, Tom was white. Dad didn't know Mo well, but said, "Both of them had charisma." Tom was twenty-eight years old with a wife and three children. My father often saw him reading in the firehouse under a dim light bulb, studying to become a pump operator.

Dad had the night off when the shift began on New Year's Day 1967. Engine 25 and three others responded to a call for a fire at a corner grocery store on Druid Hill Avenue and Lafayette Street only a mile away.

Tom was riding on the back step of Engine 25 as it hustled toward smoke in the sky several blocks ahead. Excited and eager to attack the destructive blaze, he had just said to Mo, "This place looks like it's really off," when an impatient driver darted out of the line of cars being held back, crossed the intersection and broadsided them. The engine went out of control and careened off into the marble steps of a row house, throwing both men into the air. They landed facing each other. Mo watched as Tom's eyes rolled back and he knew his friend was gone. Tom had broken his neck. Both of Mo's knees were crushed as he landed.

My father had only been in the department for a short time and was devastated by Tom's death. At the funeral, Tom's wife, a frail, sickly lady almost speechless from shock, mustered up enough strength to tell Dad that Tom had been a good family man, working hard to take care of her three children and herself. Their future, without her beloved husband, was uncertain. The errant driver was not injured and was exonerated in a court of law.

Randy didn't want to lose Bill. Randy even expressed other rather personal concerns for Bill's happiness. "And one time Randy even gave me a gift," Dad reflected.

At this point in the narrative, my father and mother always blushed, though the drive along the Jersey turnpike wasn't exactly romantic. I knew what was next. Whenever he told this part of the story, Eunice would soften and giggle with him.

As a private man who adhered to a strict moral code, my father would not openly discuss the topic of sex with his comrades, much less his children. He always carried himself with dignity and displayed the mild manners of a gentleman. He softly extolled my mother's beauty when he reminisced about how attractive she was when they met, but he never spoke suggestively of women. He didn't use profanity in the house or on the job; even his friends knew that such reticence was part of his nature. He considered the use of obscenities disrespectful to God. Even if he relayed stories in which a partner cursed, he would spell the words or disclose clues as to what expletive had been used.

"Randy bought me a book, *The Joy of Sex*, and to me that was like pornography. He knew I didn't know enough about the birds and the bees. Randy was married and figured it would be beneficial. When I unwrapped it, I guess he saw the awkwardness on my face. I was in the fire department two years before I married, and was living with my parents. I couldn't take a book like that to my parents' home. Randy grew serious. 'You need to read this now, Bill. You're getting married soon. You've got to have some knowledge about these things.'

"He shook his finger at me. 'I'm telling you, you better read this. Take it from a married man.'"

With his distrust of "whitey," it was unusual for Randy to give a white man a gift of any kind.

Segregation was the rule when my father was a kid, but race was not discussed in his home. His parents never interfered with his choice of friends; color was not a barrier. In his school years, his best friend was a shy black boy called Henry. Later, at Bible College, one of his a good friends was John, formerly a conductor for the Union Pacific Railway. The two of them had lots of laughs together. During his stint in the military, Dad cultivated many friendships with African-Americans. "In the Army, we were all in the same boat," Dad said.

He popped a piece of sugar-free bubble gum into his mouth and discarded the wrapper in the ashtray as he continued his reflections.

"At the firehouse I found it confusing that my black comrades had to use their own toilet stall, sink and cups. They could not read the newspapers that came to the firehouse until the white men had had their turn, and there were separate white and black bunks. These procedures were not discussed, just accepted. They were as senseless to me then as they are now, because, to me, we were family—we ate, worked and basically lived together. We worked in a stressful occupation requiring 100 percent cooperation in dangerous situations." Dad blew a bubble, then cracked it between his teeth.

"Thankfully, the passage of time eroded these unfair practices. But it was and maybe still is unusual for white firefighters to work in the predominantly black neighborhoods. Back then, you had to go where you were assigned. White firefighters were sent down there, but not many.

"It made me furious that the guy good enough to watch my back wasn't good enough to use the same toilet. According to some people, if you used a black man's cup it was like you were going to get a disease. I sometimes used Randy's cup. It didn't bother me, but I think it bothered him."

One time Dad was detailed at Engine 7 on Eutaw Street at Druid Hill Avenue, a mostly black section of town.

"A guy was drinking coffee from one of the station mugs and one of the white men on duty whispered 'You know that cup you're drinking from belonged to that nig—.'

"The guy slammed the cup down on the table, 'Why didn't you tell me?' His face turned red, and he started spitting all over the place, cursing and wiping his mouth. Most of the men just stood back watching his reaction and laughing. I ignored it because I felt like I didn't have any authority.

"I know Randy and the other men resented how they were treated, but most of them didn't want to make waves. Randy was something of an exception. An officer might say to Randy, 'You're doing a good job, boy.'

"'Don't call me boy,' he'd snap. 'I'm a man. Call me a man.'

"I didn't understand it, the racism. It was childish. I guess the men put up with it because they had a steady job, and maybe they thought, 'Why rock the boat?' Still, many of us resented it and could feel the presence of an underlying tension."

Dad blew another bubble and it deflated on his lips. He licked it off and resumed chewing.

We pulled up beside a toll booth. Craig and I argued over who would get to drop the change in the basket.

"You can take turns," Dad said. "There are enough toll booths on this turnpike to leave me broke. Don't drop the coins on the ground, Craig," he warned, as my brother climbed over my father's lap and leaned outside the window.

"I know, Dad, twenty cents is your pay for the week," Craig retorted.

"That's right," Dad cackled. "Drop it and I'll have to search under the car and we might cause a ten-mile backup."

After settling back in our seats, Dad picked up right where he left off. "We always had to be on guard. Lieutenant Krause baited Randy purely to nail him because he was black. I saw it happen. Randy would be watching TV all by himself, and Krause would burst in, change the station, sit down, cross his arms and then watch his program, usually a hunting or fishing program. Nothing would be said. Krause was the officer. Randy would bite his lip. Many other instances of Krause's racism occurred, not only with Randy but with other black firefighters at E-52.

"These days Krause would possibly have lost his job over them. Not then."

"What goes around comes around," we chanted in unison. The large pink bubble of gum exploded.

"Bill, can we have a normal conversation for once? And can you please stop chewing that gum like a goat? Kids, how was your last day of school?"

Our beat-up VW van didn't have air conditioning, and even my mother, who was always cold, even in the height of summer, couldn't take the heat on that particular journey. She rolled the window partway down. She pulled a pamphlet from under the flap of the Bible on her lap and fanned herself with it. "I can't breathe. It's like a furnace in here."

Craig tugged his shirt collar.

"Yeah, Dad. How much longer?" I moaned.

Dad "replied" just as we expected.

"I didn't know how to make coffee. Whoever manned the watch desk at 4:00 a.m. for two hours had to put coffee on at six. I had just finished my watch desk shift and figured that making coffee couldn't be too hard. I filled the basket to its brim with the coffee grounds, put it on the stove and let it percolate for twenty-five minutes. When Krause sauntered over to the pot that stuff was ripe, like poison. He poured a cup, took a swig and his eyes bugged out of his head. I'm embarrassed to repeat what he said so you can figure it out. 'Who made this G-D, F-in', S-H-I-T?' Randy and the other men had to fight hard to hold back their laughter.

"On another day I'd just put polish on the brass pole and, as I prepared to buff it off with a clean cloth, Krause slid down the pole. When he landed he stood there with his arms outstretched, black tarnish all over his hands, shirt, pants legs, ankles and crotch. 'G-D, look at this F-in' uniform! Who's the G-D, S-O-B that put that F-in', S-H-I-T on the pole? I got this all over my G-D, F-in' uniform! Answer me! Who put polish on the pole? I'm going to get that no-good S-O-B . . . ' I was going to thank him for wiping the polish off of the pole, but I figured the timing wasn't right."

My father would laugh so hard when he told this story that he would abandon his habitual tight-lipped semi-smirk and show his teeth.

"Bill, can we change the subject? You've talked about Krause for two-and-a-half hours." My mother sighed and wound the window all the way down.

"What's the matter, Eunice?" Dad was oblivious.

"Nothing, Bill. I'm going to escape. I'm merely trying to decide if I can jump out of the window or if it's better to open the door and just roll."

"Yeah, Dad." My brother was getting more and more restless. "Who cares about Krause the louse?"

"I have to go to the bathroom." I was the one with the weak bladder. Then, "Can we have ice cream Daddy, pleeeeeese?"

I loved when he took us to the dairy on the way to Pine Haven. It featured homemade ice cream with real bits of bubble gum in it. We'd stop in, grab an ice cream, and then he would make my brother and me sit on the outdoor cow sculpture so he could snap our photo. He took our picture there every year until we were over ten years old and bigger than the cow. We'd get back in the car, and Dad would resume his story.

"By chance, one of the other black firefighters Krause had forced out of E-52 wound up working with Krause again when Krause was made Captain and was put on Truck 10. Krause had complete control at E-52, but he didn't have the same authority at Truck 10. It must have been a promotion, but there were more black people at Truck 10. Krause couldn't have liked that.

"One time, after a fire at an old, vacant three-story row house, Krause helped himself to an ornate mantelpiece. A black guy was driving the engine when he took it. The theft was reported, only because it was Krause; otherwise they wouldn't have bothered. Krause was transferred out of Truck 10, had some of his vacation days taken away and was severely reprimanded. That's a case of—"

"What goes around comes around," Craig and I intoned.

The sight of pine trees along the street and the nearing scent of the ocean began to revive all four of us.

Smiling, Dad continued, "We were required to conduct Rat Patrol where they'd look out for people triggering false alarms. They'd send one of the men in an old red car to park near the fireboxes with the most false alarms triggered. We were supposed to call in if we saw someone pull it. Kids would throw rocks at the car. I thought, Hey, I'm a white guy sitting here at 1:00 a.m. in an old car in the worst district in Baltimore being pelted by rocks. What am I doing here?

"Firefighters painted the handles with gentian violet, you know, that purple dye that people used to use as an antiseptic, to stop people from pulling the lever. It didn't stop them. They'd just use a rag when they pulled it. Every neighborhood had a firebox. They got pulled every other day. Boxes got pulled along on Park Heights Avenue constantly. Every time we went there, crowds of people would be standing around. 'I don't know nothing' was the common response.

"One time this little kid squeezed his way through the crowd and said, 'I'm sorry.' He had stood on a bushel basket to pull the alarm. He couldn't have been any older than three. Steam was coming out of Krause's ears. We climbed back on the truck, and as we were pulling away this older kid called out to Krause 'So long, baldy,' and gave him a big goodbye wave. Krause almost lost it. He was sensitive about losing his hair. His face turned red, and he was biting his lip trying to hold his rage in. That tore me up. Randy and I were on the back step laughing our heads off. Krause was seething. Uh, hee, hee, hee, oh man, that was funny."

"Stop kicking me!" Craig shoved me.

"I wasn't kicking you."

"Yes, you were—"

"Kids, cut it out," Mom said. "We're only fifteen minutes away. I know you're both sleepy. You stayed up too late last night. Have a slug of orange juice, it'll give you a high without a low."

Craig and I refused the cola bottle she had filled with juice. By then it was warm.

"Bill, please don't talk about work any more. We're on vacation." Mom sighed and wiped the beads of perspiration from her brow.

"What happened to Krause is interesting, Eunice," Dad insisted.

"It's depressing."

"Well, when it's your time to go, it's your time to go."

"Bill, be my guest. Any time now." Mom laughed whenever she managed to slip in a zinger.

Craig and I chortled.

The sign to the entrance of Pine Haven loomed into view.

The three of us made a mad dash to the beach and left my father behind to set up the "blasted tent." This was another job he claimed to hate, but when it was completed, he would revel in his accomplishment.

We Shall Overcome

"Get your fucking ass down to E-52 immediately," Krause shouted, awakening my father at 4:00 a.m. from his Sunday morning slumber.

The night before the Baltimore Riots began, Dad was instructed, as he left the firehouse, to follow the news. "Trouble's brewing."

In the spring of 1968, President Johnson withdrew from the presidential race, and racist Governor George Wallace was winning support from southern states as a presidential candidate. Violent crime was on the rise. The "Great White Flight" to the suburbs was under way; the slumlords were getting rich buying up thousands of row houses from white homeowners anxious to sell. Most of these homes were converted into rental properties with several apartments. Well-established family-owned homes were on the decline, replaced by ill-maintained blocks of abject poverty. Segregation was evident in property ownership, education and employment.

Strong opposition to the Vietnam War, anger toward government corruption, awareness of the lack of social and economic opportunities for minorities as well as of religious intolerance, and recognition of the need for greater women's rights: all these developments signaled that it was time for change.

Then came the last straw.

On Thursday, April 4, 1968, at 6:01 p.m., the leader of the Civil Rights Movement, Reverend Martin Luther King, Jr., father of four, stood on the balcony of Room 306 at the Lorraine Motel in Memphis. He was visiting the city to support sanitation workers who had recently gone on strike. While he was speaking with members of the Southern Christian Leadership Conference, a bullet struck him in the right side of the face. He died within the hour.

The day after King's assassination, Stokely Carmichael of the Black Panther Party issued these words in Washington, DC: "We have to retaliate for the death of our leaders. The executions for those deaths will not be in the court rooms. They're going to be in the streets of the United States of

America . . . Black people know that they have to get guns."

He went on to say, "When white America killed Dr. King she opened the eyes of every black man in this country." He blamed America's leaders for failing to prosecute murderers of civil rights activists. Outraged that Governor Spiro Agnew had blamed chairman H. Rap Brown of the Student Nonviolent Coordinating Committee for causing the previous year's riots in Cambridge, Maryland, Carmichael insisted: "He ain't seen nothing . . . we'll take our troops back into Maryland . . . we'll turn that State upside down inside out."

In the weeks that followed, rebellions thundered in 140 cities across the nation. Although rioters were both black and white, the uprisings occurred primarily in urban districts with a large concentration of African-Americans.

Dad said, "For a few days, Baltimore was quiet, so I didn't tune in to the news. Your mother and I had only been married for one year, and we had had dinner with another couple in their little one-bedroom apartment in Dundalk before retiring for the evening."

Baltimore had not participated in the racially charged uprisings which had occurred the previous year, and, after King's death, it seemed that initially the city would again abstain from violence. It took nearly two days for riots to erupt in Baltimore.

Just a boy at the time of the rebellion, Paul Fairfax Evans, a black man, the author of *City Life*, said that, in the month prior to the riots, people could feel the tension in the air. Evans' church's rector, Reverend Henry J. Offer, said, "If riots come, ask the question: Who is responsible—those who have been drawn to desperation or those who drive them to desperation and violence?" Although Baltimore has been called Mobtown—ever since the war of 1812—Evans stressed that violent behavior was not part of the Baltimore inner city's fabric and that most people were quiet, hardworking and peaceful. Black Baltimoreans did not take part in the uprisings which had begun in other parts of America four years earlier. Plus, since not one outbreak occurred immediately after King's assassination, Evans had been "optimistic" that Baltimore would again remain calm. But even though people could sense that a storm was on its way, no one in Baltimore's communities, black or white, predicted or was prepared for the disaster that occurred.

In West Baltimore, on the stroke of noon on Saturday, April 6, 1968, more than 300 people, mostly black, united on Pennsylvania Avenue to honor Dr. King: to commiserate, pray and support each other. The nation's other major cities had already begun rioting on Friday evening, while in Baltimore the National Guard waited on standby, along with state police and the fire department.

It was not until dusk on Baltimore's "East Side" that glass doors and windows of storefronts along the 400 block of North Gay Street were shattered, sounding the beginning of a civil war, pitting brother against brother and forever changing the landscape of the city.

From 5:00 p.m. onward, sheer mayhem ensued—violence, arson and burglaries—as groups of youths cruised the neighborhoods in search of cash, alcohol, booze and anything they could lay their hands on. Poised to take action, police moved to cover the 400 to 700 blocks of Gay Street at 6:15 p.m.

By 6:30 p.m., two fires had erupted in the 700 block. Within the next half hour, about fifty youths ripped iron security grates from windows, broke the glass and stole goods from an appliance store in the 900 block. In the same block, just after 8:00 p.m., people robbed and burned a tailor's shop. Within the hour, the A&P grocery store and three other shops on Milton Avenue, in the east end, were devoured by fire.

Rioters closed in on another furniture store, Levinson and Klein, on Monument Street. About 1,500 police swarmed East Baltimore, but by 10:00 p.m., twelve stores were in flames. The uprising had spread to Greenmount Avenue, a major north-south street which effectively separates east Baltimore from central Baltimore, and it was advancing toward the "West Side."

White bar owners who had refused service to blacks and white shop owners who failed to employ them would soon find their livelihoods reduced to ashes. Yet, looters didn't discriminate. They were going to get the

Jews whom they accused of price gouging, they were going to show the peace activists how to win the fight to freedom and they were prepared to combat any brother who stood in their way.

They would soon ravage buildings with maniacal hysteria and the 5,500 Maryland National Guardsmen would descend upon them. Humans, black and white, would dart in every direction, like flies to raw meat. The Adjutant General of Maryland, George Gelston, ordered his men to shoot only if commanded to do so by an official, or if they spotted a sniper.

Agnew declared the obvious: Baltimore was in a state of emergency. He had already instituted a curfew from 11:00 p.m. to 6:00 a.m., in both the city and surrounding county, and threatened violators with penalties. He forbade the sale of firearms, liquor and gasoline, and rang the White House to inform President Johnson that the nearly 6,000 Maryland National Guardsmen he'd sent to scour the city's streets were not enough to stave off rioters. My father was too busy to notice the violent suppression.

As the chain of events ignited, fire would do most of the killing. The *Afro-American* and *Baltimore Sun* would report that two men, one black, one white, were found dead in a blaze at a supermarket on Chester Street.

Residents, black and white, barricaded themselves indoors and huddled in corners with their children as rioters attacked North Avenue, one of the city's largest and most traveled streets spanning the city from east to west, pillaging and burning districts in West Baltimore.

By midnight, four deaths, seventy injuries, 100 arrests and 250 fire alarms had occurred. Roughly 500 guardsmen stormed Aisquith to 25th Streets brandishing bayonets. Police cruisers were dodging snipers' potshots. Federal troops hadn't been sent to the city in nearly a century—not since the railroad strike of 1877—but now they were on their way.

Jazz vocalist Ruby Glover was singing at Buck's Bar, at the time one of the most "happening" places on Baltimore's Pennsylvania Avenue. People would travel from other states to Buck's Bar for delicious food, swinging music and good vibes. Women wearing diamonds and furs would step out of luxurious cars and head inside for an evening of fine entertainment. In a *Baltimore Sun* interview, Ms. Glover said the music was jumping and the place was packed when a sergeant burst in, saying, "It's hell outside and you all in here jamming away, and it's like walking into heaven. Well, I got to get all of you out of here safe."

Ruby said that the city outside looked like a ball of fire. "I cried all the way home, all the way home." *Baltimore Sun* reporter Carl Schoettler described the night as "aflame with years of pent-up anger and frustration."

The next day was Palm Sunday. When author Paul Fairfax Evans attended church and heard his preacher scornfully referring to "what had happened on Pennsylvania Avenue last night," Evans was stunned. At midday, thousands of parishioners exited the city churches. The churchgoers looked radiant as they strolled along the streets in the sunshine dressed in their finest attire. But shortly after their services concluded, the rioting erupted again, this time with renewed vengeance.

When Evans saw the storefronts surrounded by shards of glass with armed National Guard soldiers standing in front, rifles at the ready, he was overcome with grief. He called out, "This is stupid!" to a soldier who just looked straight ahead and made no response.

Firefighters were on their own, without the protection of the local police, who, by this time, were stretched thin. In those days, all of the pumpers had open cabs, and the firefighters became moving targets. The rioters hurled bricks, bottles, stones, sticks and garbage at the men fighting the fires. They were even fired upon.

"Fortunately, they missed me," my father commented.

Rioters wanted to prevent the water from getting to the fires. Hose lines were sabotaged, hydrants were disabled and human waves blocked streets to prevent access. One lieutenant stood at the plug with a pistol threatening anyone who attempted to interrupt the water flow.

My father has often said in jest, "I hate to admit it, but I love chaos." He'd punctuate the statement by pointing his finger in the air as if it were an exclamation point. It must be true, because he couldn't have entered the

Baltimore City Fire Department at a more tumultuous time.

Every single piece of apparatus was in use. Dad recalled, "As I arrived at the station, a fifty-year-old 1918 Bulldog Mack came sputtering up the hill toward me. It spat and popped. With hard rubber tires and wooden-spoked wheels, that primitive vehicle had probably been rolled out of the museum. A steel chain stretched from the engine to the rear wheels like a bicycle chain. Behind the driver's wheel sat Pump Operator Will Eibner wearing goggles. It was like the circus had come to town.

It stopped. "Eibner climbed out of the Mack and swiftly repaired a leak in the booster tank. He found a stick on the ground and hammered it in the hole like a piece of cork, then quickly refilled the tank with water from a nearby hydrant."

E-52 was mobbed by hundreds of rioters as the firemen slowly maneuvered down a large thoroughfare. Driver-pump operator Smitty feared for his life. Krause reached over with his left foot and stepped on Smitty's foot, pressing the accelerator. The human wave scattered in all directions, shouting obscenities and giving the firefighters the finger.

Crowds of onlookers threatened, chanted and waved their fists while the men feverishly worked to bring blazes under control. According to Dad, the scene took on a surreal atmosphere. A white couple was trying to get through the mobs in their car when the driver crashed into a police car. His wife was killed. Folk plundered their neighborhood merchants. Grocery, appliance and liquor stores were hot targets for burning and looting. As soon as firefighters vacated the gutted buildings, rioters moved in to appropriate anything usable. Many honest residents became thieves and stole any merchandise they could carry.

The fires increased in number, exhausting equipment and manpower. Most of them were attributed to Molotov cocktails, quart bottles filled with inflammable liquid with rags stuffed into the openings as wicks. Amateur arsonists would light the rags and hurl the homemade bombs into a neighbor's property. Within moments, stores became raging hells, destroying the livelihoods of heartbroken merchants. While the shopkeepers' businesses were destroyed, Bill's "business" flourished as the firefighters extinguished blaze after blaze throughout his district.

"In the midst of this chaos and confusion," Dad recounted, "I observed a small boy struggling to push an overloaded shopping cart filled with items salvaged from the rubble. All around us were people screaming and running in all directions. Fires were breaking out everywhere. He was trying with all his might to push the cart over the fire lines coiled like snakes all over the street. One of the items, a saucepan, fell to the ground behind him."

Feeling my father's presence, he turned around slowly and saw Dad standing there watching him. "Dressed in my helmet, turnout coat and boots, I must have looked like a giant and scared him half to death."

The boy began to tremble. My father bent down, picked up the saucepan and gently placed it back on top of the heap in the cart. Over the din of sirens, shouting and shattering glass, Dad said, "Here you go, kiddo. Don't want to lose that."

"Thank you, mista!" The surprised child smiled with gratitude and hurried off. My father watched him make his way up the street and disappear in the smoke.

On that Sunday, April 7, 1968, at Andrews Air Force Base (near the nation's capitol), 1,900 soldiers from the 18th Corp Airborne Artillery— some of whom were black—were loaded onto buses and sent to Druid Hill Park to put an end to what Governor Agnew declared an "insurrection."

The arrests were so numerous that police were using school buses to transport suspects and offenders. On behalf of the feds, Lieutenant General Robert H. York took over command of the Maryland State Guardsmen as well. The united forces, totaling 10,848, stampeded the streets of Baltimore.

In just over two days, citizens had called in nearly 600 reports to authorities; over fifty police and firefighters were wounded. Their beleaguered forces were bone-tired from the constant onslaught of new fire calls. Just when all seemed hopeless, my father fixed his tired eyes on a column of military vehicles looming in the distance.

"Yes! It was not a mirage, " Dad exclaimed. "The cavalry was coming to the rescue."

The men had valiantly fought fire after fire without protection. Dad was amazed by the length of the National Guard convoy comprising jeeps, trucks and troop carriers flying small American flags.

"Patriotism, honor and memories of mom's apple pie welled inside me as the procession wended its way past the doorway of E-52 toward Druid Hill Park."

The combined forces set up a tent city on the park's vast expanse of grassy knolls. The soldiers accompanied the firefighters in their jeeps and trucks as they fought the blazes. The firefighting was fast, furious and continuous, but the National Guard made the firefighters feel secure. Troops surrounded the entire area, setting up checkpoints to inspect cars for incendiary devices such as Molotov cocktails and flares. Dad said, "Some rioters masqueraded in military uniforms in order to sneak past and accomplish their devilish missions." Now and then spectators burst into a chorus of "We shall overcome." Packs of rioters continued to swell in size and fury.

At noon, a furniture warehouse on Guilford Avenue, another important north-south street, was consumed by flames. Later that afternoon, on North Avenue, a fire erupted in the 900 block, damaging four buildings. Four blocks of Harford Road (also a major north-south thoroughfare) were repeatedly ignited. Plumes of smoke steamed from East Side to West. Around 3:00 p.m. on Palm Sunday, the militia unleashed tear gas upon a group of people on Gay Street who were surrounding the American Brewery Building.

From the front steps of his house, Evans witnessed bedlam in the ensuing hours, as the police and fire department became increasingly overloaded and civil authority disintegrated. Evans spotted a beat-up car with District of Columbia tags which he described as "containing some of the most gruesome, gutter-looking people I had ever seen in my life." Like him, they were black. Leering out of the window of a car which was stuffed with as many people as it could hold, they hollered out to the neighbors,

"The next time we come back, we gonna burn all y'all niggers out." The struggle had become black against black. Evans said that at that moment he was devastated, "because I knew for the first time ever we were not in control of our neighborhood."

Somewhat ironically, West Baltimore, not the East Side where the riots began, saw the most prevalent and destructive rioting. Here, my father put out so many storefront fires that he could no longer distinguish one shop from the other. Three blocks of shops on Pennsylvania Avenue, mostly liquor stores, were pillaged, and shops nearby burst into flames.

With soldiers just outside his door, gunfire sounding throughout the streets, guardsmen shining their lights through the windows of three-story houses in search of snipers, fires erupting all over the city and a 4:00 p.m. curfew imposed by Agnew, Evans and his family were trapped indoors for days. As he watched the looters, he thought of when the French brought down the Bastille. Black fabric, including rags, scarves and even panties, hung from the doors and windows of row homes signaling to vandals and thieves that the homeowners were black and were therefore to be overlooked.

Rioting and looting were not confined to any one age group. One shoplifter, a fifty-five year old mother of six, confessed, when caught, that she had already finished her grocery shopping and hadn't even needed the items she stole. When asked why she took them, all she could say was, "I don't know. I don't know." People young, old, male and female joined in the looting. Different people stole for different reasons: some truly out of anger, while others were committing premeditated, semi-organized crimes. Many were simply caught up in the frenzy. To my father, the rioter's color was of no relevance. Then as now, he judged behavior strictly on the basis of good or bad.

Single-engine companies fought huge fires unaided. On that harrowing evening, after struggling to get past hoards of people blocking Gwynns Falls Parkway, E-52 pulled up to an oil storage depot on the other side of the railroad tracks, a mile away from my father's station. He saw a river of fire rolling toward houses and parked cars. "It was burning like crazy," he said. "All this oil was running down the hill." Apparently, some of the rioters had opened up all the valves on several tanks that stood on up on wooden platforms. The firefighters had to shut off the spigots. "I don't know how we did it, but somehow we got the situation under control."

On Monday morning, rainfall caused many youths to abandon the streets. Drivers from dairies made their deliveries, but did so later, since the curfew forbade them from starting to work until 6:00 a.m. Taxis and buses that did not have shattered windows were back in service. The turmoil, however, did not stop.

On Federal and Holbrook Streets, a warehouse burst into flames. The militia released tear gas on a crowd of several hundred looters carrying goods pouring out of a North Avenue supermarket at around 11:30 a.m. A fire broke out on Fulton Avenue. Just a few blocks away, on Baker Street, hundreds of youths threw stones and bricks at cars. People removed grids from the fronts of pawn shops, liquor stores and supermarkets. On Presstman Street and Fulton Avenue, police caught three out of a gang of ten looters. Some of them were children as young as six. Ten stores were ransacked on Whitelock Street.

Guardsmen blockaded the police station in the West Side where alleged looters and curfew violators waited to be tried.

All the firefighters were exhausted. Lack of sleep and regular meals had taken their toll, but they met the challenge. In the midst of this nightmare, a glimmer of King's dream was manifested in the benevolence of the neighborhood residents. A large group of African-American women who lived across from Engine 13 / Ambulance 4 on McCullough Street where Dad had been detailed marched into the firehouse and took over the kitchen. In alternate shifts, the women supplied the food, did the cooking, served the meals, washed and dried the dishes. After several days, they returned to their homes. The firefighters, overwhelmed by these women's generosity, expressed their appreciation by giving them greeting cards with money enclosed. The women were very grateful but insisted that it had been their privilege to care for the firemen under these trying circumstances. They presented the men with a thank-you note signed by each one of them.

In the days that followed the initial outbreak, most city drugstores closed, and the ones that remained open shut down before night. People requiring medications had to visit area hospitals. Most people who had been driven out by fires and bombs stayed with friends; a few went to local shelters. Community action agency centers collected food and other items. People needed milk, bread and baby formula, but goods were scarce. Grocery stores in districts affected by the uprising closed their doors, some indefinitely. North Avenue, normally a hub of activity, seemed to have been hit hardest by looters.

In the four days of rioting, more than 5,000 arrests, 2,000 lootings, 3,000 injuries and 1,200 fires occurred. In Baltimore, including another black man who was found dead in a building destroyed by fire, there were six fatalities. Many small businesses were burned to the ground and would never be rebuilt, leaving their owners devastated and without income. Roughly 1,000 buildings were affected resulting in $10 million in property damage.

Across the nation, riots had erupted in more than a hundred cities and thirty-nine people were killed.

Early in his career, Governor Agnew had supported moderate civil rights measures, but later he changed his stance. At the time of the riots he had been in office for two years. After the uprisings, he arranged a meeting in his office with local black leaders. When he referred to militant leaders as "the circuit riding, Hanoi visiting, caterwauling, riot inciting, burn America down type," many of the local leaders walked out. As the word spread, people criticized Agnew for abandoning the black community that had initially championed him. Ironically, later that year, Agnew became Vice President of the United States, only to resign during his second term when he was found guilty of tax evasion and accepting bribes while governor of Maryland.

When the upwardly mobile blacks, church members and civic leaders moved out of Baltimore City, the city's deterioration accelerated. The scarcity of black professionals and businessmen in the cities further weakened the black community and contributed to the social isolation experienced by Baltimore's disproportionate number of black people living at the poverty level. Evans said that, although numerous black children of the 1960s absorbed information about their rights, many did not learn about their responsibilities. After the riots, weapons sales increased.

What President Lyndon Johnson said, in response to the riots which occurred in Detroit only nine months prior to Dr. Martin Luther King's assassination, could clearly be applied to Baltimore: "The only genuine long-range solution for what has happened lies in an attack—mounted at every level—upon the conditions that breed despair and violence. All of us know what those conditions are: ignorance, discrimination, slums, poverty, disease, not enough jobs. We should attack these conditions—not because we are frightened by conflict, but because we are fired by conscience. We should attack them because there is simply no other way to achieve a decent and orderly society in America."

Baltimore, its center burned, stood as a terrible example of those conditions. My father bore witness to them. His was one of the lives that changed irrevocably as a result.

What's Going On

"This was to be the epitome of my career in the fire department, the crowning achievement, the fulfillment of my innermost desire to project my whole self into my occupation. The day had finally arrived when I was promoted from firefighter to paramedic," my father often boasted. There may have been a hint of sarcasm in his voice. But we know he meant those words. That fateful day in 1971 when Bill Hennick became a ghetto medic, as he proudly called himself, was one of the greatest days of his life. He sometimes added that it was a pinnacle mostly because his career went downhill from there. For the first five years or so, Dad was content to be a firefighter. He enjoyed the unpredictability, the danger, the camaraderie. As time passed, however, he became aware that people in the community were living in Third World conditions. He felt the need to become involved in alleviating human suffering.

While working at E-52, Dad had sometimes been detailed to be an ambulance man or "first responder." Whenever he drove to the fire station and passed a street boundary on the West Side, Dad saw a wasteland. The largely black area, the so-called ghetto, stood in direct contrast to the way of life Dad knew. He was raised around European-American, blue- and white-collar families who were assured that their dreams and goals could be realized through hard work and perseverance. The West Side did have hardworking residents, to be sure, but it was populated in overwhelming numbers by impoverished people and welfare recipients. The music, food, language and everyday life in the area were totally foreign to my dad, and if he were going to serve the people, he would need to adjust.

Criminals, prostitutes, mentally disturbed individuals and the occasional bohemian in search of an "alternative lifestyle" wandered Baltimore's beleaguered streets at night wearing their invisible armor, as they had to—that is, if they did not own a bulletproof vest or pack a handgun. They had to be looking to their left and right with a gangster's gaze, refraining from making eye contact in the dark. My dad imagined that even the birds seemed to be haunted with a spirit of doom, scavenging the city, their wings tattered, their "song" sounding more like curses than chirps. Nobody seemed to have the same last name, Dad reflected. Many single women were raising several children, and the men in the houses were often referred to as "uncles." The same mother might have five children with five different last names. The fathers were not held accountable. Children became street-savvy at an early age. Many ran around in packs at all hours of the day and night when they were as young as eight or nine. Some of the children trod barefoot over the broken glass in the street, even in the winter. Some of the mothers appeared drunk or stoned. My father would ask them why their children didn't listen, why they just did whatever they pleased.

"What can I do with my boy? He just leaves," was a weary refrain. According to my father, many of the parents tried to steer their children in the right direction, but the kids too often just got sucked into the environment. Countless residents of the area could not read or write. Patients whom my dad was assigned to help had the right to refuse service or procedures. When forms were required to be signed by patients who could not sign their own names, my father would point to the line on the paper for their signature. The person would write an "X," which would then be witnessed by someone who was literate.

Ghetto dwellers spent tremendous amounts on lotteries and other quick-money schemes, whether trying to win a better life or simply to have fun and keep hope alive, but, as Dad would say, "Spending their money this way left them stagnated in a useless existence." Because they were vulnerable and poor, they were easily exploited. Corner grocery stores often sold their black customers inferior and outdated food, including tainted meat. Car insurance was sky-high and usually provided coverage on a day-to-day basis. TVs, radios, stereos and furniture were rented out monthly at exorbitant rates.

Although Baltimore City was my father's mission field, Prairie Bible School could never have prepared him for a career as a ghetto medic. In fact, nothing but his own eagerness to serve prepared him.

In the 1960s, ambulance men were given nothing but first-aid training. The term "swoop and scoop" was used in reference to the way they worked. The first responders swooped in to apply basic first aid, then simply scooped the victim up, placed him or her on a litter and rushed to the nearest hospital. All firefighters were required to fill in if an ambulance man was absent, and most of them did so grudgingly. "They considered details to the medic unit worse than a trip to a bad dentist." But Dad loved it.

The early 1970s marked the beginning of a new era. Ambulance men were given state-of-the-art information and equipment and were referred to as Emergency Medical Technicians (EMTs) or Cardiac Rescue Technicians (CRTs). After completing an intensive training course, they were assigned the title of paramedic. Eyes gleaming, Dad said, "Nothing equaled the satisfaction I felt in being the initial caregiver on the scene, providing comfort and lifesaving technology to the victims of disease and trauma. I relished calling the shots, stabilizing the patients, delivering them to the closest hospital. Euphoria went with the accomplishment of a job well done. I had the best of both worlds, in that I went out on both fire and medic calls.

"Departmental regulations had to be adhered to, but I alone was responsible for my actions. As a firefighter you're with a group. As a medic you're on your own. The ghetto was my workplace, and I felt comfortable in its confines."

When the opportunity arose to become a paramedic, my father didn't hesitate to seize it.

Medical specialists volunteered without pay to instruct the trainees who, for the first time, were taught at hospitals. My father had the privilege of being instructed by Dr. R. Adams Cowley, a world-famous pioneer in the burgeoning field of emergency medicine, who presided over the Shock Trauma Unit at University Hospital in Baltimore, Maryland. The unit was later named after him. In-class show-and-tell might include the placenta from a recent baby delivery or a bucket of human hearts. The "telling" would be done in medical language explaining the causes and effects of heart disease. Dad was allowed to observe cardiac surgeries. He also trained for several days at the Spring Grove Hospital to learn how to work with mentally ill patients.

Fully prepared to deliver emergency care to the sick and injured, Dad became an Emergency Medical Technician in 1971 and moved on to the rank of Cardiac Rescue Technician a short time later. At that time, only fourteen ambulances serviced the entire city of Baltimore with its population of over 900,000 people. My father was assigned to an ambulance in the same area that had been his home during several of his years in the fire service.

As a medic, my father received a slight increase in pay from the fire department, "Maybe $500 a year," he estimates. Unlike firefighters, however, paramedics were locked into the same rank with little chance of promotion. To Dad, the money didn't mean much. One of Dad's all time favorite one-liners, which he delivers with one index finger raised to reinforce the point, is "Medic 4 was a place for men who wanted to start at the bottom and stay there."

The ambulance known as Medic 4 was located in a modern one-story firehouse, Engine 13, which also contained a ladder truck and a fire engine. Nearly a dozen firefighters, a battalion chief and the chief's driver worked out of the same premises. While E-52 was on the fringe of the ghetto, Medic 4 was in West Baltimore, deep in the slums.

With his head held high, Dad recalled: "When I transferred there my fellow workers at the firehouse bade me a fond farewell with a flurry of congratulatory remarks such as, 'You'll be sorry,' 'I thought you were smarter than that,' and 'Now, I know you're crazy.' I ignored the jeers and taunts. I walked out of the door of old E-52 for the last time and took my prestigious position as a paramedic on Baltimore City Medic 4."

Bridge Over Troubled Water

It was his first day on Medic 4. My father was "cruising through the 'hood" in the passenger seat with his first partner, Larry Burch, who lived in the district which the ambulance covered. Larry was a large black man with a mischievous grin, a crooked Afro and a passion for the harmonica. He sang in the fire department glee club. He would play the harmonica and sing love songs popularized by Otis Redding, Lou Rawls and Ray Charles while driving the ambulance. That day he was singing in a suave, booming voice.

"I'll let no one nobody, nothing, nothing separate us, Honey, when this whole world comes to an end, I'll be standing there holding your trembling hand and I won't let nothing, no, no, separate us, nothing in the world . . ."

Although Dad had worked as a firefighter on E-52 on the north end of the district, at Woodbrook and Liberty Heights, near Mondawmin Mall, he hadn't driven the truck much and wasn't familiar with the streets. Medics didn't have time to fuss with maps. Larry suggested that Dad come down into the area when he was off-duty to study the street locations. "Ain't no way" was Dad's response. He was convinced that any white man coming into that area with civilian clothes on would be mistaken as a bill collector and would disappear, never to be heard from again.

Larry knew the district. Dad learned to trust that, with Larry at his side, no one would mess with him. Larry was an amateur boxer with powerful arms. He knew ghetto psychology, how to read people, and had a sixth sense which could not be learned from books—invaluable in tough situations. So there was my skinny white father, dressed in his uniform, entrusting Larry with his life. When Larry finished the tune he turned and fixed Dad with a stare. "Where's the 1800 block of School Street?" his bass voice boomed. Larry returned his eyes to the road and began snapping his fingers, impatiently demanding an answer.

Dad squinted in concentration like a contestant on "Jeopardy."

"I don't know."

"Most people don't. It's a tiny block buried just below North Avenue. That's all right. You got Burch here showing you the ropes. I got a feeling 'bout you, Hennick. You a quick learner. Etting Street?"

Dad didn't hesitate. "Behind the bus parking lot, above North Avenue."

Larry laughed. "Not bad, kid. See, you gonna be all right."

My father would soon know Etting Street as a catwalk for cross-dressers with barefoot kids in rags playing in their midst.

Every day on his way to Medic 4, my father cruised off of the expressway at Mt. Royal and made a right on McMechen Street in Bolton Hill, a still elegant-looking neighborhood of stately nineteenth-century homes and mansions. Seconds after rounding the corner, he would pass a stalwart old building called The Beethoven. Local news celebrities lived there. The Beethoven Apartments on Park Avenue, like its neighbors, was built in the nineteenth century. Five stories high, the ten brownstones it comprised were built in Second Empire style with a stucco façade, mansard roofs, and ornately decorated windows and cornices. Daily my father admired this beautiful structure. Many times he would pause to reflect on what it must have been like to live in a century Baltimore seemed to have now forgotten.

In the nearby Mount Vernon neighborhood, the monument to George Washington (long pre-dating the District of Columbia's Washington Monument) stands 178 feet tall in a cross-shaped park replete with trees and flowerbeds. The Peabody Conservatory of Music, the Walters Art Museum, and the Enoch Pratt Free Library—the world's first public library, and one of the first public buildings to explicitly state a mission to serve people no matter what their race or creed—are little more than a stone's throw away. Ironically, they are an equally short distance from the direly poor area my father served as a paramedic.

Baltimore has many nicknames. "The Monumental City" provides some indication of Baltimore's values, struggles and ethnicities. It is home to the Korean War Memorial. Fort McHenry, near which Francis Scott Key wrote the song which became our national anthem, is a national monument and historic shrine. Maybe, my father sometimes speculates, these grand monuments giving Baltimore the appearance of invincibility were like life rafts in a tempest, serving as reminders that hope is never lost.

"Baltimoreans," he often says, " if they have nothing else, will hold onto their pride as if their lives depend on it, and perhaps they do."

Pennsylvania Avenue, sometimes called simply "The Avenue" by West Side locals, is one of Baltimore's most historically significant yet long-neglected thoroughfares. It lies in the heart of the district my father routinely visited on Medic 4.

In the early to middle twentieth century, Pennsylvania Avenue was alive at night with loud music and bright lights. Swarms of people scurried along the sidewalks heading toward restaurants, hotels, clubs, moving picture theaters and the occasional brothel. Venues such as the Schanze Theater, The Regent, and the famous Royal Theatre featured tap dancing, chorus lines and vaudeville skits suiting tastes from cultured to bawdy. The 1,350-seat Royal, originally the Douglass, premiered drama, films and music. For decades, fans were mesmerized as glittering suede or sheer curtains opened to reveal some of the world's greatest black stars, including Ethel Waters, Pearl Bailey, Count Basie, Sarah Vaughan, Duke Ellington, Dinah Washington, John Coltrane, Miles Davis, Cab Calloway, Ella Fitzgerald and Louis Armstrong. Comedians like Slappy White and Red Foxx played there; later Red Foxx owned an eponymous nightclub in the area, featuring such top jazz groups as the Modern Jazz Quartet. Some graced the stage solo. Others fronted big bands decked out in tuxedos. From ragtime to scat, Dixieland to bebop, all the hepcats would be jiving, swinging and swaying to the cool vibes in every lounge, club and barrelhouse on the Avenue.

During WWII, with the addition of visiting soldiers and defense workers, the Avenue drew as many as 20,000 people on a Saturday night. In the 1950s, jazz was pumping. The Avenue was anchored by the Royal Theatre at the south end and the Sphinx Club to the north. Locals called it the "Chitlin' Circuit." The strip is reputed to have had roughly fifty liquor licenses. The Tijuana Club on the upper end hosted such luminaries as Billie

Holiday, Miles Davis and John Coltrane. On Fulton Avenue Chet Baker, Ahmad Jamal, Gig Gryce, Russ Freeman and others attracted jazz aficionados, both black and white. Although at that time Baltimore was largely segregated, everyone shared in the energy of the Avenue. In the sixties, right up until the riots following Dr. Martin Luther King's assassination, there were still some noteworthy happenings there—in the Comedy Club, Club Tijuana and the like—such as an impromptu battle of the saxes between Sonny Rollins and Sonny Stitt, pianist Horace Silver sharing his piano bench with lady customers on a crowded night, or Rahsaan Roland Kirk demonstrating his uncanny ability to play several wind instruments at once with the help of his nose. Among the black clientele were many whites. The jazz joints were particular favorites with writers from the various area newspapers—at that time, there were several dailies.

In Pennsylvania Avenue's heyday, men dressed in suits and ties shook their fine tail feathers, romanced the ladies and toasted the entertainers. Women wore their finest clothes as they swooned, crooned and strutted their stuff. Every Father's Day, during an annual Cadillac parade, stars would wave as they floated by in flashy cars. The Supremes, The Temptations and Nat King Cole graced the Avenue. With their presence, they anointed the once-dusty road lined with slaughterhouses and barns, transforming the Avenue into a great, nationally known cultural center. Spectators came from many outlying neighborhoods, white and black, to sit in their cars and watch the annual Halloween Parade sent down Pennsylvania Avenue at midnight.

Back in the Roaring Twenties, business had flourished in the daytime with the opening of numerous offices, including legal, medical and financial firms on the West Side. The Great Depression, however, devastated Penn-North as a location for business sites and middle-class residences. As employment opportunities for black people grew scarce, houses were purchased by landlords who converted them into apartments, which, through neglect, turned into slums, giving rise to sanitation and health problems. From 1950 to 1970 the area's decline grew steeper, and about one-third of the population fled the district. Previously successful industries closed. In

1953 arsonists torched the Lafayette Market, the district's prime shopping center. While significant revitalization efforts are now under way, not much music is heard today other than police sirens, gunshots and the sound of the wind blowing through empty lots of grass dating back to 1968, when the riots effectively ended the sense of comfort which middle-class people felt in the clubs and theaters.

"Not only was Pennsylvania Avenue famous for its rich cultural heritage, but it also held the distinction of having the highest crime rate in the city." Dad was sad to see its deterioration as, in the sixties and seventies, he watched it fall into more and more neglect and disrepair.

On the corner of Lafayette Avenue and Pennsylvania Avenue, a bronze Billie Holiday still stands eight and a half feet tall. For a time, Baltimore was home to the legendary singer. In a strapless evening gown with gardenias in her hair, her mouth parted in mid-song and one arm outstretched to Baltimore, she is poised with bliss in her eyes as if gazing at a heaven no one else can see.

Dad recalled that, during his Ambo-4 days, folk would gather around the Billie Holiday memorial across the street from the Frolic Club to drink malt liquor, rum or the ever-popular Thunderbird. Thunderbird's jingle went: "What's the word? Thunderbird. How's it sold? Good and cold. What's the jive? Bird's alive. What's the price? Thirty twice."

"Pimpmobiles" were a common sight. They might be pink, or painted in a checkerboard pattern. Each car had its own distinct personality. "They were as colorful as floats in a circus parade."

Behind the firehouse was a well-attended church. Every Sunday morning a beautiful gospel choir sang, boosting my father's spiritual morale before he had to exit the station on a mission of mercy. Just across the alley from the firehouse bunkroom was an old red brick building housing the Elk's Club. Folk would climb rickety stairs to the second floor on hot summer nights and enjoy the sounds of saxophones, drums and piano. The music permeated the darkness until two or three in the morning. Dad lay on his bunk in the heat for brief periods between runs listening to the soulful sounds of jazz which still echoed through the district at the time. A lone man with his saxophone would play tunes on one corner; a quartet of young boys would sing in harmony on another. Although the musicians might now be unknown, their jazz and blues poured from the heart.

Dad's mentor Larry was a pool shark; he frequented the many watering holes on the Avenue. He would bring his breakaway pool stick to the station in a black case lined in red velvet. At the end of each night shift, Dad would watch him polish the wood, chalk the stick and head off to one of the back-room clubs on the Avenue. Speaking in awe of Larry, my father said, "He could run 115 to 120 balls without missing a beat. He had a hard time finding people who didn't know him. Everyone on the Avenue knew Larry. It was hard for him to get a game."

As a pool shark, Larry was also a con man. He would lure victims who'd never met him into playing against him by seeming to be no good and initially giving them the upper hand. Ever the calm, cool expert, Larry kept his private life private, which only enhanced his mystique.

Whenever Dad and Larry walked into a house in the ghetto, Larry would assess the situation and instantly know what he was going to do. On one of their first calls, a man was lying in fetal position on a soiled hardwood living room floor.

Dad rushed to the man's side and began checking his vitals. Larry held his hand up, signaling Dad to stop.

"Boy, get up off that floor and act like you grown," Larry ordered the patient.

The man coiled on the ground opened his eyes and held his stomach. "I ain't doin' so well," the man groaned. Dad started to reach for him but then glanced at his partner, confused.

"You don't got no problem other than that there Colt 45. Take a couple of aspirin, and leave that malt liquor alone. You know better than to drink that stuff."

The man stood and puffed up his chest. "You mean you ain't going to take me to the hospital?"

Larry opened the door and started to leave while the man continued to rant. Dad followed Larry's lead.

"I'll fix you, motherfucker! Who's your boss? I'm a give him a call right now."

"Come on, Bill, let's go." Larry nodded his head toward their belligerent patient. "There ain't nothing wrong with him."

Dad could still hear the man shouting as they closed the door behind them.

Working with Larry taught my father how to function in West Baltimore. Larry educated Dad about the realities beneath the surface. For instance, he told my father that there were three or more snowball vendors to a block. Drug dealers hoping to expand their clientele sometimes put a powder packet in the bottom of the paper cone. "Ten bucks, no change."

"They didn't have a state lottery until 1973, so illegal lotteries flourished all over the city. Larry would stick his head out of the window of the ambo and call, 'What's the number?' The people knew the winning number."

Larry pictured himself as a ladies' man. He had that smooth way about him, an impressive self-assurance. He would flash his smile and croon, "How you doing, baby," or "You're looking good today." Once in a while he would pull over at one of his lady friends' houses in the district and leave my father waiting in the medic unit. Larry would say, "Keep the motor running." My father would listen for incoming calls and get impatient, then go bang on the door. "Larry, break it up, time to go."

"Be there in a flash." Larry would call out from the other side of the door. He never got rattled. And he didn't miss a beat. Nearly an hour would pass; then he would come out with a big grin and a sandwich. "Let's get back in service. I'm ready."

My father and Larry shared an affinity. There were no courses on how to work in that district. Larry didn't follow protocol, and Dad didn't like protocol much either. In fact, there was no way they could adhere to any kind of protocol in the area they served.

To my family, Dad's stories about Larry Burch were like biblical parables. If the fledgling ghetto medic had received his initiation from a less caring and skilled partner, he would have been killed within the first year of his new job, he is sure. And if God had conducted a search for the best guardian for the job, Gabriel, Michael, even Lucifer before he fell from grace, would no doubt have refused the assignment. My dad was completely convincing on the subject of Larry.

It was the archangel Larry who protected my father with his insight about life in places such as the notorious George B. Murphy Homes and Lexington Terrace. Although they were both bad, "the Murphys" regularly hit the papers and were probably the worst of the "projects." According to Dad, the Murphys were bastions of fear, ignorance and depravity. Low-income housing projects, the Murphy Homes, built in 1963, consisted of four fourteen-story government-funded high-rise brick buildings located on the corner of George Street and Argyle Avenue, the south end of my dad and Larry's district. Shootings, stabbings, domestic violence and contagious sicknesses ran rampant in those blocks. Dad was ill at ease if police were not yet on the scene when he arrived, but knowing time was critical he would often go in anyway.

Dad first went in to one of these buildings after a shooting on the fourteenth floor. He walked into the small, trash-strewn lobby, pushed the button for the elevator, and leaned against the wall contemplating whether he should wait for it or take the dark and foreboding stairway. After several long moments, the door slowly slid open and Dad was greeted by the lifeless hulk of a man slumped on the floor of the elevator car with a bullet through his heart. Someone had casually snuffed out the victim's life during a party on the fourteenth floor and lowered his body to Larry and Dad as if to save them a trip.

The younger occupants sometimes threw rocks and bottles at Dad and Larry from their balconies, striking their hard-hats. Urine would rain from above. Once they were called to the Murphys to retrieve a dead man from the top of an elevator car. No one knew the body was there until a woman got into the car and saw blood dripping through a ventilation grate.

Someone on one of the upper floors had stabbed him several times, forced open an elevator door, and dumped his body down the shaft.

On another occasion, they received a call reporting an unconscious person on the fourteenth-floor stairway. Entering the building, they stepped over the garbage to reach the elevator only to find it was inoperable. At the time, Dad was secretly relieved. His apprehension was not from fear of the unknown but from the knowledge that he could not hold his breath for fourteen floors on the slow-moving, creaking elevator. He called the elevators at the Murphys "the world's largest moving vertical urinals." A stench of urine, feces and vomit always permeated the cars. This combination would bring tears to Dad's eyes and "clear my impenetrable sinuses cavities." There was also a real fear of the elevator floor caving in, since most of it had been eaten away by human acid. Often, a Murphy elevator did not work at all.

Dad gladly followed Larry to the stairwell at the end of the building. They climbed the poorly lit stairs, huffing and puffing, until they found an apparently unconscious black man about eighteen years old on the eleventh floor. Concerned, Dad leaned down to administer aid. The youth suddenly swung at him. Dad dodged the punch, which narrowly missed his jaw, but the momentum of the swing caused the thug to lose his balance and tumble down several concrete steps. Instantly, four tall black youths appeared, sealing off Dad and Larry's only escape route. From the size and stature of "the dudes" Dad sensed the two of them were in big trouble. As "the goons" grouped together, Larry performed his magic.

He slowly removed his coat, folded it neatly and placed it on the concrete landing. He took off his glasses and placed them carefully on top of the coat. As he rolled up his shirtsleeves, he fixed "the hoods" with a cold stare and calmly asked, "All at once or one at a time?"

Dad had no recourse but to go along with Larry's plan of action. He began to sweat. The old Martha and the Vandellas classic "Nowhere to Run" began to pound inside his head. His life flashed before him as he prayed for a miracle.

Larry and the five men continued the staring contest for a few seconds until, to my father's complete astonishment, the hefty young fivesome backed off. "I'm sure glad you were here," Dad said. But the words sounded weak. Larry had, in fact, saved his life. Dad realized that he still had much to learn in order to survive as a paramedic in unwelcoming surroundings.

Larry introduced my father to soul food, too. If they were hungry after some frenzied activity, they'd stop up the street at Leon's Pig Pen on the Avenue for some ribs or a pork chop sandwich (bone-in). There were several Leon's throughout the city. A sign over the front door boasted, "We only use meat from pigs that make hogs of themselves." Dad said, "If a fire had broken out, Leon's would have gone up like a torch. It was worth skidding across the greasy floor to the counter for some of the best soul food in Baltimore. I loved the sensuous feel of the fat dripping down my chin."

Sometimes they'd drop by a real hole-in-the-wall Chinese-food joint. Larry would order ya-ka-me (pronounced yokimy), a pork mixture served in a cup with a hard-boiled egg slapped on top. It wasn't available outside of the ghetto. The pork was tender, but my father's suspicions mounted when he noticed an absence of stray cats and dogs in this block. He and some of the residents were never sure about the products used in the cuisine from this particular neighborhood carryout.

Then there was Covington's for good chicken and coleslaw: a "cut above," located near Herb's liquors on Laurens Street just three blocks up from Medic 4. While operating his "lucrative business," the proprietor of Herb's Liquors, a white man, wore a sidearm "to discourage the criminal element." Dad regularly stopped in to see him. He was not one of Herb's customers, but whenever somebody got intoxicated and passed out, or a fight erupted outside of his place, Dad and Herb would get talking. Herb kept the locals fuelled. Everybody knew where Herb's was. At one point every house on the block was torn down for renovations, but nobody touched Herb's place. As far as Dad knew, he never got shot: "Herb could take care of himself. But you never know what an addict or drunk is going to do. You just hope they don't get violent."

"Local people ate fish called lake trout. It's whiting, a low-end fish.

Then, as now, neighborhoods with a high percentage of black residents were riddled with lake trout carryout shops, often next door to bail bond emporia. Back then, many of both kinds of establishments made house calls." Dad would normally carry to work a paper bag containing sandwiches and fruit, along with a homemade dessert. Most firehouses had candy and sodas available. Before vending machines, "coonskins" were the source of candy, crackers, sodas and so on. I'd like to hold out hope that "coonskin cap" was all the term stood for, but given the neighborhood, and knowing that "coon" was then one of the more common derogatory names for a black person, one must suspect otherwise. Each shift had its own coonskin—a tin for collecting pocket change—managed by someone who would keep the supply of snack items well stocked, usually from his locker. When the men wanted a treat, they'd put their donation in the tin. If enough profit was made, they would purchase a TV, toaster, microwave, coffee pot or radio. Thieves stole these items so frequently when the men were out on runs they had to be bolted down.

After speeding to the aid of a possible heart attack victim on Harlem Avenue, my father jockeyed Medic 4 into a parking space and grabbed his case. "You feel sickly, we come quickly" was the motto printed on the bright red case containing his emergency supplies. He had also neatly printed in black marker the slogan "Feeling poor, call Ambo 4," and stuck a white medic cross that he made from medical tape on the other side of the case.

Distant sounds of anger and malice gone out of control came from the third floor. Screams of "motherfucker-this" and "goddamn-that" echoed. It seemed that everybody was calling everybody else "nigger." My father and Larry took the stairs two at a time, wondering what awaited them. They pushed the partly open door, but it wouldn't open fully. Someone was hiding behind the door, and half a dozen or so people were crouched behind sofas and chairs throwing dishes and knickknacks at each other, oblivious to their arrival. An elderly woman lay motionless in the middle of the floor. She needed immediate attention, but it was going to be difficult to remove her from the war zone.

Dad crawled to the unconscious victim and dragged her across the floor to the safety of the hallway. The woman was breathing and had a slight gash in her head. As Dad and Larry gingerly carried her down the outside marble steps, a plate crashed two feet to my father's right, followed by a barrage of dinnerware. Their friends upstairs had now united to attack my father and Larry. As glassware shattered all around them, they loaded the victim on the litter and beelined for the ambulance. Articles continued to crash onto the unit as they sped off.

Dad often said, "Dodging bullets while working is part of my routine. It doesn't faze me." This was just one of the times his unflappability came in handy.

One eerily quiet, pitch-black night, Larry and Dad parked Medic 4 next to an injured black man lying on Ashburton Street near the Lutheran Hospital. The lights of their ambulance illuminated his motionless body. When Dad knelt down at his side, he discovered that the man was still breathing but was comatose due to loss of blood from a gunshot to the torso. As they lifted him from the street onto the litter, Dad and Larry heard gunfire followed by the pings of bullets against the side panel of the ambulance. "Get in the ambo," Larry said. Someone was taking pot-shots at them with a small-caliber gun, probably a .22. "Get in the unit now!" As they raced off, bullets continued to strike the vehicle.

Larry bluntly refused service to nonemergency patients and reprimanded clientele who wasted his time. To him, a real emergency was something life threatening. Residents, however, had their own interpretations of what constituted an emergency. People would request medics for small cuts, stomachaches, headaches, constipation, diarrhea, sore toes and other minor complaints to get a free ride to the ER. Catering to such nonemergency whims would remove a vital medic unit from the district and possibly spell disaster for a heart attack or stroke victim. Shootings and stabbings might have to wait until emergency services arrived from farther afield.

Dad didn't blame Larry for his seemingly rash decisions. "Larry was direct in his approach toward African-Americans, even though many of them did not appreciate a black brother telling them how it is. And if Larry was going to attend to you, you better be legitimate. If he thought you were lying, he'd treat you like dirt.

"If they declared they couldn't walk, Larry would say, 'You mean to tell me you got injured in front of the house and you can't walk? So how did you get all the way up here in the rear of the third floor?' The guy might have been shot in the chest, but Larry would say, 'Next time you get shot, stay in front of the house where you belong.'"

Then Larry would turn to my father. "If he wants to go to the hospital, he'll walk down those steps." Then he'd turn back toward the patient. "I'm leaving, I'm gone. I'm not carrying you."

Dad would say, "You can't leave him here."

"Can he walk down the steps?"

My father would give no answer.

He soon discovered "That man can't walk" was a popular phrase. The victim would claim to have been injured on the street and somehow always end up on a top floor of the apartment building. If Dad tried to assist the person in walking back down, a friend, family member or even a complete stranger would protest. "That man can't walk." In order to keep the peace, many times my father would then remove the patient on a backboard or a fixed litter, a back-breaking job if the patient happened to be overweight. Dad always strived to control the scene and not provoke outbursts or anger bystanders. "The ghetto was a tough place to live. Its inhabitants were always on edge. You had to understand this as you worked this job."

If a man was curled up in a ball on the floor, Larry would tell Dad, "He just drank too much. Make sure his head is turned to the side in case he has to vomit. Don't let him lie flat on his back." Sometimes Dad was stunned by Larry's behavior.

"He'd say stuff that I wouldn't dare say. We'd often revisit the same places. The clientele didn't like Larry because he didn't mess around, and he didn't care whether they liked it or not. And he could con people into believing they didn't need to go to the hospital. Most times he was right. However, if an important call came in, he wouldn't slight anybody. You'd think he would have been fired a hundred times over, but he always got out of trouble. He could finagle his way out of anything. He'd conjure up stories to make it so it looked like the other person was at fault, not him. He always had the last word."

Larry was constantly at odds with Battalion Chief Martin C. McMahon, head of the medical bureau at the time, for refusing to adhere to standard operating procedures. Dad sided with Larry. Larry didn't follow the book. He did what he knew he had to do. The Chief tried to make him stick to the rules. This conflict between them remained until they both retired. Chief McMahon made occasional trips to Medic 4 to confront the team about some allegation about what Larry had done or didn't do.

My father told me, "I would be hauled in too, because I was his partner. I wasn't going to lie to protect Larry, but I wasn't going to volunteer any more information than I had to. I needed Larry down there. And the way I saw it, McMahon was a white guy, totally unrealistic, with absolutely no idea how the neighborhood functioned."

Most of the charges concerned the blunt way Larry spoke to people. Larry didn't make idle conversation. The higher-ups sometimes took away his vacation days, but that didn't matter to him. He would just call in sick and head down the road with his cue.

"Larry grasped the situation the second he laid eyes on someone. He wouldn't pacify people who talked to him with disrespect. Larry wasn't racist, either. He would never bring up black or white. He always looked out for me, defended me out there."

But McMahon couldn't stand him, and Larry knew it.

Larry stayed quiet when McMahon lectured him. Then Larry would say something like: "Well, that man came after me with a knife. I did the best I could do."

On several occasions, McMahon accused Larry of pocketing patients' cash. According to my father, "Larry wouldn't rob an innocent victim, but

Larry didn't like the thugs. So if he found a drug dealer lying wounded in an alley, he knew the victim's family wouldn't get the money. I really don't know what he did. But Larry always came up smelling like a rose."

McMahon grew more and more frustrated. No matter how hard he tried, he couldn't get Larry fired. And then one day McMahon broke down. My father never forgot it. Chief Schamberger, an intelligent, aloof man who headed up the 4th battalion, was stuck in the middle. Dad told me, "McMahon was this big man and it was a sight to see: he just fell apart and cried in front of Chief Schamberger. He spoke fast, his face turned red as a beet, and his voice kept going up higher until it began cracking. 'This man, I can't stand this anymore,' McMahon gibbered. 'I get these complaints coming in and . . .' Then the tears poured down his face. He stood there bawling in front of the three of us '. . . I just can't deal with it any more.' Larry gave a little smile as if to say, 'I won.' I just calmly stood by and enjoyed the show."

Dad recounted a time when the screams of a woman in distress pierced the tranquility of an otherwise peaceful evening. It was close to midnight when Larry and Dad arrived at the scene. Larry maneuvered the medic unit curbside. Dad started out of the ambulance. Larry gently gripped his arm. "Hold up until the police get here, Bill."

My father shot Larry a questioning look. When he got worried about Dad's safety, Larry called him Hennick. "Don't go in there, Hennick. Something's not right. I'm telling you."

Dad paused. The screaming grew louder. He found it impossible to sit outside and do nothing when a human was suffering only thirty feet away. In his zeal to help, my father started in, ignoring Larry's warning.

Through the glass panes of double doors Dad could see a large woman lying on her back screaming hysterically in the vestibule. As he entered, a tall threatening man wearing a French beret and a pair of oversized sunglasses emerged from the dimly lit hallway and assumed a karate position. Just as my father began to contemplate his next move, Larry suddenly appeared at his side. He and the thug locked eyes.

Larry sighed. "Think you'd best back off, brother, and let my partner here attend to his business," he said in his bass voice, standing there "real casual, like he wasn't worried about a thing."

Ignoring his advice, the man turned toward Larry, struck a threatening pose as if preparing to attack, and snarled, "You think you all that? Let's go, motherfucker."

Larry's second warning was to no avail. With his left foot, "the dude" in the beret struck Larry's left elbow. Without flinching, Larry retaliated by thumping the attacker in the chest with his heavy hand. The impact hurled the man several feet backwards into the plaster wall. Dazed and in pain, he slumped to the floor. It turned out that this was the thug who had savagely beaten the screaming woman earlier. Larry and Dad attended to the two people's injuries until helicopters appeared overhead and police arrived to take him into custody. The assailant served time while several broken ribs mended.

Dad often said, "If I had been with someone else it would have been a disaster. Because Larry risked his own life in order to save me from harm, I learned not to be hasty and to listen."

Dad was sure Larry must have been thinking, "'I told that dumb white man not to go in there.' But he was quiet about it. He didn't say much throughout the rest of the shift." My father knew Larry was right. After many lessons, Dad gradually felt more at ease and confident, but also less likely to take risky chances. He always said, "The things that Larry taught me I could have never learned from a book."

But there were some things Larry couldn't teach my father; he had to learn them for himself.

We Are Family

Often, after working a day shift on the medic unit, Dad would burst through the back door of our semi-detached suburban home, pinch our cheeks, say "And how are my little crumb snatchers today?" and immediately start firing stories about his many "lessons."

First, though, he would walk over to the stove where my mother was cooking, lift up the lid on the pot of stewed tomatoes, look at my brother and me, and murmur, "What's this? Last night's gar-bahj?" My brother and I would giggle.

"Bill," my mother would sigh. She was accustomed to his humor but, as she would later recall, "It was like Martha Stewart being married to Mel Brooks." She wanted perfection, and Dad wanted a laugh. "Move it," she'd snap. He'd step aside so she could check the roast in the oven. Sometimes she'd crack a smile at his jokes, but she didn't like to encourage him. She was still dressed from having been out shopping, but by now her blue shirt had come untucked from her wrinkled skirt and a smudge of makeup was visible on the inside of her collar, unbuttoned for comfort as she shuttled between the stove and table. The curls in her hair, which had been carefully ironed into existence that morning, had softened into loose tresses.

My father always began his stories as if we hadn't already heard them a thousand times before. He would laugh uncontrollably, shake his head and say, "I'm telling you, these guys were characters, straight out of a movie."

Although I had never met most of the medics or firefighters he was referring to, I felt as if I knew them. When starting to reminisce about his earlier days as a paramedic, my father would hum an unrecognizable tune as if revving the engine. One of the people he liked to talk about was a man whom I'll call Milo. We loved hearing stories about this hippie firefighter who drove an old beat-up van.

Milo had a sugar-sweet smile and intense blue eyes. He had long blond hair when he went into fire school, but he had to have it cut in order to fit the respiratory mask. He practiced yoga and would put a rug at the watch desk, where he'd then stand on his head. Milo was friendly to black people and tried to create a bridge between the races, almost as if to show them that he was "different from other whiteys." He reminded Dad of the white cop in "Sanford and Son" who always tried to connect with black people and show that he wasn't like the other "honkies." Nobody understood Milo, according to my father.

"One night we went to an area near the Murphy Homes," he said. "This guy was caught by his clothing on a chain link fence. He'd been gunned down when trying to outrun his assailant and ended up falling on the fence. Pieces of the chain link are sticking out of him and he's hanging there limp. Milo starts smiling and talking to the poor guy. The victim had been shot four or five times and was moaning in pain, but to Milo it was an opportunity to talk to a bro'.

"'What's up, Bro'? How you doin', man?'

"'Milo, 'I said, 'the guy's been shot five times. Why don't we get him down off the fence and take him to the hospital? You can talk to him later.'" Dad went on. "Milo ate garbage. Garbage, not gar-bahj. The first time I saw it was when a firefighter threw the last few bites of his sandwich into the trashcan.

"'You don't mind if I have some of that, do you?' Milo said. He reached into the bin, unwrapped the sandwich from the balled up napkin and ate it."

Milo waited around for the men's leftovers, grabbing scraps of food from their plates and the sink, a real scavenger. "One Christmas," Dad recollected, "some men made a Christmas tree for him with old hamburger bits, dried up hotdog pieces and rotting fruit as ornaments. I gave him a plastic plate I'd found at a five-and-dime shop. On it was printed a dog and the words 'Eat it up quick or Milo will get it.' Uh, hee, hee, hee."

As long as Dad was telling stories, he was as bright as the morning sun. Singing "To the dump, to the dump, to the dump, dump, dump" to the tune of "The Lone Ranger" theme song, he'd gallop over to the Mr. Coffee machine and pour himself a cup from the cracked glass pot.

"Bill, put the empty pot in the zinc, please." Mom didn't really speak the Baltimore dialect, but she occasionally used some of its colloquialisms. "Bawlmorese" is famous for the way it rolls words together as if the speaker has marbles in his or her mouth. Often you'll hear the dialect in a nasal "Bawlmore" or "I'm goin' downy ocean (pronounced 'ay-shun')" or "put da kebab on aluminum fool, while I warsh the tray in the zinc, Hon. Youse can dry it with summa them paper tales." In general, Baltimoreans are unpretentious and have a do-someone-proud dignity. However, you will know if you are not welcome.

"What about the grocery cart story?" my brother would plead. Dad would clasp his hands together against his abdomen and smile.

"Oh right, the story with Heath, now he was a character. We're preparing to leave for a run and pull out on the ramp. The Lieutenant says, 'Heath, go back and close the door.' Heath strolls back inside, closes the door, then stands there scratching his head through his helmet, looking out at the engine from behind the window. We had to be precise when giving him instructions. If he was driving you might say, 'Hey Heath, turn right.' He would then keep on making rights until judgment day. 'You can stop turning right, Heath, just go forward.'

"'Right, all right, I got it.'" Dad would roll his eyes toward the heavens. "I'd think to myself, 'It's going to be a long night.'"

"Bill, are you going to just stand there talking about the good ol' days all night or are you going to set the table?"

Dad looked at my brother and me, and, purely to get under my mother's skin, said, "And another thing . . ." Craig and I would giggle till we snorted.

"Bill, you're not at all funny." Mom slid a mitt on her hand and opened the oven door.

"The Hennicks thrive on depression," he would retort, as if his highly individual sense of humor were genetic. He often spoke about his funeral or lifted his hands toward the heavens, semi-smirking, and pleaded, "Take me away, I'm ready and waiting." He would say that the high point of his life would come when he was being wheeled around in a nursing home, "staring, drooling and making puddles. And your mother can play shuffleboard with the other fellas." My mother would just shake her head. He would joke about the pressures of the job, but we all knew from his whistling and the glint in his eye that he was genuinely happy.

"One time Heath and I are called to one of the old stately six-story apartment buildings on Charles Street near Johns Hopkins University, which is a relatively low-crime area. As we ride the elevator to the third floor, I feel confident the call about an injury will be strictly routine. We rap on an apartment door.

"'Ambo,' I call out. The door is ajar. I can see a young male crumpled on the floor just inside the doorway. He's been shot twice in the torso and is unconscious. His breathing's shallow. I stabilize the victim and realize that although I have the medical bag, the stretcher is in the medic unit. Just as I'm about to tell Heath to go for the litter, I reconsider. He just might become lost. Time is of the essence.

"Then I recall that I'd seen an old grocery cart at the end of the hallway as we rushed in. Necessity being the mother of invention, I quickly grab the cart and lift the victim into the wire basket. I lead the way to the elevator with Heath in close pursuit, pushing the cart for all he's worth. Surprised neighbors stare at us as we speed down the sidewalk to the waiting medic unit.

"We quickly transfer the patient to the litter and transport him to the closest hospital. Thankfully, Heath follows my instructions, and we arrive at the hospital in time for our human cargo to be saved."

"Bill, if you piped down for a second, you might hear the dog yelping to go outside." Dad egged our pet poodle on. "Speak," he exhorted, "or forever hold your pee!"

Mom narrowed her green eyes and sighed at steaming-kettle volume, not at all amused. Craig and I snickered. Dad opened the screen door, and Snuggles raced out. With rapidly fading patience, Mom said, "Bill, I thought I asked you to set the dinner table." Dad scratched the five o'clock shadow around his chin, undid a few top buttons on his blue shirt and headed to the silverware drawer.

In many ways, my father was like TV without the commercial breaks. He was almost always on. But we could choose the channel and select from several programs: Name that Gloom; Wheel of Misfortune; This is Your Death; The Hitler, Holocaust and World War II Mini-Series. Some tales could last for an hour and a half nonstop; these were more like feature length films: Calamity Bane; Lust for Death; and his favorite: How West Baltimore was Lost.

Once my father began telling stories, we were likely to suddenly become preoccupied with other things. My brother Craig would play with kitchen utensils, usually two eggbeaters, and, with his vivid imagination, he would transform them into helicopters, jeeps or men on horseback. Making radio static, siren and chopper noises was his specialty. My mother, however, would become engrossed in the sermon coming from the radio and in the carrots she was chopping. I would fixate on the picture hanging on the kitchen wall: a bald guy with his head bowed in prayer and a crust of bread on his plate. I'd innocently wonder: Why didn't God give him more food? Where is his family? Why do Grandma and Aunt Sharon have the same painting on their kitchen walls?

Dad's storytelling style oscillated between that of a university lecturer and that of an off-duty serviceman—switching from generalized commentaries to outrageous anecdotes in a matter of moments. From time to time we might listen, but we knew his stories so well that any of us could recite them ourselves.

We knew that the district where my father worked had an above-average level of human suffering. The row houses were mostly two and three story, built of red brick with flat tar roofs, now in various stages of disrepair and neglect. Many had dilapidated wooden rear porches atop rickety stairways. Inside were vestibules where moldy umbrellas or stinking overshoes lay on doormats. Whether the dwellers were white or black, the same smells greeted Dad's nostrils: a combination of grease, urine, mold and bug spray. Old food was often left to rot on tables and countertops. In filthy kitchens, he could smell the vinegar in which people cooked cheap meats like hog jowls and pigs' knuckles in order to make them tender enough to eat. "Soul food at its most basic," Dad said. Paint peeled from the walls. Many times windows had been nailed shut, locking the stench inside the home. Soap operas and "Soul Train" emanated from televisions set at ear-shattering volume. Dirty rooms contained soiled cheap furniture, maybe a few crates and an armchair or couch with the stuffing coming out. Bedrooms were occupied by three or four people sleeping on filthy mattresses surrounded by piles of old clothes and trash, a perfect environment for fire and disease.

The high-rises were like derelict stables. Drug dealers ran them. If Dad wanted to know what was going on in the Murphys he would talk to Popeye the Drug Dealer. If he was responding to a call to the building for a shooting and didn't know where the victim was, he only had to knock on Popeye's door. Popeye knew about everybody, who they were and what they did. He wasn't a big guy. Dad said, "He was a skinny dude with a goatee and eyeglasses, but he sure had a lot of pull." His apartment was on the third floor at the end of the hallway, which was always crammed with clients. It was common knowledge in the building that he was "The Man." People would tell the medics, "Popeye knows." My father relied on him. The police left him alone. Everyone needed him.

Mom cocked her head and fixed a stare at Dad, who was standing just inside the room. "Knock it off, Chicken Little." This was one of Mom's pet names for Dad. When he wasn't talking about the ghetto he was forecasting disasters—the next big stock market crash, the conquest of America by China or the ultimate annihilation of the human race in a nuclear holocaust. And that was on a good day.

Dad rolled back his eyes, and in a low ghoulish voice imitating Lurch, the Frankenstein-monster-like family butler in the TV show "The Addams Family," he intoned, "You rang?" He then pulled the handkerchief from the left breast pocket of his shirt and loudly blew his nose. "Stress gets me congested," he unnecessarily explained (we all knew that). "Ugh, [loud nasal snort] I couldn't wait to get off of that meat wagon today."

Dad moved so fleetingly through people's lives that he seldom learned whether they had survived or not. He often pitied the ignorance of those he tried to help. He frowned and shook his head. "We respond to a sick case on the sixth floor of the Murphys. When we get there, an emaciated ten-year-old girl opens the heavy metal door. Obviously in shock, she stands there all tense—wide-eyed and perspiring.

"'What seems to be the problem?'

"'It's my mother.'

"'Can you tell me what happened?'

"The girl leads us into the kitchen. So depressing at best—those inside walls of all the rooms in the Murphy units are plain concrete block. Anyway, a heavyset woman, maybe in her early thirties, is sprawled out on the floor, lying face down on the linoleum. We rush over.

"'She drank this stuff,' she whispers.

"'Drank what? What did she drink?'

"The little girl points to a series of bottles lined up on the kitchen counter. Between painful moaning and gagging, the mother says that her daughter earlier made a bet with her that she would not be able to drink a glassful of a concoction consisting of ammonia, Clorox, and five to six other household cleaning solutions. Apparently the daughter prepared this 'Mr. Clean' cocktail which her mother promptly chug-a-lugged." Dad paused, "We take the woman to the closest hospital. But we'll never learn if she survives." Dad furrowed his brow and began placing the silverware on the table.

"Bill, you're full of doom and gloom," Mom said.

"Eunice, I love the doom and gloom, the doomier, the gloomier, the better. And it's a good thing, otherwise I would never be able to tolerate working down there." My father always referred to Baltimore City as "down there." He continued, "And working down there has enabled us to afford this luxurious lifestyle." He opened his hands, inviting us to look around the kitchen. The floor had a large mark on it from the time my mother dropped a hot dish of apple cobbler on it, the red wallpaper with yellow flowers had begun to peel, and the brown refrigerator, purchased a decade earlier, moaned as if in excruciating pain.

My parents joked about being poor, but in reality they couldn't have cared less about renovating the house or buying new furniture and linens. They were "people people." Although they readily admitted that my father's job strained their marriage and tested their faith in God, and they had to budget carefully to make ends meet, they provided Craig and me with a comfortable childhood. He and I were never hungry. We always received more Christmas gifts than anyone we knew. Mom and Dad bought us good clothes and all the latest toys and gadgets. Never spending money on themselves, they enjoyed taking us on excursions or trips to the movies. Their partnership was built around God, my brother and me. They were amazingly content.

"Enough, Bill, the food is getting cold. Who's going to pray?"

"But Eunice, Rachel asked me to tell her the story about Krause."

"Yeah, Bill. That was three days ago and you haven't given it a break."

In reality, Dad was not monomaniacal. He would gladly help us build a tree house, sculpt an igloo or take us sleigh riding on "Suicide Hill." This was a grand slope on the grounds of the Baltimore Country Club, which is situated in Roland Park, a leafy neighborhood with huge old houses. He helped my mother host a combined birthday party for my brother and me with forty-some neighborhood kids as guests. One Halloween, he dressed up in tights as a musketeer—even at home Dad was a Superhero. He played soccer with my brother in the back yard. He helped us with our homework. He took out the garbage without being asked, cleaned up after himself, took us to medical and dental appointments. But, like most kids, Craig and I took his good fathering and husbanding for granted.

Our neighbors always turned to him when they needed emergency medical help. Whenever my friend Christopher had an accident—Christopher was a little German boy who lived two doors away—he'd shout through the streets, "Mr. Hennick! Mr. Hennick!" till my father came running. One time his big brother, Marc, shoved Christopher against a cabinet so that its corner nearly sliced off his ear. It was my Dad who bandaged up the wound.

Another time, during a pool party thrown by the people who lived behind us, a young man was drowning. Our family happened to be outside. When we heard the screaming, my father jumped the four-foot fence between the two yards in what seemed to be a single bound and saved the man's life.

I remember one day, while he was unpacking groceries, he casually told me that, earlier, at the supermarket, "some punk" stole an elderly woman's purse. My father chased the thug down the street, shouting, "If I get my hands on you I'm going to kill you!" The thief dropped the bag. Dad promptly returned it to the grateful lady.

"Look, Eunice, I'm trying to tell the kids how it is down there in the ghetto."

"Bill, you *live* in the ghetto. And since you insist on talking, why don't you pray before we all starve to death?"

This was another of Mom's efforts to stop the storytelling for the time being. It tended to work, though only briefly. My brother and I would refuse to say grace, and my father was overjoyed to be asked to speak. He was a fervent believer in the scriptures and the teachings of Christ, although his faith was tested time and time again. He respected other people's beliefs and would not discuss religion at work. Although at home he always joked about serious topics including religion, praying was no laughing matter to him. Dad spoke to God as if he were addressing royalty. We would all fold our hands and close our eyes. My father would bow his head and rattle off a prayer in high-toned English which we assumed was from the King James version of the Bible, though he spoke so rapidly we couldn't understand him.

During dinner, my mother would flash him stern looks to remind him that we were "only children" and did not need to hear the "gory details" of his work. "Not at the table, Bill," she'd chide.

Nevertheless, she often praised my Dad to Craig and me. "He's a wonderful father to you kids. He knows how to play. Think of how he dresses up the dog and makes you both laugh. When he rehashes those stories about blood and guts, he has you two laughing until you both are almost falling off of the chairs." More seriously, and half to herself, she'd add, "I try to teach you kids etiquette because that's how I was raised. I never understood how a person could laugh about death but that's how your father copes." Mom herself coped by turning to Jesus.

Throughout their marriage, my father worked two jobs at a time. For a while, in addition to his job as firefighter and paramedic, he worked in the Army Reserves, in the insurance industry conducting basic medical evaluations and as a limousine chauffeur. Mom said, "He couldn't sleep much when he was home anyhow. He was always too keyed up."

After he'd worked fourteen or even sixteen hours, at night Dad would come home and want two hours' sleep. When my brother and I were toddlers and Dad was working night shift, Mom would keep us up late so that we would sleep late in the mornings and not wake him up. We watched Johnny Carson. We watched the United States flag appear on the screen with "The Star-Spangled Banner" playing. We watched till the static appeared and the stations went off the air. Neither my brother nor I noticed Dad's absence. My mother managed the household in such a way that my father was able to share time with us. Mom later told me, "When he was with us, he was really with us." He wasn't the type to go out drinking with the guys; in fact, he didn't drink at all.

I was never frightened when Dad wasn't home at night. I was sure that Mom would kill an intruder without flinching if that's what it took to protect her cubs. She never needed to sleep with a club or a handgun. According to Mom, she had something stronger to protect her entire family: Almighty God Himself. When I was much older, she confided, "I was alone a lot, and as a woman, I had a need for intimacy. So, I developed a wonderful relationship with God. It fulfilled me." Often, when my father started one of his stories, my mother would try to drown him out by singing a few bars of the Hallelujah Chorus or reciting Bible verses. It didn't faze my Dad; his soliloquy just rose louder.

"Lord for thy, blah, blah, blah, bless this food for our bodies, blah, blah, blah, in thy name we pray, Amen."

Very recently, I asked my mother, "What was Dad saying when he prayed?"

"I have no idea," she replied.

Nightly we dined to the morose tune of Baltimore's social ills which my dad insisted didn't trouble him and my mother felt were unsuitable for the dinner table. Roaches, maggots, lice, assorted vermin—Dad said, "I was always on the alert for anything crawling near me." He often saw folk eating dinner without reacting at all to roaches actually on the table and in their food. Roaches were on the beds, walls, floors and ceilings, in the cupboards. They even crawled deep into people's ears at night. My father would find the victims of such an invasion delirious and screaming. The effect was described as an unbearably loud buzzing: "A plane is taking off in my head," one woman cried. They had to be taken to the hospital where the physician would administer a thick waxy solution to suffocate the roach, making removal easier. Dad had to be careful not to inadvertently carry vermin home with him.

Sipping his iced tea he'd say, "In fires, the roaches and rats all would beeline for the exit and scatter across the ceilings and walls. The heavy smoke alone would kill most of them."

"This is lovely dinner conversation, Bill. Honey, you're not eating your liver."

"But I hate liver."

I sometimes cut it up into pieces, put it in my pockets, excused myself to use the bathroom and flushed it down the toilet.

"I'm sorry, Precious." I loved it when Mom called me "Precious." "We have some leftover chicken, you can eat that instead."

"How was school today, honey?" she asked my brother while placing a few drumsticks on my plate.

"Fine."

"When's your next soccer match?"

"Saturday."

Blithely Dad would describe rats "the size of housecats." Rats were abundant in Baltimore, particularly in the poor areas where Dad worked.

Norway rats, which can be huge, predominated. People, especially babies, were often bitten by rats. Periodic garbage strikes encouraged the rodent population to proliferate. Rats would feast on mounds of garbage left uncollected in the streets and alleys. The emergency lights of the ambulance would be reflected from the eyes of countless predators as the medics responded to nighttime pleas for help. "Oooooooohhhhh, Dad, stop it." Coming from my brother and me, that cry served as encouragement.

My mother spooned some peas onto our plates.

"The rat droppings look just like those peas you're eating there."

"Okay, Dad, enough." Craig had a weaker stomach than I did. Dad would stifle a laugh, his head bobbing up and down.

"Well, I've got to make sure your uniform is washed. Your Dad's on night shift so he'll make the game. I've got to take Rachel to Brenda's birthday party and then I'll be there. Do you want Doritos in your lunch tomorrow or Cheez-Its?"

"Doritos, Mom, and don't starch my uniform, it makes it stiff."

"Mom, remember that math test that Dad helped me study for?" I hated math and Dad often helped me with my homework. "Oh yes. I was praying for you, honey. How'd it go?'

"I got a B."

"Amen. Eat your peas."

Much more intelligibly than when he rattled off dinnertime "blessings," my father spoke of Martin Luther King's death as if the civil rights leader were one of his comrades. His eyes would widen and the pitch of his voice would climb higher, as if he were reaching for an answer. "If I was upset by King's loss, I know black people must have been devastated, to feel like you'll always be oppressed, to be hated for your skin color. It's hard to imagine the overwhelming grief that people must have felt."

Dad fought with all his might to save the poor people of Baltimore City. As a child I saw my father and the city as one, inseparable. Like Baltimore, he was quirky, had a rich history and was struggling to survive. The more I understood about the history of his district, the more I realized the significance of my father's life's work.

"There's no reason for all this suffering," my father would sometimes comment after a night of attending to senseless suicides, homicides and assaults. "Why do so many of the black Baltimore City residents live in squalor?" Like my father, I have hungered for the answers and turned to the city's long history for them.

After the Civil War, former slaves were drawn to Maryland and settled in northwest Baltimore, the city's previously German and Jewish enclaves, making it America's most heavily populated African-American district. Amid protests from white politicians and neighborhood associations, free black professionals, craftsmen, barbers and ministers began to move into Druid Hill Avenue, McCulloh Street, Madison Avenue, Eutaw Place—sections which, at the time, were wealthy and white.

Some of Baltimore's influential business leaders and politicians promulgated the idea that black residents would cause property values to decline. They underscored their arguments by scaring residents with the threat of "black diseases." These were deliberate strategies to divide people by race, and they succeeded horribly, creating a division that some would say rivaled South Africa's apartheid.

On December 20, 1910, Mayor John Barry Mahool approved the West Segregation Ordinance, named after Baltimore's City Council member Samuel L. West, to divide the city blocks by the race of its residents. Whites or blacks could be fined for living in the other's territory. Impressed with Baltimore's "success" at dividing its black and white residents from one another, cities across the United States began to pass copycat legislation. Although the Supreme Court declared such legislation unconstitutional in 1917, variations of the law continued to be passed in Kentucky till 1940. In the early 1900s, as neighborhood petitions and newspapers exaggerated depreciation rates, white Baltimoreans began to beat a retreat from old West Baltimore.

Education for blacks was essential if they were to advance. This necessity precipitated the burgeoning of Maryland's black academic institutions in the late nineteenth and early twentieth centuries with African-Americans entering the legal, medical and other professions. However, discriminatory practices by private industries continued, and most blacks, if employed, were given menial jobs, low pay and little hope for promotion. A few blacks held political positions, but blacks did not receive fair and equal representation. Although not as reactionary as some cities farther south, by the late 1960s Baltimore was not a racially progressive city, either. Blacks and whites seldom mixed socially; and when they did get together it was apt to be for the express purpose of developing strategies to increase blacks' economic and political opportunities.

After the riots of 1968, the Great White Flight began in earnest. Blacks earning higher incomes moved out too, taking with them old Baltimore's black communities' economic diversity, services, and quality products, as well as most of the children's role models. The time was ripe for these upwardly mobile blacks to move into the predominantly white enclaves, to seize what they had always been denied and to ascend by claiming America's greatest status symbol: property. The poorest of the poor were left behind, and, as their communities' needs changed, Baltimore did not adapt.

"Oh, come on Eunice, come on. Please Eunice, please Eunice, please, please, please. One more, Eunice. Let me tell one more. One more."

Dad liked to push my mother's buttons, and she knew it. She could push his too. Mom snatched the spatula from the serving pan and waved it at him, causing liver grease to spray the table.

"Hennick, read my lips, Si-lence."

"Kids, call the police. Your mother's gonna beat me to death with a spatula."

"Police? Ha. You're gonna need the undertaker in a minute."

Dad compressed his lips and, after only the briefest pause, began: "The other day, I happened to go to Union Memorial Hospital and bumped into a medic from the next station over from mine, Medic 16 at North Avenue and Mount Royal Avenue. 'Do you know a Captain Krause?' the medic asked.

"I said, 'Yeah, why do you ask?'

"'Well, he's in that room there.' He pointed to a room across from my partner and me. 'He died on the way to the hospital.'

"'What happened?' I asked.

"The other medic misunderstood the question. 'He raised his head up a little bit, smiled, put his head on the pillow and passed away.'"

Dad's deep-set eyes bugged out, and his usually placid voice rose an octave or two. "I'd heard Krause was sick, but I thought he was on the mend. I didn't realize it was that bad. As far as I know he never smoked. There was a trailer set up at the Timonium Fair where medical personnel were taking chest X-rays. They found a spot on his lungs. He received the notice in the mail several weeks later. He went downhill quick.

"I went in. He was lying dead on the gurney just inside of the hospital room. They just shoved him in there until they could take him to the morgue. No one was with him."

My father was clearly shaken. All the anger he once felt was gone. I could hear empathy in his voice. He would never forget how tiny Krause looked lying on that gurney. "He had shrunk to a third of his normal weight. He looked like a miniature version of himself. I thought of what the medic had said and pictured his expression. He raised his head from the pillow, gave a smile like he was relieved the pain was gone and put his head back on the pillow. He'd suffered agony. Death must've been a relief. I couldn't help thinking that if Medic 16 had been out we might have picked Krause up ourselves, because he lived close by, in Hampden."

The other firefighters were less empathetic than my father about Krause's death. "'Could've had his funeral in a phone booth,' one guy said. 'Payback's a B-I-T-C-H.'

"Another guy said, 'What goes around comes around.'" My father admitted, "I felt a tinge of sadness, but I didn't miss him. I don't think most of the brothers did."

Because it takes a lot to rattle my father, Craig and I became uneasy at the slightest tremor in his voice. My father rarely seemed to take anything seriously; whenever he grew solemn, it discomfited my brother and me to the point where we would try to lift his mood with the kind of humor we'd acquired from him. Sometimes, but not always, we could snap him out of his pensive reverie. My brother would croon a sorrowful ballad and passionately play his air-violin. I would snort until my laughter erupted all over the room like shattered glass. Lost in thought, Dad sometimes appeared not to notice. This was one of those times.

"Institutionalized racism in the fire department began to fade just about the time that Krause did."

Dad rose to help Mom with the dishes. "Don't ever worry, little beast," my father would affectionately say, pinching my cheeks. "Life," pregnant pause, "will only get worse. And one day," (he patted my brother on the head) "it will hit you like a ton of bricks."

It may be hard to believe, but my Dad would say such things while flashing a smile. He said these kinds of things with so much optimism that I cherished every moment of my life. In fact, statements like that gave me the same sense of comfort that I would later find in a line from a geology textbook: *The Earth is a dynamic and ever changing planet.* I learned about the horrors of nature: earthquakes, volcanoes and tsunamis. And, from my father, I learned about the power of fire. Geology and my father sent the message loud and clear: Be prepared for anything, because the worst can and does happen. This is life.

But sometimes life brings change for the better. In April 1970, black firefighters united and the Vulcan Blazers of Baltimore City launched a social and legal attack against racism and bigotry. They struggled to gain opportunities for equal treatment and advancement in the workplace and encouraged more blacks to join the fire service. Whites have always been welcome to join the Vulcan Blazers.

Louis R. Harper became Baltimore's first black captain in 1970. In 1971, of more than 2,000 firefighters, fewer than 300 were black. That year, four Vulcan Blazers won the first major case in America for black firefighters against employment discrimination. The City of Baltimore and the Civil Service Commission were found guilty in the class action suit.

Women had been fighting fires as volunteers in America for two hundred years. America's first female firefighter was Molly Williams, an African-American slave in New York, in the early 1800s. In the 1970s, at last, women were starting to receive pay and were permitted to become career firefighters. Baltimore's first female firefighter, Andrea McFarland, was also black and would not be appointed until 1987, but eventually, black men— and women—were regularly appointed to high-ranking positions within the department. This too was life.

Ball of Confusion

For a time, medics were forbidden from declaring anyone dead, no matter how obvious it might be. One time Dad had to take a victim of a horrible fire to Maryland General Hospital. A few of the medical crew were eating pizza in the break room. Dad lifted the sheet from the body, which was still in a crawling position, and hoisted it onto the litter.

"Doc, can you declare this man deceased?" Dad asked. The other personnel threw their pizza slices back in the box.

"Yeah, he's gone. He's a crispy critter," Dr. Haupt said, and continued eating his pizza. Nothing fazed Haupt. Gesturing with one hand to re-cover the body, he sipped his coffee from a mug shaped like a gargoyle.

Eventually, after receiving his EMT training, my father was given the authority to declare a victim dead, but he still needed the final word from a hospital physician before ordering the body transported to the morgue. He took corpses to the morgue himself only occasionally.

At first he felt painfully awkward in the face of death. He consulted God about how he might appropriately deliver the bad news to patients' loved ones. He even rehearsed his tone and posture so that he would come across as diplomatic, tactful, yet strong. No matter how hard he practiced, in the early days, he wasn't prepared for the reactions he received.

In response to an anonymous call for an injured male, Dad went with another medic to an old three-story building. They walked to the end of a dark hallway and turned the corner. As Dad headed toward the spiral staircase, he nearly walked into a man's knees. Looking up, he saw a man's body hanging from the ceiling by a rope tied tightly around his neck. The body gently swayed back and forth in the center of the staircase. After a quick inspection, Dad knew that he and his partner could do nothing to revive the poor man. Clearly he had died well before they arrived.

Hoping to obtain information, my father swung the body slightly to the left in order to reach an apartment doorway. He banged on the apartment door behind him. The door slowly opened. A frail lady with huge eyes greeted

Dad. She was trembling as she leaned out and looked at the body.

"Is he?"

"Yes, he is."

"You mean—?"

"I mean just what I said."

"He's dead?"

"I'm sorry. Do you know the gentleman?"

She stretched her neck up and gazed on the face of the victim, as if she was trying to recollect his identity.

"Great Googa Mooga!" she cried as recognition set in.

This was an exclamation popularized by Maurice "Hot Rod" Hulbert, Jr., a black DJ imported from Memphis on the recommendation of Buddy Deane, the white DJ whose failed efforts to racially integrate his dance-party show became the background of John Waters' Broadway show and movie "Hairspray." "The Rod" was the first black radio personality to work full-time at an all-white Baltimore station. "Great Googa Mooga" enjoyed minor national popularity, but in Baltimore it was huge. The phrase always purported amazement—usually in a context very different from the discovery of the suicide of somebody near and dear. Today it's still hard for my dad to tell this story without a moment's amusement, despite the horror and pathos of the scene.

On one late-night run, Dad was called to a party where a man was stretched out on the living room floor. He leaned over him and began to check for vital signs: blood pressure, pulse, respiration. His heart had stopped, he was not breathing and his pupils were dilated. The fingernail beds, instead of being pink, had turned completely white, indicating that the blood was no longer circulating through the man's body.

"A dozen people were hovering over me waiting for the verdict. They thought he'd fainted or had too much to drink. They had stepped around him all evening. They figured he'd just passed out.

"Somebody asked, 'Is he? Is he?' "

My father scanned a dozen faces which were anxiously awaiting his response. He dreaded being the bearer of the wretched news that their dear friend had not passed out but passed on. This was the first time Dad had ever told a group of people that their loved one was dead, and it would be the last.

"Yes," he sighed. "I'm sorry I can't do anything further. He's dead." Dad looked at his medic partner Larry, who rolled his eyes, shook his head and cupped his face as if he couldn't believe what Dad had just said. In a flash he understood why.

Pandemonium broke loose. Everyone began howling, "Oh my God, Oh my God—you sure?"

"I'm sure."

"Oh Lord, Lordy no!" A few people ran down the steps and out into the street. One man knocked over a table as he dashed out of the back door. Others threw vases, ashtrays and lamps against the wall. People screamed uncontrollably. One woman rolled around on the floor and began pulling out her hair. Dad worried that his hasty declaration could have caused additional injuries or even another fatality. "I took a mental note. The word 'dead' is a trigger. Don't pull it.

"After this, I would never indicate to someone that their loved one or they themselves were dying, knowing it would cause panic and make the situation unmanageable. This news would be better delivered in the confines of the hospital."

If someone was already dead, he would direct his attentions toward the living relatives and friends. Dad would administer routine medical care and remove the dead person to the closest hospital to be pronounced deceased in order to "keep the lid on a potentially explosive situation." He said, "A death was a delicate matter that had to be handled with utmost concern and compassion. From that point on I quickly learned to say, 'Let's see what we can do.'"

Dad probably would've been a terrific guest star on that popular TV show *Emergency!* about a Los Angeles County paramedic team which made its debut not long after he became a paramedic. Dad had the sideburns for the job and he could put on a convincing act whenever necessary.

My father's partner, whom I'll call Sid, was an intelligent man who used to be a teacher. He had a well-trimmed moustache and spoke with a slight nervous stutter.

A police officer was dutifully compiling his report on a deceased elderly lady who had died of natural causes on the third floor of an old apartment building. Suddenly he smelled smoke drifting in from the hallway. The smoke grew thicker. He called for the fire department and left.

Dad and Sid arrived at the scene with Medic 4 just before the fire units. They quickly entered the building and went door to door to get everybody out safely. The other firefighters arrived soon after them and began search-and-rescue. Dad checked the apartments on the second floor, found them unoccupied, and returned to the lobby on the first floor.

Within seconds, in a haze of smoke, Sid came running down the steps into the lobby with a frail old lady in his arms. He stuttered, "I f-f-f-f-found this w-w-w-w-woman."

He was excited about his daring rescue. As they approached the exit, Dad caught a whiff of decomposing flesh. When he touched the patient's body, it was "as hard as a rock."

"What are you doing?" he said. "She's a corpse. She's as stiff as a board. She's been dead for hours, Sid."

In his honorable haste to help the damsel in distress, Sid had thought she was merely unconscious due to smoke inhalation.

"Sid looked so upset. His eyes widened. 'She's d-d-d-d-d-d?'"

The crowd of onlookers had swelled to almost two hundred people by that time. When reenacting the scene, Dad would always scan our kitchen as if seeing an imaginary crowd. "We had to make ourselves look good. Lights were flooding the building. All the people were watching the fire scene. This could get to the news. The evacuees were looking. Passersby, police officers, the media were looking. It was like being on a Broadway stage. We couldn't turn around and run back into a burning building with a corpse."

Dad said, "Follow me. We'll put her in the medic."

"While the crowd watched, we charged toward the unit as if it were a real rescue. We placed the corpse on the gurney, pretended to attempt to revive her and put her in the ambulance."

Unbeknownst to them, after the fire, the cop returned to the apartment to finish his report about the deceased person he had located before smelling smoke. He was decidedly puzzled. He thought she must have gotten up and walked out. Instead of the standard Dead on Arrival report, he was contemplating a Missing Person report. Baffled by the subject's disappearance, he approached my father and asked if he knew where she was. As much as Dad was tempted to lead him on with a fictitious account, he opted for the truth. "We got her in the back of the medic unit. We didn't want to be famous for rescuing a cadaver."

Heaven Help Us All

Mom agreed with scripture that Sunday was the Lord's Day. To my brother and me, Sundays were hell. We had to pry ourselves out of bed bright and early. My mother would struggle with Craig to get him to put on his dress pants. "I'm going to count to three," she would say. That's when I knew my father would step in and take command. My brother would emerge from his bedroom grumbling about how he hated those "stupid dress pants," hated church and hated the oatmeal my mother had served him in bed. She'd hoped to cheer him up with a red tray and an orange slushy.

I was next. Before my mother could count to three, I threw on the yellow ruffled dress with its loathsome prairie collar, bawling all the while about the itchy shoulder pads. She would clip a wad of chewing gum from my Dorothy Hamill hairdo—I'd sometimes fall asleep while chewing gum, and it would slip out of my mouth and get tangled in my hair—and I'd scream about how the hairstyle made me look like a boy.

My father was next. Dad looked sharp in his black suit.

"You're not wearing the red tie, Bill. Put on the blue one."

He grumbled about how he detested the blue tie as he put it on, then, at her request, closed the fastener on my mother's necklace.

"Let's go." Mom looked stunning in her cream suit, matching shoes, gold necklace and earrings.

My father told Craig that Snuggles, our aging black poodle, couldn't come with us. "Poor Snuggles, pooooor, pooooor Snuggles," he whimpered in jest as the pooch lapped his face.

To save a few bucks Dad always trimmed the dog himself, with the result that Snuggles ended up with several bald patches and a mangled pompadour.

"Bill, don't shave the dog any more."

"She looks perfectly fine, Eunice."

"She looks like she fell into a blender. Now help me carry this."

My mother always insisted on taking a cooler filled with several cans of Coca-Cola, bananas, apples and a few bottles of orange juice. The church was only twenty minutes away, but Mom, like my father, had to be prepared for anything.

"The Lord is so good," she sang. After we all piled into the white Comet, my brother and I were still scowling through the sleep in our eyes.

"Let me tell you what the Lord taught me this week," Mom would begin. "When all hell breaks loose we are on the verge of a miracle."

As a family, we were always "on the verge of a miracle."

In a given week my father might have had a knife held to his throat, I may have broken an arm, Craig was likely to have been sleep-deprived from a torturous case of hay fever. My mother's week generally went like this: playing nurse and referee to my brother and me, doing the laundry and ironing, cleaning the house, cooking the meals, packing the lunches, throwing a party, doing the shopping, feeding the dog, and praying. Mom had a "Prayer Hotline" on which people would ring her nonstop for counsel and "a word from the Lord." My mother offered this service free of charge, and our phone rang so frequently that she had to take the receiver off the hook to get a break. Mom is a woman of keen insight, and the accuracy of her messages from heaven never ceased to amaze even my skeptical father. "It's unbelievable," he'd say to me "but sometimes your mother's messages from the Lord are true."

It was God, Mom told us, who decided that she should marry Dad and not the former boyfriend who had just proposed to her by mail. She was nineteen and Dad was twenty-four. Bill and Eunice met at their church group, "Youth for Christ."

Mom and Dad's dates consisted of a soda pop after church at the local hamburger joint. Mom later recalled, "Bill used to come over to our house for parties and sit in the corner reading a comic book while we played spin the bottle. I liked him because he was faithful and consistent, and he had a strong work ethic."

Dad told her about the year he lived in Germany where his father was once stationed. Mom thought he was exotic because he had spent time overseas.

Yet, in the eyes of my father, with her striking beauty, she was the exotic one. My mother described her great-grandmother as "dark skinned with kinky black hair." People often questioned her mother's nationality. My maternal grandmother was a perfectionist who refused to divulge her family's history. A proud Baptist woman with youthful silken skin until the day she died, Grandmother Elsie often spoke about how she tried to proselytize local Jews. Not long after her funeral just a few years ago we learned from a distant cousin that her own grandmother was in fact, a German Jew. My grandmother kept this a family secret.

Even though he was shy, Bill was popular and well liked by everyone. He proposed to mom one evening after church. They were in her parents' living room. The house was full of people. "Your dad leaned over and asked: 'Will you marry me?' There was nothing at all romantic about it. I said, 'Get out. You need to leave right now.' To me, marriage was a decision for eternity. Still, he had integrity, nobody handed him anything, he always worked for what he had. I admired that in him."

That same week, she had received a letter of proposal from her previous boyfriend, but eventually God told my mother that Bill was the one. It took God three years to get around to sending her the message.

"I am so on fire!"

When my mother said this, she was referring not to earthly passion but to being high on Jesus. My brother would loudly clear his throat and rub his red nose, while Dad applauded Mom's excitement.

My father got excited about greed. He despised it. He quoted Matthew 19:24: "It is easier for a camel to go through the eye of a needle than for a rich man to enter the kingdom of God." Questioned about God, Dad would embark on a sermon, so we rarely asked. But car rides to church were another golden opportunity for my father to preach. The car rides varied greatly in length and direction, and so did Dad's homilies. The family went to all kinds of churches: Baptist, Presbyterian, Assemblies of God. We attended inner-city churches where we saw people "filled with the spirit," so we knew what he was talking about when my father described parishioners in his district.

"The people in the ghetto reach out from their anguish and despair to praise the Lord with singing and preaching. These folk are united in praise during worship services that usually continue for hours. You can see it for yourself where we're going today. In a black church there's a lot more audience participation than at churches with white congregations."

For a split second Dad released both hands from the wheel and shouted "Hallelujah!" Then he continued: "People are uninhibited and enthusiastic. They have great appreciation for being sustained through terrible situations. After a horrible fire in the neighborhood, I watched people leave the churches on Sundays with smiles on their faces."

He continued, "It seems contradictory that the presence of churches on every corner didn't seem to have much effect on the surrounding community and still doesn't. The drug problems still exist. I don't know why, given how many churches there are." But he knew that one answer was this: "The people have to be careful because the thugs know where they live. If they report them, they'll fire-bomb their houses, beat them up, threaten their lives. It still happens.

"Whenever the community bonded together down in my district to protest against drug activities or inform the police, good citizens got killed. People become frightened. When the police or the medics arrive on the scene, the scared bystanders say, 'I don't know nothin'.'"

My father's words were proved a few years ago when Angela Dawson reported to police the rampant drug dealing in her neighborhood. The dealer torched her house, killing her, her husband Darnell, and their five children. Their home is now a memorial: the Dawson Family Safe Haven Community Center, offering computer and arts courses as well as general tutoring services to children in the district.

More than 600 places of worship exist in Baltimore today, and they are as eclectic as the row homes. Churches from the Victorian era still stand in Mount Vernon, and more modest storefront churches are scattered throughout the city.

"Although church attendance didn't end the crime, the services recharged the people, gave them the power to stand strong. To survive from week to week. Despite the challenges, the people kept the faith.

"They didn't take church casually. They may only have had one set of dress clothes, but they'd dress up for church, because that's what you do when you're going to the House of the Lord." Dad described how the men wore suits, ties, impeccably ironed white shirts. The women often wore white dresses with white stockings, high-heeled shoes and coordinated pocket books. "Church hats," whose glamorous and fanciful shapes might be trimmed with fruit or feathers, have been the subject of dissertations and at least one gorgeous coffee-table book. The choir was resplendent in flowing robes. In their finery, the women and men wore smiles on their faces matching the joy in their hearts when worshipping the Lord. The singing and preaching were exuberant and heartfelt; sometimes Dad could hear the music and praise pour out of open doors and windows as he made calls. Congregations ranged in size from four to four hundred. Attendees gathered together in whatever venues were available; then as now, these ranged from old storefronts and former movie theaters to ornate churches, many of which dated from a bygone era when the congregants were affluent whites. Even those which had been abandoned by their former congregants were beautiful structures that had stood the test of time.

My mom handed my brother and me one pack of orange Tic-Tacs each. She would wave a banana in my father's face hoping he would take it and shut up for the rest of the ride.

"Wait a minute, Eunice. You gotta hear this."

"Dad, are you going to tell us about the lady who—" My father cut me off, but I had guessed correctly again.

He said, "One Sunday, my detailed partner and I respond to a call at a large African-American house of worship, specifically the New Metropolitan Baptist Church. Now, I don't really know what happened before we arrived, but based on our regular attendance at inner city church services, I imagine it went something like this: The preacher's delivering his sermon, 'Yes, Lord, this is a beautiful Sunday morning and the good Lord has given us this holy sanctuary to praise his name and worship the Almighty. Turn your head to the brother or sister next to you and shout, God is good!' The congregation follows the instruction, but a few people notice that one sister, slumped over in her seat on the fifth pew, is unresponsive. 'Let us all pray for our fallen sister while the head usher calls for the paramedics. She needs our prayers, love and support and most of all, we need to praise the Lord for all he has done.'

"The men from E-13, along with me and my partner from Medic 4, burst through the rear door of the sanctuary with our medical equipment. As we wheel the gurney toward the unconscious elderly woman sprawled in the pew, the preacher continues. 'My, oh my, the Lord is good.'

"He keeps wringing his handkerchief and wiping his brow every couple of minutes. 'And we pray for God's anointed blessings on our paramedics as they attend to the needs of our beloved sister in her present circumstance.' Her pupils are fixed and dilated. She isn't breathing and has no pulse. The minister is at fever pitch and everybody is right up there with him. Remembering never to use the word *dead*, I glance at my partner and whisper, 'Start CPR.' Meanwhile, the preacher doesn't stop. We feign an attempt to revitalize the deceased woman.

"'And I'll tell you, brothers'—the preacher gasps, then continues—'including our brothers working on our sister, that our Lord has given us this day to celebrate his name . . .' All the people are calling, 'Mmm, hmm' and 'Amen' and 'Yes, Lord.' 'We all need to pray for our blessed sister in the pew there . . .'

"After establishing an IV, I secure her to the gurney and place a small backboard under her so she won't sink into the mattress. My partner steers the gurney as I walk alongside giving closed chest compressions.

"'Give these anointed men a handclap as they roll our sister up the aisle and transport her to the hospital. We know that the will of the Lord is being done. Praise you, Jesus!' Everybody's clapping, waving their hands in the air, jumping and shouting. A lot of churches would stop the service. Not in this neighborhood: nothing stops the praise.

"I can still hear him shouting, 'The Lord bless our brothers for helping our dear sister . . .' as we head down the aisle and out of the sanctuary. I don't let anybody know that she's gone, since the preacher is going on like everything was fine. I figure that maybe he knows something that I don't.

"Despite our valiant efforts, the beloved sister was pronounced dead on arrival at Maryland General Hospital."

We pulled into a parking space near the front door, and before my father had even turned off the engine, my mother was out of the car.

"Praise the Lord, we're here at last," she groaned.

Help Is on Its Way

One evening, just before dark, my father and his partner were careening down 33rd Street past the old Memorial Stadium on a "mission of mercy." As they parted the traffic by flashing the emergency lights and sounding the siren, pedestrians and motorists shouted and waved at them. My father thought they were excited to see the men in action. Then he noticed that everybody on the sidewalks wore worried expressions. They were pointing anxiously at the ambulance. Dad and his partner pulled over and were horrified to see a five-foot flame shooting out from the transmission housing under the unit. The citizens of Baltimore enjoyed the show until the fire department arrived to attend to one of its own.

Baltimore was not unlike other municipalities when it came to budgetary constraints. The city almost always had to opt for the lowest bidders when purchasing emergency equipment. Less than desirable tools of the trade resulted. The units ran incessantly, so breakdowns were commonplace. In the early days, my father used to do temporary repair work on Ambulance 4. Taking a unit to the fire department shop, which was always inundated with units in various states of disrepair, was the last resort. Dad would try to fix minor things himself to avoid having to use a replacement unit that might be in even worse condition.

Duct tape could be used to repair a hose and cover holes in seats, and wire held exhaust pipes more or less in place. Dad spent a lot of time under the hood, jerry-rigging hoses, wires and carburetors. On one occasion, my father's foot went completely through the rusted floor on the driver's side. He covered the jagged hole with a coffee can lid to stop his foot from scraping on the macadam. "I didn't want to propel the vehicle with my feet like Fred Flintstone," he laughed.

Although most ambulances had automatic transmissions when he became a paramedic in 1971, a few old stick-shift units were still in use; these provided a real thrill ride for the medic and patient in the back. Sudden bone-rattling stops and starts were common when a nervous, inexperienced driver ground the gears.

Before the transition to larger, better-equipped medic units, the men had to make do with ambulances my dad termed "Spartan." The 1965 models were impractical. The front cab was a small box with a tight-spaced, suffocating medic module attached to the back of it. The divider between the two compartments made it impossible for the driver to communicate with his colleague in the rear. Dad's cramped red module had bloodstained curtains on the rectangular windows. "That must have given patients confidence," he said.

Doors would unexpectedly pop open. The red bench doubling as a stretcher would sometimes come loose from its restraining brackets. Air conditioning units were a luxury. Even if an AC unit had been fitted into the bare-bones vehicle, it might not work, so the trucks were nearly unbearable on stifling hot summer nights. The back of the medic unit was akin to a boiler. Once, on such a night, a male patient vomited rum. The stench, the closed space and the heat made Dad ask himself, "What am I doing here?"

My father privately initiated an ambulance-decorating contest during the Christmas season.

"A little levity went a long way in relieving stress."

Christmas cards and messages were stuck onto the interior walls. Pine boughs protruded from the air vents. My father's message was "Jingle Bells, Jingle Bells, Jingle all the way, Oh what fun it is to ride in #4 today." He added another message on the ceiling just over the head of the litter which simply said, "If you can read this, you are still alive." Another medic stenciled "Season's Greetings" inside the plastic dome covering the revolving emergency lights.

Low bidding played a role in the purchase of several new, "state-of-the-art" ambulances from a company outside of Maryland. Medic 4 was fortunate to receive one of these units as a replacement. All was well except for one problem. If the frame bolts were not constantly tightened, the modules tended to jolt back from the cab six to eight inches when the driver accelerated. It was even possible for the module to detach from the cab section completely, slide backwards along the frame, and land in the street. My father told me, "I imagined the module stranded in the middle of the street with a paramedic inside administering CPR (cardiopulmonary resuscitation) while the driver arrived at the hospital in the cab." As a remedy, the lieutenant handed my Dad and his partner each a wrench with which to crawl beneath the medic units every morning and tighten the bolts.

On one occasion, the medic unit broke down with no other ambulances nearby, so the medics had to call for a pumper. They went up in the hose bed and worked on the patient there while the fire engine transported them to the hospital.

In the early seventies, a lot of people were doing LSD, PCP, and sniffing glue as well as shooting up with heroin. Dad said that sometimes it was hard to detect exactly what drug patients were "on." In case of a drug overdose, medics were supposed to send an electrocardiogram directly to the emergency room, so the physicians could look at it and advise proper treatment; unfortunately, the EKG equipment often broke down. At that time, the EKG monitor was a large, bulky brown box wired to a radio—another big, heavy box—with an antenna. They would flip open the top and attach three leads with suction cups or round adhesive discs to the person's chest. To transmit the read-out, in theory they simply pushed a button. But there were often bad connections; the read-out was frequently "squiggly" and the radio transmissions were often unreliable.

My dad developed an alternate procedure. From the microphone in the unit or from the handheld radio set, my father would simply call the doctor at the emergency room of whatever hospital was involved and describe the patient's symptoms. The physician would then instruct my father on the administration of appropriate medications.

"I loved to invent new tunes on the Federal Interception Siren," Dad confessed.

The siren control had a series of buttons you could push to make different sounds. If you held them at a certain angle you could change the pitch of the notes. "We'd go up and down the scale. Kids on the side of the road would dance to the beats. It was fun to get the children involved."

One of my father's favorite hits was Three Dog Night's "Joy to the World (Jeremiah was a Bullfrog)." It was on the top of the charts in 1971 and reminded Dad of when he first became a medic. The original medical units did not have ordinary radios, but by the time the new ambulances came in, around 1974 to 1975, radios were standard equipment. Whenever Dad heard "Joy to the World," he'd crank the Medic 4 radio up to top volume. He told me he'd "see men giving each other high fives, women skipping into church holding their children's hands and clusters of teenagers dancing on the corners. I'd watch people enter the greasy spoons and billiard joints, buying snowballs and drinking on the stoops. I'd see the beauty of the people around me and remember that moments of joy can be experienced even in the most appalling circumstances. I'd remember that this is a community worth protecting, worth fighting for. These people are special because of how, despite adversity, they appear to love life."

Sadly enough, the radios were eventually disconnected by the fire department shop on the grounds that they might drown out incoming medic calls.

The medics' supplies could never keep up with the demand. Some weeks my father would go through hundreds of four-by-four inch gauze pads, mostly on head wounds. "Those really bleed!" He had to spread the patient's hair apart, but, he added, "When it's in an Afro the hair springs back into place. That makes it difficult to find the source of the bleeding and stop it." The medics regularly attended to hundreds of head wounds. "People stabbed, shot and clobbered each other, and they almost always attacked the head. To play it safe I sometimes wrapped the entire head, including the Afro. That took a lot of bandage!" Until my father spoke up about the shortage of supplies, he never had enough pads, kling (roll bandage) or even Band-Aids. When they were short on supplies, if he didn't have a splint and gauze, he'd take a magazine or an old board, place it against the leg, and wrap string or gauze around it to immobilize the ankle.

A few leaders like Howard Owens, Superintendent of the Fire Board, really cared about the community. Owens went out on the street with the medics and saw that they needed additional units and more equipment. "You're going to get it," he said, and they did. Owens put an emergency light on top of his own car so he could respond to calls along with the firefighters and thus get a genuine understanding of how they operated.

The media often praised Fire Chief Martin C. McMahon and the medical community for contributing significant improvements into the training processes of emergency care workers. McMahon was associated with the high-profile doctors. My father thought that although McMahon projected well when he taught a class and was always as enthusiastic about his work as a military drill sergeant, he seemed to feel threatened that somebody might steal his thunder. Dad suspected that McMahon didn't like to give subordinates the new equipment. The guys at the station believed McMahon's red car was full of hoarded items such as backboards that were supposed to be distributed to the medics. Dad said, "A captain told us that he couldn't even get equipment for demonstration purposes from McMahon. And this captain was the guy at the top, the guy who ran the show.

"You pandered to the chief to keep him out of your hair. He was harmless enough, but he was full of himself."

McMahon always made a big deal about this great invention that he and a doctor developed together. It was an S-shaped tube called the "resuscitube" to be used for CPR. It was undoubtedly a clever idea. However, my father didn't realize the resuscitube's shortcomings until he and Sid were administering CPR in a life-or-death situation. Dad started doing chest compressions while poor Sid placed the resuscitube into the person's mouth and blew into it. The person's stomach contents came up, erupting through the shaft. Poor Sid's eyes grew big.

"I got a m-m-m-mouthful!" he sputtered, wiping his moustache.

"Apparently this drawback was not foreseen by the great inventor," Dad wryly commented.

My father secretly bided his time for the right moment to convey the unit's needs to the Chief of the Medical Bureau. All he needed was the opportunity.

One soon presented itself.

"It was midday. My good friend Sid and I were cruising through downtown Baltimore. Sid had the dubious distinction of being detailed to the medic unit on this particular day. I was happy about that. He was a pleasure to have on board, as he never complained and was always the gentleman. He used to greet me, 'Dr. Doom, I presume.'

" 'Okay, you've got me pegged, but in truth, I'm Dr. Death, I confess.'

"Sid would also refer to me as 'Cecil B. De Doctor.' I took it as a compliment. As we ribbed each other that day, University Hospital loomed into view, and my brain registered but one strong signal—hot dog! This hospital cafeteria had the most succulent wieners in the known world. I had to have one. I asked Sid to pull our meat wagon up to the main entrance.

"Stops like this were against regulations, but Sid was happy to comply. I had promised to buy him one of these mouth-watering delights.

" 'Mustard, onions and relish!' he shouted as I took off.

"I negotiated my way down the crowded hallway to the cafeteria. I hurried to the line, scooped up two dogs and two sodas. After paying the cashier, I turned and saw Sid rushing toward me, wide-eyed and obviously distressed. 'What seems to be the problem?' I asked. Sid blurted, 'Ch-Ch-Ch-Chief Mc-Mc-Mc-Mahon is outside and he w-w-w-wants to know why we are p-p-parked at the main entrance of the hospital.'

" 'Not to worry. Go out and tell the Chief that I'll be right out.'

"I needed to act quickly. I decided to exit the building via the emergency room. En route to the ER, I wolfed down both dogs, destroying the evidence. My hands were then free to pilfer two or three packs of 200-count four-by-four gauze pads and some kling from the storeroom.

"As I approached the unit with the booty, it dawned on me that at last my golden opportunity had arrived. Chief McMahon was poised to verbally assault me for temporarily deserting my ambulance, despite the fact that I had a portable fire radio with me in case a call came in.

" 'What are you doing here at University Hospital?'

" 'Chief, we do not receive even the basic medical supplies we need, so we have to supplement our stock by frequenting hospital ERs.' It wasn't a lie.

"He was completely taken off guard. My Chief then commended us for our interest and concern. As we chatted, the radio transmitted an emergency run to Medic 4.

"The last thing I saw in the rear view mirror was my boss trying to temporarily hold back traffic for his men. What a guy! As I engaged the siren and apologized to Sid for consuming his lunch, I let out a long, satisfying belch. I savored our small victory. From that point on, we began to receive additional supplies upon request."

Daddy Sang Bass

In the darkness, my brother and I hear a noise. Craig clutches my arm.
"You go first," he says.

"I'm not going first," I whisper, "Why don't you?" If we scream, the intruder might hear us. And if we don't, no one will help us. We can hear it breathing from behind the linen-closet door.

There is no way out. Behind us are only the bedrooms, where this monster will get us for sure. No, we must pass the closet to reach the stairs and escape from the house. Together, we suck in our breath and hope the creature won't hear us. We inch our way forward gripping each other tighter with every step. The floor creaks.

It's too late. It leaps out from the closet and stands in our path.

"Oh no, it's the Pantyhose Monster!" The stranger growls. The Monster turns on the flashlight and holds it under his chin. Flesh-colored nylon distorts its face grotesquely.

"Run!" we scream.

The Monster tackles and tickles us, and we laugh until we can hardly breathe. Daddy sure looked funny with the legs of the pantyhose swinging from his head, making him look like Eeyore, the floppy-eared donkey in *Winnie-the-Pooh*.

When Craig and I were around eight and seven, the Pantyhose Monster was one of our favorite games. We would play it until bedtime, and, then, of course, before tucking us in, my father would tell us medic stories.

Mom preferred to read us children's Bible stories from glossy picture books, the pages crammed with cartoons of Jesus, his disciples and followers. We learned about Jonah being gulped down and trapped in the belly of a whale, about how everyone on the planet except Noah and his family were wiped out in a flood, and how, although Jesus was perfect and spent his life saving everyone, he was eventually betrayed by his friends, ridiculed, tortured, and murdered by the very people he tried to rescue.

By comparison, some of my father's stories seemed almost cheerful.

While some children listen to fairy tales before going to sleep, my bedtime stories were all about characters battling poverty, prejudice and addiction in Baltimore City ghettoes—that is, if my father was home to tuck me in and not out in the streets engaged in that battle.

He would deliver his adventures comically, as if to ease our fears about the dangers of his job. He stressed that "the Golden Rule, doing unto others as we would have them do unto us, is what life is supposed to be about." As he recounted and acted out the scenes, he taught us to see beauty in tragedy. Wide-eyed at the end of each story, he would shake his head as if befuddled, and momentarily grow silent. These people in the stories were not strangers; they were people in crisis who touched his heart.

When Craig and I were around four and five years old, as a special treat we were sometimes allowed to sleep in the same room. My brother had a four-wheeled fire engine bed, painted red, with a real bell and a wooden wheel that he could steer. His room was wallpapered with a print of firefighters in action, Dalmatians standing faithfully beside them. We had several toy fire trucks. One even had a hose and a pump with which my brother liked to drench my Barbie Dream House. He would then rescue Barbie by flinging her face down on the sidewalk.

Once we were nestled under the covers, Dad would march in like a monster with his arms extended stiffly in front of him. He would slide out his three-tooth partial plate with his tongue and grip it between his lips to make himself look as if he had only one tooth.

Craig and I would scream with laughter and clutch each other, pretending to be terrified. Or Dad would spin around like Julie Andrews in *The Sound of Music*. He'd turn his back to us and muss up his hair so it stood straight up, then he'd turn around and belt out, in a shrill falsetto voice, "The hills, they're alive, Aaaahhhhhhh!"

After the monster yell, Dad would stand in the doorway of my brother's bedroom hoping to prolong his exit. He was on a roll. But before he could begin another tale my mother's voice called from downstairs

"Biiillll! The kids are going to King's Dominion tomorrow. Please don't keep them up."

"Eunice, they're sound asleep."

"Don't lie to me, Hennick. You've got ten minutes," came the response from on high.

"Aye, Aye, Captain." Dad saluted in Mom's direction.

Craig and I roared with laughter while we fought over the covers. "How 'bout Jungle Man, Daddy?" We loved hearing about the man who grazed in one of the city's few parks.

"Bill," Mom called out, "the kids need to get to sleep."

My father pretended to resist. "You don't want to hear that do you? You've got to get to bed."

"Please, Dad, please." Jungle Man was one of our favorites. We never tired of that story.

Dad obliged—softly, so my mother couldn't hear him. "They called it Harlem Park, a small green patch on Harlem Avenue surrounded by row houses. One of the residents was a small, skinny, middle-aged black man affectionately dubbed Jungle Man. Jungle Man liked to lounge in the center of the park and eat grass. When I encountered him, he was surrounded by about half a dozen teenagers, and he was chomping away with the chlorophyll dripping down his chin.

" 'Everything all right?' I ask. No response. 'You okay?' He looks up with his big eyes and keeps on chewing. 'Can you walk?' Not a movement. He just kept grazing. Every once in a while he rolled his eyes up as if to say, 'I see you, but I don't want to be disturbed.' Jungle Man just looked at me with his big hollow eyes. As gaunt as he was, I pegged him for a wino whose mind had gone.

" 'What's his name?' I ask the onlookers.

" 'Jungle Man,' the kids say. They went on to explain that he ate grass in the park every day.

" 'Well, Jungle Man doesn't look so good.'

" 'What's the matter with him?' they ask.

" 'Well, if he eats grass every day and nothing else, maybe he needs something more in his diet.' I point to some weeds, 'Like these dandelions over here.'

"'What do we do?" they ask. They knew I had to be kidding about the dandelions.

"I can see by the looks on the kids' faces that, to them, he isn't a drunk; he's their neighbor. I can't just leave him there. I try to make it clear that I have Jungle Man's best interest at heart. I can see that they're eager to help him. He needs hospital care, but I can't wheel him out across the bumpy ground on a litter, because it might tip over.

"I run over to the medic unit and retrieve a backboard used for people with neck and back injuries and return to the kids hovering over Jungle Man.

"'I know you all like Jungle Man, and I'm sure he'd appreciate it if you could help get him out of here to where he can get some care and some better food. You all can help him. Are any of you strong here?'

"All the kids cry out, 'Yeah, we strong. We can help.'

"I gently hoist the patient onto the board. Six boys, three on each side, lift Jungle Man. Then there is a procession leading to the medic unit about three hundred feet away. The scene takes on the appearance of a metropolitan safari as we wend our way across the park. Even as they carry him to the medic unit, Jungle Man is still chomping away on a wad of grass. The young neighbors are pleased that he's hospital-bound and delighted to have had an active role. As I deliver Jungle Man to the closest emergency room, I can't help but wonder if he will hold out for grass over hospital food."

"All right, kiddos, time for beddy-bye."

Then he'd kiss us, say "I love you," and turn out the lights.

We weren't afraid of the dark. Dad had taught us that, even in the depths of fear, laughter is the light that will lead us safely home.

Love Child

Once my father walked ten miles to work in a blizzard when his car was snowed in. He lay on the couch suffering from bronchitis the whole following week. I later learned, when I was old enough to know where babies came from, what had happened the day of the snowy ten-mile hike.

Dad had arrived in time to begin his shift at 7:00 a.m. The second he stepped into the firehouse, exasperated and half-frozen, the medics received a call and headed out. Despite having put chains on the wheels of the medic unit, they got stuck in a snowdrift. Several residents helped to dig them out so they could respond to a woman who was about to give birth.

When they arrived, the mother-to-be, who must have weighed 350 to 400 pounds, was having contractions three to four minutes apart. They managed to transport her to the hospital. Dad struggled to stay awake through the rest of the day. At about four in the afternoon, a call came in for the same address. It didn't occur to my father that this call could possibly be for the same maternity case. However, they pulled up in front of the same residence they had visited ten hours earlier.

The medics entered the front door amid confused shouts from the occupants. Dad was perplexed. The same full-term mother-to-be they had delivered to St. Agnes Hospital was back home standing in the middle of the living room floor.

"What's seems to be the problem?" he asked.

"I went to the hospital and they told me to go home. They told me it wasn't time yet. I still got pressure in my belly, it hurts." In the 1960s and 1970s, prenatal care was unknown to many pregnant women in the ghetto, and my father frequently helped mothers to birth their children. Sometimes the women hadn't even known that they were pregnant.

Before Dad had time to question her further, the tip of an upside-down newborn's head emerged from beneath the hem of her muumuu. The infant bounced gently up and down, suspended by the umbilical cord.

He pointed to the new arrival, "Well, looks like it's time."

"Oh my goodness. Oh my goodness."

She was in shock. With the help of family members, as my father cradled the infant, they lowered the new mom onto the tile floor. The baby wasn't breathing. Still holding the infant in his arms, Dad stuck a syringe into each of the child's nostrils to remove the fluids and clear the airway.

Dad told me, "If that hadn't worked, I would have breathed the slightest puffs of air into his mouth and used two fingers to administer CPR. I had done that a number of times. I gave a sigh of relief when I heard a cry from his fragile little body."

When the umbilical cord stopped pulsating, my father tied two pieces of string around it, and in the gap between the ties he cut the tough, fibrous cord with surgical scissors. He then presented the newborn baby to the mother and, tired as she was, she smiled and softly whispered those first bonding words to her baby, kissing the top of his tiny head.

They waited for the placenta to be expelled. According to Dad, "The placenta resembles a big liver. I always placed it in a plastic bag like a fish and took it to the hospital where the physicians could examine it for diseases and determine whether the infant had been infected. I always hoped for the best."

Of course, one baby story led to another. "The most unforgettable birth was when I rushed to an apartment and found the mother-to-be lying on the bed watching a soap opera," my father told me. "Her contractions were down to one minute apart. The water hadn't broken yet, but delivery was close.

"'We need to take you to the hospital. Your baby is on its way,' I had said.

"'No. Hold on. I got to see the end of my story!'

"'But your baby could arrive before the next commercial.'

"'I told you to hold on just a minute. I like this one. This is the big day. I've got to find out what happens.'

"'It's time.'

"'It's time for me to find out what happens on this program. Now you wait, I want to see this. Wait ten minutes. It will be over in ten minutes.'

She had a big frown on her face."

My father continued, "She was a big woman and I wasn't going to argue with her. I sat down, and we both watched the last ten minutes of the television drama. Her water broke just as it ended, and she delivered a healthy baby boy. Now that's what I call a dedicated fan of the soaps!" Dad said, bursting into his typical cackle, "Uh, hee, hee, hee. Oh man, that was funny."

According to Dad, "Black women seemed to experience less difficulty in giving birth than white women did. I know it may sound racist to make a generalization based on race, but I have to say that by comparison, the women in the ghetto were more subdued during the pain of childbirth and much less likely to scream, panic or complain. I believe it was because they'd experienced greater hardships and become resilient."

These babies survived, despite being born in the worst of conditions. I sometimes wonder what life's work lay ahead for all of the precious infants my father delivered over the years. I shudder to think that many of them may eventually have ended up as addicts or dead at a young age. But I hope others grew up to be good parents and hard workers. Maybe they found the means to provide a better life for children of their own.

Living for the City

"We can take this act on the road!" my father said as he beat his belly like a drum. The rhythm escalated furiously. I tap-danced harder and harder on the brown linoleum of the basement floor, improvising steps in my imaginary tap shoes, pretending to be Shirley Temple performing with Bill "Bojangles" Robinson, swinging my arms left and right.

I picked up my moves from the classic films Dad and I would watch together on Sunday afternoons when he didn't have to work. We played this game regularly, but we didn't have a name for it.

"If times get tough, I'll put on a pair of shades and grab a tin can and we'll stand on a corner and rake in the cash," he'd joke, accentuating his punch line with a drumbeat. "But listen to your old man. Marry rich."

I'd twirl and twirl to see how fast I could spin around without getting dizzy, then stop to watch the room spin and feel the blood rush around in my head.

"It doesn't matter if he's rich, honey, as long as he loves the Lord and you," my mother would call out from the kitchen.

"Ah, no," he'd stage-whisper, "What you want to do is sit by your private swimming pool all day." He'd give a drumroll and then add, "And don't forget to buy your aging father a hot tub."

Dad saw so much poverty that he didn't want his children ever to be in need. He always worried about money. He would often eat little but eggs and toast so he could buy soccer cleats for my brother or new eyeglasses for me. But Daddy was wealthy in spirit.

My father wanted to save the world. He didn't think he was perfect. Highly self-critical, he often berated himself for working long hours and not earning much money. He thought maybe he should have accepted the lucrative management position which the American Automobile Association had once offered him. "I'm not any kind of a hero," he'd insist. "I'm just doing my job." I don't think he could have lived any other way even if he had wanted to. He followed the convictions of his heart. My mother said, "Some people are called to be teachers, housewives, or gardeners. Your father was called to be a ghetto medic."

But there were some people he couldn't rescue. And though it wasn't his fault, he never got over losing Charlie.

He told us Charlie's story. "It was a hot, steamy July afternoon the first time that I took notice of this little black boy about five years old trying to make a go in the ghetto by giving shoeshines to passersby on Pennsylvania Avenue. He stood out. He was a little kid, but he was seriously working. His oversized shirt and pants hung loose on his small body.

"I was on a run, and I remember thinking to myself that whoever is looking after him is doing a good job. He showed maturity beyond his years, real potential. He seemed to put his heart into his work and gave the pedestrian clients great shoeshines for the small fee he charged. Yet I felt sorry for him, because I knew that he had a labyrinth to get through if he was going to survive."

On that same day, toward evening, Dad was called to return to the same corner where he had noticed Charlie earlier. After the unit screeched to a halt, Dad got out of the ambulance and made his way through the crowd. There lay Charlie, still at his post, only now he was writhing and twisting on the ground in the relentless throes of a full-blown grand mal epileptic seizure.

My father knelt down, slid off his jacket, and put it under Charlie's head so he wouldn't smash his skull on the concrete. He tried to put several rolled up gauze pads in Charlie's mouth to stop him from biting his tongue, but his teeth had already clamped down. Gripping him firmly but gently, my father and his partner tried to protect Charlie from harming himself on the broken glass and debris surrounding him on the sidewalk. Dad held his hand and monitored his airway until the crisis passed. After several minutes, his exhausted body relaxed.

Dad and his partner examined him. Charlie had numerous cuts and bruises, along with the temporary loss of memory that always follows seizures. He was weak and fatigued but conscious as they transported him to University Hospital. The physician attended to his wounds and declared him fit to return to his home, which was located in a high-crime area several blocks west of Medic 4.

This was the first of many encounters Dad had with Charlie over the years. Charlie was always shining shoes, selling newspapers or sweeping sidewalks in front of the small storefronts along Pennsylvania Avenue: anything to earn a few dollars. Dad wanted to see him succeed but knew his chances were slim in that environment.

The next time Charlie had a seizure, Dad met the boy's grandmother at the hospital. She was young, probably in her forties, a stocky woman with thin ankles. She wore a plain housedress. Her pulled-back hair was untidy. By her account, his seizures were on the increase, and taking care of Charlie was requiring more and more of her time.

"I could tell she didn't take time to do anything for herself," Dad said.

She mentioned that she didn't have transportation to the hospital, but she had to be there with Charlie because he was a minor. Dad said, "I knew she had her hands full. I respected her and empathized with her situation. I told her that when it happened next I would take him to her house first." She lived in an area known today as Sandtown-Winchester, an area south of North Avenue and west of Pennsylvania Avenue.

In the late 1800s, Sandtown was a diverse suburb of working-class, professional and rising-middle-class residents. Rich and poor lived side by side. Both whites and blacks had moved to Sandtown to improve their status. Back then, it was a neighborhood where children played football and basketball in the streets while their mothers kept a close watch on them. A few people can still remember when Sandtown was a close-knit community offering gleaming marble steps, flowers on windowsills and countless social engagements. But by 1970, most incomes in the area had fallen below the federal poverty line, and the place was the site of a thriving drug market. Back in Charlie's time, the area was sick.

Still pounding his "drum" while I danced, Dad continued. "It deviated from protocol, but the next time Charlie had a seizure I went by his grandmother's place before going to the hospital. It was a corner house next to an alley on Riggs Avenue. The neighborhood was pretty rough. While my partner attended to Charlie's injuries in the back of the medic unit, I knocked on the door. His grandmother opened it.

"'We found him on Pennsylvania Avenue. He fell down and hit his head on the pavement.'

"'I appreciate this, you coming by, I really appreciate it. What do you think?'

"'He needs to go to the hospital.'

"I waited for her so she could ride with us. She moved quickly: grabbed her coat, instructed several other kids on proper behavior, phoned a trusted neighbor to watch them and headed out the door."

My father told me that he developed a routine. He would attend to Charlie on the street and then stop by his home with the ambulance to notify his grandmother of the boy's condition and potential need for hospital treatment. More often than not, after looking at the cuts and bruises, she would want her grandson to remain at home under medication and allow time to heal the wounds.

Dad said, "She impressed me as a hardworking woman with tremendous inner strength and an unselfish love for her grandchildren. Quiet and serious. She tried to keep him motivated, busy and out of trouble. His welfare was paramount to her. She saw great possibilities in Charlie. She wanted him to reach manhood and make something of himself. She always wore an expression of great concern as she attended to his needs. Over the years, I continued to marvel at the determination and devotion that this woman freely bestowed on her loved ones."

As time passed, the frequency of Charlie's seizures increased relentlessly. Dad saw Charlie more and more often.

And then he disappeared.

From time to time Dad called on Charlie's grandmother to check on him, but, by then, even she had no idea of his whereabouts. It later transpired that Charlie was spending more and more time with the neighborhood alcoholics. Drinking and seizures don't mix. My father was later to learn of

Charlie's tragic end.

"I missed him." Dad said quietly. "I tried to keep in touch, but he just dropped out of sight."

Looking back, it's amazing that I did not twirl and twirl until I lost consciousness to escape the heartbreak that throbbed in some of these stories.

My father and I had nicknames for each other which we used once in a while. He was "Chumps." I was "Little Nanakabutski." I never knew what it meant, and he didn't either. It was just a word he made up. He usually pinched my cheeks when he said it.

"I missed him, Little Nanakabutski," he repeated, almost in a whisper.

I extended my legs as if I were in a chorus line, lifting my invisible hat with every kick. In my heart, I believed that, even if our family somehow became destitute or one of us got some kind of disease like Charlie's, we would survive. I knew I was lucky. We had a father who would stand by us no matter what. We would never go hungry. We would never be without medical care. Daddy would simply pound his belly and I would dance my heart out until the money poured in.

Stayin' Alive

"You ain't taking me to Provident." The big unshaven man with cuts from head to toe spat.

He and Dad were on their way to the hospital. The man had gotten into a fight at a McDonald's on Reisterstown Road and ended up crashing through a window. When Dad arrived, he was lying on his back hemorrhaging, with six- to eight-inch shards of glass spearing his body.

Dad pointed toward the window and said, "See the block numbers? They're going up, not down. Don't worry, we're going to Sinai."

"He must have weighed 250 pounds. I think if I had been taking him to Provident he would have mustered up the strength to let fly at me," Dad said.

With integration, diminishing community interest and a growing upwardly mobile black population, the number of black-operated hospitals fell from well over a hundred in the 1950s to around a dozen in the 1980s. When Dad was working as a paramedic, Old Provident Hospital on Division Street—originally constructed in 1894 to serve the African-American community—did not have a good reputation in the district. In those days even the best hospital emergency rooms were small and inadequately staffed, but conditions at Provident, as widely reported by patients, staff and journalists, were appalling.

By the 1960s, medical practitioners and insured patients preferred to go to "better equipped" white-operated facilities. Provident Hospital had accepted significant state loans in 1968 for construction of its new building; however, by the mid-1970s, with immense debt, poor cash flow and insufficient patient numbers, it was already in financial difficulty.

My father said, "The local residents all knew someone who had either received poor service or died there." The hospital was dirty. The nursing staff were reputed to make mistakes and either ignore patients or give them a hard time. Sick and injured patients were tolerated instead of being treated with compassion.

Once, Dad saw a man sitting in the hallway swaying back and forth holding a compress on his arm. "He'd been stabbed, and the knife probably hit an artery because blood was pouring on the floor. The pool was already three feet across and growing. He was going to die." He was barely conscious when Dad questioned him.

"How come you're sitting here like this?"

"The nurse told me to hold this compress on my arm, and she never came back." My father got somebody to help him immediately.

Provident Hospital was located near the shopping center created in the late fifties, Mondawmin Mall. The city and community had had high hopes for Mondawmin. Dad frequently sang the old advertising jingle:

Mondawmin, Mondawmin,
A better shopping day is dawnin',
Just park your car, and there you are,
In beautiful new Mondawmin.

"Catchy but inaccurate," Dad said. "Back then I thought to myself, if you had a car to park, you had to pray it would still be there when you finished shopping. I worried that it might be a good shopping day for shoplifters, car thieves and hold-up men."

Mondawmin was once a 45-acre estate, including stables, manse and slave quarters, located in northwest Baltimore on Reisterstown Road and Liberty Heights Avenue. It had belonged to venerable physician Dr. Patrick Macaulay, director of the Baltimore and Ohio railroad, member of City Council, and colleague of hospital founder Johns Hopkins. In the early 1800s, the poet Henry Wadsworth Longfellow visited the new country home of his friend Dr. Macaulay. The red brick house sat atop a hill on the rolling terrain, surrounded by a rose garden, rhododendrons and native forest trees. Together the two gentlemen stood on the porch gazing onto an expanse of corn. Dr. Macaulay asked Longfellow to assist him in choosing a name for his abode.

"You have the name right before you—Mondamin, the spirit of the corn," said Longfellow.

He was referring to a name that appears in one of the songs belonging to his epic poem *The Song of Hiawatha*, written about northern American Indian tribes.

More than a century later, investors arranged for the demolition of the buildings on the estate to accommodate Mondawmin Mall. (The name had been slightly amended.) Built in 1956, it was, at the time, the most advanced shopping center in the United States and the first to be built in a residential district of a city.

As blacks began settling in the area in the 1950s, whites started to move out. After the race riots in the sixties, a mass exodus of whites and many middle-class blacks occurred. The number of customers decreased. Sales plummeted. Merchants vacated their stores, giving the mall an air of degeneration. In 1973, with the exit of its "anchor," Sears & Roebuck, the mall further deteriorated. By 1977, Mondawmin Mall was 25 percent vacant and the government declared it a distressed property. It became known for its open-air drug markets with up to fifty people at a time waiting on corners for deliveries. The run-down feel of the mall was matched by that of Provident Hospital.

Eventually, under the new management of Rouse Company, renovation efforts began. A physical makeover, new tenants, increased police presence and added mall security aided the successful transformation, which nearly doubled previous sales within five years and reduced vacancy to 3 percent. Mondawmin has shown great resilience and, in the hands of General Growth Properties, it is thriving today.

Not all Dad's comments about Provident were negative. "There were some good medical practitioners there, such as Elijah Saunders. Dr. Saunders was a well-respected cardiologist who later became the head of the Division of Hypertension at the University of Maryland Medical Center. When good nurses and doctors worked there, they usually didn't stay long; they couldn't tolerate the conditions. It was as if many of the personnel just didn't care about the people."

The political hierarchy in the city chose to ignore Provident's shortcomings. The belligerent shard-studded man was just one of the numerous people who begged my father to transport them to a hospital other than Provident. The rules required him to take them to the closest facility, but, regardless of that, Dad would go somewhere else whenever he could.

He told me about an incident that occurred when there was a horrible car accident. Three cars were totaled, and five or six people lay injured on the street. Dad called the hospital, explained the extent of the injuries and told them to get ready. When he arrived, the nurse was just sitting at the reception desk, head resting on her hand. At any other hospital, in a situation as horrific as that, staff members would be at the door ready to assist the victims. She had not even bothered to call anyone to be on the alert.

"Oh, was that you who phoned? Okay, whatcha got there now?" was all she said.

Pick up the Pieces

"Attending to people in wealthy areas was like stepping into another world," Dad said. And in areas such as Bolton Hill, homes occupied by the wealthy and the destitute alternate between streets. He had to adjust immediately from handling the derelict drunk on the street to tending the socialite in the mansion. Although the rich might have had well-kept homes and expensive furnishings, they and their less well-off neighbors sometimes had a common bond. While the derelict was drinking himself to death, the socialite was using prescribed medications as a ticket to the next life.

On one occasion, a woman from one of the expensive homes had just experienced a major heart attack. When Dad wheeled her toward the back of the medic unit, she fired demands: "Is my door locked? Did you turn the heat down? Make sure my purse isn't on the table . . ." Saving a few dollars was more important to her than her own life.

Bolton Hill, named not long after the Revolutionary War for an English estate, is also known as the Gin Belt—a name assigned by the artists, writers and other bohemians who moved there in the 1920s. The district lies between central Baltimore and Druid Hill Park. It is where F. Scott Fitzgerald wrote his acclaimed novel, *Tender is the Night*. It is the location of the Maryland Institute College of Art, the Meyerhoff Symphony Hall, the University of Baltimore, and the Patricia and Arthur Modell Performing Arts Center. Streetcar tracks are still visible among the cobblestones. The old alley houses on the 1300 block of Rutter Street still exist and today are home to art students.

Bolton Hill's nineteenth-century row houses, all elegant whether simple or ornate, were once owned by art collectors, philanthropists and Confederate war veterans. Carriage houses, mansions and brick cottages stand alongside modern town houses and brownstones. Some display wrought iron ornamentation, terra cotta carvings and deep bay windows. Others have stained glass windows and rusticated stonework, arched entrances, and marble fireplaces. Eutaw Place, one of several tree-lined Bolton Hill boulevards, boasts fountains, monuments and urns filled with flowers.

Dwellings built by affluent Baltimoreans on hilltops allowed for distant views of the harbor. African-Americans worked as domestic servants in the mansions of wealthy physicians or politicians, either as live-in servants or occupying small alley houses. However, in time, people began to leave Bolton Hill; some could no longer maintain mansions like those on Eutaw Place, while others left their city dwellings for county houses surrounded by acreage. In the mid-1900s, numerous homes were converted into apartments for WWII defense workers. Although much of "posh" Bolton Hill has been preserved at the western end, roads such as Linden Avenue and Eutaw Place deteriorated into slums and have only recently begun to show the revitalization efforts which began in the 1960s.

At least once a week, for six months to a year, my father would drive Ambo 4 north on Linden Avenue to assist his friends Harry Lee, Leroy and Lucille. According to Dad, Harry Lee looked like an adult version of "Buckwheat" from the TV show *Little Rascals*. He sported a scraggly beard and an Afro. Leroy was a taller and thinner version, more nondescript in appearance. Lucille was a huge woman who wore her black hair combed back severely. They were all around 40 years of age. They were drinking buddies, and Thunderbird was their beverage of choice.

The threesome were the best of friends most of the time, but once in a while an argument escalated into violence. Harry Lee would stab Lucille, Lucille would hit Leroy over the head with a bottle and Leroy would shove Harry Lee down the steps. They'd beat each other with household appliances and kitchen utensils. That's when Dad would appear on the scene to bandage their wounds, administer intravenous drips and hope for a successful trip to the ER. Most of his clients he would see only once a year. Because these three were "regular," Dad and the trio got to know one another. A friendship developed. He grew fond of these folk. Eventually they addressed each other on a first name basis. Every week or so, when Dad got called to the address, he would try to guess which one of them was hurt.

One night he was attending to Lucille's knife wounds in the back of the medic unit.

"How you doin', Lucille? What happened this time?" he asked.

She spoke slowly. "Oh, you know, Bill." Then she smiled and propped her head in her hand, resting her weight on her elbow. "Isn't this some mess?" She narrowed her eyes like she was trying to make sense of it. "Ain't this somethin'? That man stabbed me again."

"You gonna file charges?"

"No." She squinted her eyes tighter. "I'll get that S-O-B."

On my father's next visit, he arrived on the scene to find Lucille clutching an eight-foot two-by-four. She'd nailed him. Harry Lee lay motionless on the ground in a large pool of blood. Dad hesitated before approaching him. Just as he did, she raised the board over her head, looking a bit wild in the eyes.

"You better back off right now, Bill, I'm tellin' you—you next, I'll kill ya, hear? I ain't foolin', I'll kill youse both."

"But Lucille . . ." my father crouched and shielded his face and head with his hands, "Harry Lee might survive if I can get him to the hospital right away."

She froze, breathed loud through her nostrils and then slowly lowered her weapon. My father knelt down beside Harry Lee and examined his gaping head wound. "Lucille, he's going to die if we don't stop the bleeding and get him to the hospital ASAP."

Slowly Lucille nodded her head in agreement. She stood there trembling and sweating as my father established an IV and tried to control the severe bleeding. He bandaged the wound with a thick stack of gauze pads and wrapped a roll of kling around Harry Lee's head like a turban.

My father said, "We all rode to the hospital together, united in the desire for a positive outcome in the welfare of our mutual friend."

I Can't Get it Out of My Head

Baltimore dubbed itself "Charm City" in 1974 when copywriter Bill Evans attempted to turn around the city's poor image. "Decaying wharfs, rats, hoboes. That was downtown Baltimore," Evans himself once said. Natives quickly came to refer to Baltimore as "Harm City." Their dark comedy was a salve for the city's seemingly insurmountable problems.

One of the later medic units had a seldom-used speaker designed for crowd control mounted on the roof. There was a microphone in the cab. One guy rigged it so that when he turned his portable tape recorder on and opened up the microphone, the William Tell Overture would resound as they sped out of the door.

As the last strains of the overture faded one night, the unit arrived on Gilmor Street in response to a call. Just a few yards from a small neighborhood watering hole, a man was lying on the concrete sidewalk mumbling incoherently. A small crowd of onlookers had gathered to watch.

Bending over the seemingly intoxicated man, Dad asked "What seems to be the problem?"

"Arrooh, eeeooch, slahsha." My father had no idea what he was trying to say. He examined the man for a possible injury or a severe medical condition warranting transport to a hospital, but he was injury-free, and his vital signs were stable. As the man lay only a short distance from the bar and had no other visible problems, my father thought he was drunk.

"Where do you live?" my father asked.

"Arrooh, eeeooch, slahsha." Dad repeated the question over and over and each time received the same incomprehensible answer. Unable to make any headway, he turned to the onlookers.

"I think he say he live at that house," ventured a young man, pointing to a place a few doors away and across the street.

To save putting him in the emergency room for something that wasn't an emergency, my father and his partner, a detailed firefighter, put the mumbling inebriate in the wheeled litter, rolled him up the street and carried him up the marble steps to the doorway of the old brick town house. The door was ajar.

"Ambo," Dad called out several times but received no response. He eased into the foyer and noticed a neatly made bed in a sparsely furnished room to his left. They gently transferred their friend onto the bed. He smiled and sighed, seeming to affirm that he was home. They rechecked the man's vitals to ensure he would be okay before bidding a fond adieu.

A little later, as they were leaving, my father noticed several blue lights of police vehicles converging on Gilmor Street. Dad and his partner returned to work, and two or three hours after this incident, my father saw a police car coming down the cross street. He knew the cop. When he pulled over, my father asked him what the commotion had been about on Gilmor Street.

The police had been called to the same house they had visited earlier. The elderly lady who lived there had returned from the corner grocery store only to find a man in her bed, muttering and throwing up. They apprehended the man and charged him with trespassing. No one could understand him. As they drove him to the lockup in the paddy wagon he was shouting "Arrooh, eeeoooch, slahsha."

"People are trapped in bottles. Like genies." I heard my father say this time and again. "Driving under the influence of 'the bottle' and other drugs is common for people in my area who happen to have cars. Often they don't have car insurance, and if they do they pay for it by the day."

One night, as my father and his partner approached the scene of an accident, they could see three damaged vehicles. They screeched to a halt. A taxi and a second car had been stopped at a red light when both were struck from behind by a speeding '66 Oldsmobile. The entire back end of the taxi was crushed all the way to the rear windshield. Dad expected the worst as he poked his head through the side window. All three female passengers were conscious and complaining of neck and back pain. The paramedics slid backboards under them, put soft collars around their necks and checked their vitals. They then called for two additional medic units to assist in treating the victims and transporting them to the hospital. The second car in the group contained one male. He had minor abrasions and contusions. However, his car got folded like a concertina when the Oldsmobile forcibly shoved it into the taxi.

The driver of the Oldsmobile, a short, stocky, black man in his early thirties, was standing on the median strip with both hands in his pockets. He gave the impression of being oblivious to his surroundings and totally unconcerned with the mayhem he had wrought. My father made an unsuccessful attempt to talk to him and was greatly relieved to see the police pull up.

"What happened here?" an officer asked.

"I ran into the back of that car!"

The officer rephrased his question. "Well, how did it happen?"

"I couldn't find the brake pedal." Since the brake pedal on the Olds was about eight inches wide, the cop immediately suspected that the driver was drunk. He demanded proof of registration. The driver pointed to the glove compartment, confessing that he had borrowed the car for the evening, and gave the name of the rightful owner.

My father was still on the scene compiling information when a tall, well-dressed black man appeared. He was visibly shaken and, with trembling lips, tried to express himself. In a voice fraught with panic and disbelief, he asked his ex-friend, "What happened?"

Silence.

"You understand it's going to cost me hundreds to get this car fixed?" The ex-friend continued to stare into the distance with both hands in his pockets. The distinguished owner of the car took a more realistic approach. He said calmly, "It's going to cost me fifteen to twenty dollars to get my car towed. Are you taking care of that?"

Slowly and methodically, the driver removed his hands from his pockets and began counting some loose change into his right hand. He kept rubbing his eyes, adjusting his focus and swaying. After a few moments, he nonchalantly drawled, "Well, all I got on me is two dollars and I need that for cab fare."

A few months later my father was in the district on a run that turned out to be a false call, so he had a few minutes to spare. Dad hadn't heard anything from the crew on Linden Avenue for a while and wanted to see if they were okay, so he popped by.

Lucille opened the door and smiled. "Bill, how have you been? Come on in. I want to show you my apartment."

"Well. This certainly looks a lot better than it did before, Lucille."

Previously, it had been a trash heap.

Harry Lee had survived the head injury dealt by Lucille's two-by-four and, not long afterward, had proposed to Lucille. They became man and wife with Leroy in attendance as best man. My father later said he could just picture the look on Lucille's face when she said "until death do us part." Lucille had become a homebody and proudly took him on a tour of the old house, which she had cleaned and decorated with loving care. My father was never called to his friends "on business" again.

Almost Lost My Mind

Back in the seventies, before lunatics started lacing children's candy with cyanide and stuffing apples with razorblades, Halloween in any Baltimore neighborhood was a sight to behold. At night, droves of children masquerading as monsters, witches, goblins, movie stars, cheerleaders and athletes knocked on strangers' doors to collect assorted goodies. My brother and I greedily accepted Mary Janes, Smarties, Twizzlers, Gobstoppers, and Starbursts; already parents were warning children not to accept treats that didn't come in store-bought packaging. Each year, my father drove us to other suburban neighborhoods with row homes. There we could easily dash from door to door, fill our plastic pumpkins and even pillowcases with candy, and empty them in the car where Dad waited before racing to another section of houses. He wouldn't have to buy us candy for about five months.

When we got home Craig and I would dump it all onto the dining room table, creating a candy mountain. Mom would give us a few dozen bowls of various shapes and sizes, and we would sort the treats accordingly, dividing chocolate, chewing gum, caramels, licorice and hard candy. Dad would sneak a few pieces himself when he thought we weren't looking.

My mother, a gifted costume designer, meticulously sewed our outfits from scratch. We were "matched sets" like Raggedy Ann and Andy in grade school; in later years Donny and Marie (with perfect plastic teeth), Luke Skywalker and Princess Leia, or Danny and Sandy from the hit movie *Grease.*

We would wait to carve the pumpkin on a night when Dad was home from work. He would slice off the top while Craig and I argued over who got to dig out the mush—we both loved the creepy feel of the slime squishing between our fingers. Mom exhorted us to take turns. After we picked out the seeds she would spread them evenly on a cookie sheet and toast them in the oven.

"Dad, can we go to the haunted house at Putty Hill Shopping Center?" Craig asked.

"If you kids want to see some haunted houses, I'll take you to downtown Baltimore."

"Daaaaad, I'm serious."

"So am I. I'm telling you, some frightening things are going on down there."

"Tell us about Wolfwoman," I would plead.

"No. You don't want to hear that, do you?" Dad would tease his audience by launching into a different story, reserving Wolfwoman for the finale. My exasperated mother would begin singing the hymn "How Great Thou Art."

O Lord my God, When I in awesome wonder,
Consider all the worlds Thy hands have made;
I see the stars, I hear the rolling thunder,
Thy power throughout the universe displayed.

It wasn't at all unusual for Craig and me to listen to Dad talk about death and destruction while mom sang about salvation.

"Down there it's Halloween every night. How some of those folk survive, I don't know . . ."

As an adult, I learned the frightening facts about the mentally ill whom my father served. In Maryland, after deinstitutionalization became policy, roughly 30,000 mentally ill people were discharged into the community. Nobody kept track of their whereabouts. Although deinstitutionalizing began in 1955 as a humane idea to incorporate psychiatric patients within society in less restrictive environments, for many the consequences proved cruel. All over the U.S., hundreds of thousands of people in need of psychiatric care became homeless; many were jailed, and others, if not rehospitalized, were placed in public nursing homes. They were frequently suicidal or violent. Some have become part of the city's landscape as they mutter to themselves and verbally abuse pedestrians while digging through street bins, dressed in filthy rags.

Nationwide, nearly 1,700 murders are committed annually by chronically mentally ill patients, many of whom are suffering from untreated schizophrenia or manic-depressive disease. More than 388,000 homicides have been reported in the United States over the past two decades and people with extreme mental illnesses committed 10 percent of these murders. Negative public perceptions of the mentally ill are exacerbated by reports of violent crimes committed by those who cannot look after themselves and don't take their medication. Baltimore contributed substantially to these statistics.

Dad discarded the jagged remnants of the pumpkin as he carved deep lines in its skull with a knife, following the lines he had drawn earlier with a pencil.

"Mom, are the pumpkin seeds ready?" Craig asked. She handed us each a few to try.

"They're still mushy, Mom."

"Give them five more minutes."

"What about Wolfwoman?" I egged Dad on. The hymn of praise recommenced.

When through the woods, and forest glades I wander,
And hear the birds sing sweetly in the trees.
When I look down, from lofty mountain grandeur
And see the brook, and feel the gentle breeze

"Then can we go to the haunted house?" Craig asked as he wiped the sticky pumpkin residue from his hand onto my forearm.

"What about Wolfwoman?"

"You don't want to hear about that."

Mom continued even louder.

Then sings my soul, My Savior God, to Thee,
How great Thou art, How great Thou art

"Sometimes mentally ill people were simply incapable of asking for help. At other times they didn't want to be rescued. And once in a while someone like 'Wolfwoman' would plain scare the crap out of me."

The incident Dad was about to launch into occurred in East Baltimore, at the time a mostly white district with low-income earners of Polish, German, Greek and Italian descent. The mixed ethnic backgrounds led to highly eclectic decoration of the houses. Some residents used old tires as outdoor flowerpots, while others placed plastic flowers, colorfully painted Madonnas or pink flamingos in their front yards. Windowsill scenes made up of plastic or ceramic figurines—often including the Virgin Mary—were displayed. Row houses might have window screens painted with scenes of cottages, windmills, mountains and lighthouses; theoretically this was done to prevent passersby from seeing into the houses, but historians now take Baltimore's painted screens very seriously as folk art.

Attempts were made to disguise the underlying structure of the houses. Sometimes the brick facades were painted a brighter "brick red" with bright white lines painted over the mortar to make the brickwork look brand new. Some of the homes were covered with faux stone bearing brand names such as Formstone and Permastone, creating what John Waters, the famed Baltimore filmmaker, termed the "polyester of brick." Waters captures the Baltimore knack for transforming trash into art in his movies *Hairspray, Pecker, Serial Mom* and many others.

"You can go to a dinner party and hear people talk about Waters' early movie, *Pink Flamingos*—one scene shows the late drag queen Divine eating dog feces—with the same regard they have for their city: a mix of shame and pride, love and hate," Dad marveled.

"One night, I'm working on the East Side on Medic 13. All seems quiet as we pull to the curb in front of a row home. The door is half open, and I peer inside calling out 'Ambo, Fire Department.' Me and my partner Vince, who's gentle and always diplomatic, stand there listening. Eerie silence for a moment. Then we hear a low, barely audible, growl. Both of us agree that the source of the strange noises sounds like a woman as we cautiously edge our way to the kitchen.

"We stop abruptly at the kitchen doorway. Seated at the table is an obese, disheveled, white female with stringy hair, a craggy face and half a dozen teeth missing. She keeps growling and peering at us angrily from eyes narrowed to slits. She turns up the volume on a small radio as if to let us know that she wants to be alone.

"'Well, Miss,' I venture, 'what seems to be the problem?' She growls even louder.

"'Ma'am, would you mind turning down the volume for just a moment please?' Vince asks politely.

"Without warning, she grabs the radio and throws it in our direction. It shatters as it strikes the wall to our immediate left. As she lunges for a butcher's knife on the table, we both do a rapid about-face, and in our hurry the two of us get momentarily jammed in the kitchen doorway. We break away and race for the front door.

"On our way out we greet the cops. They've been called by a neighbor because the woman has thrown a bed, in sections, out of the second-story window, narrowly missing a passerby.

"'You step around that corner and you'll be in trouble,' I say to the officer in the lead. 'We got it, boys,' he scoffs and looks at us as if to say: 'You just couldn't handle it.'

"As he steps into the living room, a sugar bowl soars past his nose and crashes into the wall behind him.

"The woman darts out of the kitchen, picks up the dining room table, holds it up over her head and prepares to heave it at us. She is big and unbelievably strong.

"'Back out, men, back out. Get the cattle prods, the net and the shields,' the burly sergeant orders.

"They return and after struggling to get the net over her, they finally haul her outside to a waiting paddy wagon. Even now I can still see her wild expression as she glares wide-eyed through the small grated window. Her mouth is partly open and saliva drips down her chin. She begins growling with more intensity as she stares at the full moon hovering over Patterson Park. And then she bays at the moon."

At last Dad held up the demented face of his hollowed out pumpkin shell and howled "Aaahhhwuuuuuuuuuuuuuuuuuuuu . . ."

Blowin' in the Wind

Although he had been a military man most of his life, my paternal grandfather had possessed great humaneness, and perhaps Bill inherited from him some of his joy in caring. My grandfather, Captain William Phillips Hennick Senior, helped out many destitute veterans, including the real-life, much-written-about Sergeant York, the most decorated hero in World War I. In later years, when York fell ill after a cerebral hemorrhage and needed help, all of York's work had been long forgotten. Captain Hennick sent a letter to the U.S. Congress on York's behalf and took up the cause of the many veterans who did not know they had rights. He would pound away at his typewriter every night trying to summon up aid. Maryland's chapter of Veterans of World War I made my grandfather their commander. But brave Sergeant York died destitute.

I think maybe my grandfather would have liked Dad to secure a full-time position with the Army. An American German, William Senior fought in three wars: the 1914 Mexican Border Wars, World War I and World War II. As a military police captain during World War II, he processed over 500,000 German prisoners throughout Africa, Germany, Italy and France. He tracked down escaped foreign and U.S. prisoners and brought them back to their designated holding cells. He fought on the front lines and often confiscated the prisoners' weapons, a dangerous job considering a captive could have hidden a hand grenade on his person. He was right behind the lines in the six-week, bitter-cold Battle of the Bulge that took place during the winter of 1944–45 in the Ardennes Forest. The U.S. Army honored Captain Hennick with at least fourteen medals, and my dad inherited a two-inch thick book of certificates and awards that were given to his father.

When he was eighteen, Dad enlisted, and, after training at Fort Knox, he held a job as a clerk typist at Fort Meade Headquarters in Maryland for a couple of years. He often said, "I'm not like my father. I don't care for the military, they brainwash you to conform. So the first time I joined just to get it over with and later, when I worked in the Army Reserves, it was because military work was permitted as a second job for firefighters who needed to boost their income."

However, William Jr. administered care to numerous veterans, many of them African-American, during his work as a medic in West Baltimore.

He recalls one of the times when he and his partner were called to an injured man in a back alley. When they arrived at the scene, he hesitated for a second before stepping into the darkness. He heard a faint cry in the stillness of the night.

"Help. Somebody help." Stifling his frightened sense of foreboding, he headed in the direction of a low-pitched moan which seemed to come from somewhere in the middle of the alley, perhaps fifty feet away. Again he heard the faint voice but couldn't see anything. He tried to find his way under the moonlight, but clouds kept going over, giving him alternating moments of dim light and complete darkness.

"Somebody help. I need help. Somebody help."

In a few seconds he was hovering over a black man about thirty years old. Whoever had called the medics to assist him had left. They probably wanted to help but didn't want to be involved. The victim was fully conscious but confused and desperate.

"You're going to be all right, everything will be okay," my father reassured him as he strained to see him more clearly in the darkness.

"They broke my legs. They broke my legs," the man kept repeating hysterically. Dad expected to splint the legs. He moved his hands to the femur and followed the course of the leg down to the knee, being careful to pause on occasion to check for swelling and tenderness. His examination ended abruptly at the knees. The pant legs were empty from the knees downward.

"They broke my legs," he moaned.

Dad was confused. "I don't know how to ask you this, but—where are they? Your legs?"

"They threw them over the hedge."

Dad wondered how in the world they could throw them anywhere, unless they'd cut them off with a buzz saw. He walked over to the bushes, and, in the glow of the moon he saw shoes attached to artificial limbs which were sticking out from the foliage.

Astonished, he asked what had happened. The patient had been attacked and knocked to the ground. He had begged his attackers not to harm him. At this point, they tore both artificial legs from this poverty-stricken war veteran and threw the limbs into a nearby yard.

"It was pitiful. He already had terrible problems. How could someone be that cruel? When it comes to people wanting drugs, alcohol and money, there are no limits."

My father's detailed partner arrived on the scene with a flashlight, and, in the thin beam of light, retrieved the artificial limbs from the bush. Dad turned again to the man on the ground. In a barely audible voice, he said, "They not only broke my legs, but they got my last two dollars."

Good Times

"Can we change the station? This show really irritates me."

After Dad got home and changed out of his uniform, he would descend the basement stairs wearing his red, white and blue striped pajama pants. It was 1976, America's bicentennial, and patriotism was all the rage. He'd kick off his slippers and slide next to us on the tattered brown and orange colonial style couch splattered with printed eagles and U.S. flags. The paneled walls were bare, but a large black iron eagle was perched on the brick mantel of our faux fireplace.

"But daaaaddddd, it's *Good Times*." I loved the sitcom depicting an African-American family living in the "projects" in the 1970s. I think it reminded me of my father.

"Yeah, Dad," Craig chimed in. "We like J.J. Dy-no-mite!"

He would surrender. We'd try to watch the show while he interjected stories about "the way it really is down there."

"Down there, drug addiction is a problem, but alcoholism is equally devastating to the community. I was aware that alcohol dulled the senses, but in my wildest imaginings, I had never considered the total effect booze could have on an individual."

"Sssshhhh, Dad we're trying to watch the show." Craig didn't take his eyes from the screen. My father would quiet down until a commercial break.

"I'll never forget one day when spring had sprung and my fancies had turned to pleasant thoughts of a slow day on the ambo. Taking full advantage of the sunshine, my detailed partner Bob Lechner and I cheerfully cleaned and polished the module inside and out. Bob was an excellent firefighter on Truck 4. He was good-hearted, congenial, a hard worker, dedicated to his job. Married. Had one child. Bob was a musician; he played the Cordovox, and he often brought his instrument into the station and played it between runs. The Cordovox resembled an accordion but had a smoother and richer sound.

"Fact is, Bob hated being on the ambulance, but he didn't complain, and he shared my empathy toward patients. Problem was, he had a weak stomach. But he overcame it enough to do his job, because he cared for people. I found it ironic that Bob always seemed to get assigned to the unit when I encountered some of the most nauseating experiences that I've ever had in my career.

"I had almost completed checking the equipment when I heard the distinctive beep on the communications set. Bob retrieved the run ticket, and we dashed to the location only four blocks away from the firehouse.

"When we arrived on the scene, I saw five black men congregated on the corner. One of the men was seated on a chair, reclining back against the wall, basking in the warm light. His friends told me that he had foot trouble and needed medical attention. I stooped down to remove the shoe and found it to be immovable, as if it were part of the foot. I took the shoe in both hands and pulled with more vigor, causing it to slip off of the foot. The sight that greeted our eyes was horrifying. The front half of the right foot was eaten away by gangrene and the maggots had made a fleshy cave out of the rest of the foot.

"Bob had just eaten a Polish sausage with sauerkraut for lunch. I instinctively held my breath to avoid the stench. Bob began gagging and went into uncontrollable dry heaves. The guy just continued to lounge back, smiling and humming. He didn't have any feeling down there. The alcohol had destroyed enough of this man's nervous system to make him impervious to the pain of severe infection.

"I washed the mutilated foot with sterile water and carefully bandaged the affected area. I later learned that the entire foot had to be amputated. This man was just one of thousands in the district with a near-lethal drinking problem."

"Okay, okay, it's back on."

I knew my father needed reminding when the ads were finished; otherwise he would have talked through the rest of the program, and I wouldn't find out what happened until the next rerun.

Dad would patiently sit with us until the next commercial break. My brother and I had a sneaking suspicion that he only watched TV with us so he could talk during those breaks.

"Kids, Bill, do you want anything? Something hot, something cold to drink?" my mother called from upstairs.

"Chocolate milk," I said.

"Craig?"

"I'll have a Sprite, Mom."

"Bill?"

"Iced tea, Eunice, thanks. Hey, kids, get your feet off the table." Craig and I had reclined on the couch with our feet propped on the edge of the coffee table so often that it was lacerated with vanilla-colored lines. Dad walked over to the television and turned the knob.

"Hey, turn it back." Craig protested.

An ad for WJZ news flashed on the screen. "What's an Oprah?" signs were plastered all over the city in a publicity stunt before the young news anchor moved to Baltimore that year. It was a brief stint before her rise to stardom.

Dad turned the TV dial back to our program. J.J. sauntered across the screen. "Death is a stark reality in the daily life of a ghetto paramedic," he interjected. "Needless shootings and stabbings snuff out so many lives. There's no way to rationalize these murders to the loved ones." In fact, he never got used to any of the deaths he encountered almost daily.

He described how crib death—SUID, Sudden Unexplained Infant Death—kills infants between three to six months, how it left him dumbfounded, unable to explain to the young black mothers he served why they would never again hear the lusty cries of their newborns. But sometimes the mothers were the victims.

"I vividly remember the night when I came across a lifeless young alcoholic mother. She was lying in bed with her two toddlers next to her cold body. They were playing, unaware that mommy's voice would never again be heard."

"Bill, the kids don't want to hear that junk, and neither do I."

My mother would place our favorite red tray with cookies and drinks on the coffee table in front of the couch where we were all lounging. She would stay there to rifle through the freshly laundered clothes which spilled out on the faded and scratched billiard table. She'd begin ironing, a chore she said she loved. For her the scent of the steam and the act of smoothing out the crinkles were a meditation. She even pressed and folded our underwear.

"Nobody wants to hear it, but it's the truth, Eunice. That television program *Good Times* aggravates me. I'm working down there in the ghetto and I know what's going on. *Good Times* does look good next to what I'm seeing in real life. They don't show it the way it is: the hunger, the incredible hunger, the depravity. In the show, James and Florida have a close, loving relationship. J.J. is an artist. His brother Michael is going to college. They left out a lot of episodes in that program. J.J. didn't have maggots crawling out of his foot due to alcoholism. Papa was home."

A friend of the family once said to me, "You know why your father doesn't drink? Because if he did, he'd never stop."

Later in life Dad amended his thinking about *Good Times*: "Looking back on that program, it was probably helpful. Maybe people in the Murphy Homes could have seen that show and not given up hope. But there was nothing like *Good Times* down there."

Eleanor Rigby

Baltimore's rich cultural diversity is reflected in its architecture. But many of the city's row homes which look fine on the outside are rotting within. After only a short time as a paramedic, my father began to see all of them as looking the same: one dilapidated house after another. Although some residents didn't have the funds or inclination to maintain their homes, those who tried often had their homes vandalized or burglarized. Others, particularly the elderly or disabled, had neither the means nor the strength to keep their homes maintained.

The city is famous for its row houses. Although many of them have been converted to offices or apartments and others have been knocked down and replaced with modern houses, the city's ethnic past is still reflected in their varied architectural designs. Front steps made of marble are perhaps the most famous features of Baltimore row houses. Years ago, residents could be seen on their hands and knees armed with scouring powder and bristle brushes, scrubbing their marble steps weekly—sometimes even daily—until they gleamed. But by the time Dad became a paramedic, many seemed to have other priorities.

Dad often said, "The parts of the city where I work have a lifestyle of their own." Inhabitants had to expect the unexpected—fires, fights, and violent crimes threatening their very survival. Occasionally, something unimaginably grotesque and frightening intruded on the daily life.

To my father, the song "Eleanor Rigby," released by the Beatles in 1966 and further popularized by singer/pianist/composer Ray Charles, captured the spirit of the Baltimore ghetto. "Every time I heard it, I thought of how truly alone people are in those communities with absolutely no one to care for them." He thought of "Aunt Alice," as her neighbors called her.

Aunt Alice was an elderly black woman, well established in the neighborhood, highly regarded by all on her block. The neighbors told Dad about her ready smile and gentle disposition. Aunt Alice always had a friendly greeting. Her cheerful demeanor was an inspiration, they said. Folk in the area would do her shopping for her and try to help in small ways.

"She was not rich in worldly goods," Dad recalled, "but she was that rare kind of person who was able to show unselfish love to all she encountered. Aunt Alice knew pain and anguish most of her life, but she maintained warm feelings for everyone in the community."

On a brisk day in early spring, my father and his partner responded to a routine call not unlike thousands of others they received in the course of a year. A "sick case" can run the gamut from a drunk on the street to a cardiac arrest. According to Dad, "Not knowing, at first, the severity of the case is part of the fascination and challenge of the job."

They arrived on the scene in under three minutes, pulled the medic unit directly to the front of a neglected dwelling on Argyle Avenue and ran up the marble steps. The front door was hanging by only one hinge, making entry for the medics a cinch. Nothing could have prepared him for the sight that would greet his eyes.

My father peered into the living room. Garbage was piled two feet high throughout the entire first floor of the house. Shielding his mouth and nose with the palm of his hand in a futile attempt to avoid the unbearable stench, he trudged through the trash across the rotting floor. In the center of the room, the lifeless body of a seventy-year-old black woman lay face down in a crawling position. Half of her face was gone—down to the bone—and the torn, bloody flesh of her arms and legs indicated that a savage attack had been inflicted upon her. Both eyes were intact and open wide, registering the terror brought about by a horrible death. Aunt Alice had been the victim of an army of hungry rats.

"I assumed she had suffered a stroke. She had apparently tried to drag herself to the front door to call for help but, with ten more feet to go, she could go no further. By the look of anguish and horror on her face, she must have been conscious when the rats found her, defenseless and immobile.

"It was daylight," Dad continued. "Rats come out at night. A quick check upstairs revealed numerous rats' nests in a pyramid of trash constructed like a miniature volcano." Dad envisioned rodents the size of house cats coming after her like a pack of tigers. Aunt Alice had become senile and was unaware of the danger lurking in the confines of her own home. Neighbors apparently were oblivious to the severity of the squalor. My father told them only that she had had a stroke and died.

"All that remained of Alice were memories of a warm smile and a kindly word. Come to think of it, that's not a bad legacy to leave behind."

Play the Game

Christmas Day 1975. Mom woke Craig and me at 4:00 a.m. We raced downstairs to gobble sticky buns and orange juice and almost choked while reading a garbled letter from Santa scrawled in Dad's print. The note, which complained that he preferred chocolate chip to Fig Newtons, was left beside a plate of crumbs. "Santa" went on to say that he was underpaid, overweight and getting too old for chimney sliding. Dad stood at the top of the stairs and declaimed a passage about Christ's birth from the King James Bible, while we sulked and beckoned him to hurry.

We dashed down the stairs and tore through the basement like a pair of hurricanes, shredding paper and wildly abandoning one toy for the next, until Dad kissed us goodbye and headed off to work at five. Craig and I played until we were cranky with fatigue, and Mom sent us back to bed for a nap. She lined the mantel with little stocking-stuffer sized gifts wedged between model fire trucks and that black iron eagle. We were permitted to open one of these presents (and only one) each day after Christmas. She wanted our joy to linger.

Between Christmas and New Year's Day Dad would find time to join us in a board game. Craig slid the Monopoly box out from under the Christmas tree and wiped the fallen pine needles from its surface. We spread the board on the beat-up coffee table in the basement. By the late seventies, we were finally old enough to play the game previously reserved for our parents and were just beginning to learn its complex rules. We kept the television turned on so we could catch snippets of our favorite shows during breaks.

Dad sometimes delivered his stories with the formality and the rhetorical flourishes of a presidential speech. "As the first days drifted by, I began to learn my way around this distinctive area held together by welfare checks, cheap booze, and the efforts of the fire and police departments. I had to modify my approaches and responses to care for the afflicted and to gain the confidence of the people. At first I followed everything I learned in class, but I had to throw most of that out to get the confidence of the people."

He sneaked a piece of licorice from our candy bowl while we set up the pieces. "Instructors just tell you the medical procedures, and those are really incidental. If the person is bleeding use direct pressure, tie on a tourniquet, put in the IV . . . They don't teach you how to develop a rapport. The instructors didn't discuss the interpersonal aspect of the job. You better learn that. But you don't learn it until you're out there on your own."

"Dad, it's your turn to roll." Craig snapped.

"Remember, you're the top hat, Daddy, Craig's the wheelbarrow and I'm the Scottie dog."

"Yeah, you are a dog," my brother teased.

"Jerk. Pass me the M&M's."

"Hey, what's over there?"

Dad pointed to the window. Craig and I turned to look, and seeing nothing, turned back again to catch Dad grabbing another handful of licorice. He resumed talking with his mouth full.

"You have to show you're sincerely interested in helping people out, because if you're uninterested they pick up on it. If you're comfortable, people trust you even in difficult situations. I moved around down there like I'd lived there my whole life, and it didn't bother me who they were. The mayor wouldn't receive better or worse treatment than someone lying in the gutter."

"Roll, Dad," Craig pleaded.

Dad cupped the dice, shook his fist and spilled them onto the game board. He slid his top hat across several spaces and stopped. "Pennsylvania Avenue, I think I'll pass. I'd be taking my life in my hands if I bought property down there." Of course, he was referring to Baltimore's Pennsylvania Avenue, not the green-trimmed square on the Monopoly board.

"You can't buy anything anyway, Dad. I've got two houses and a hotel there. Hand over the rent, buddy." Craig was ruthless.

Dad tossed him several pastel bills and continued talking. "I hate the comment made by some of the black residents, 'If he was white . . .' implying that I treat patients differently according to skin color. In reality, I believe in caring for all of my patients with the same interest and concern. I don't differentiate between the man in the gutter or the socialite in a half-million-dollar home. Both need help, and both occupy the same wheeled litter at different times on their journeys to the hospital.

"I might recruit one of the onlookers to assist me. This person will then assure the others that this white man is trying to help. I enlist people to carry things, direct traffic and clear the way for the medic unit. In the absence of police, if I have an unruly patient, I have several folk hold down the person's arms and legs. I want to get patients away from the scene without too much contention because it can put my life in jeopardy. When the public and I work together with a shared goal it eases the racial tension. We don't have time to think about black or white."

"It's your turn to roll again, Dad." I handed him the dice.

He rattled the dice and dropped them. "Oh nuts, I'm in jail."

"It's okay, Daddy," I said. "You're just visiting."

"That's what they all say down there." Dad's jokes were sometimes lost on my brother and me, but we were glad to see him happy.

Dad leaned back against the couch. "When delegating positions, I look for people who will be helpful and who can control everyone else. Then they will tell the others, 'Leave him alone. Don't bother that man,' referring to me. They police their own people. A cop with a chip on his shoulder can cause a riot. But most of the time the police are good, and I hear few complaints."

When the police went on strike in 1974, Dad carried a loaded .38 pistol in his medical bag in order to feel safer. The small nickel-plated revolver had belonged to his father and was so old that Dad did not even know if it would fire. "We still had to work, and protection wasn't available. I had to defend myself. Although I never used it, I felt much more secure."

The Fraternal Order of Police was a weak union at that time, and the officers relied on the fire department's efforts. The firefighters' union, Local 734, was stronger. When firefighters got a pay raise or better conditions, the benefits tended to flow on to the police because of the parity between the two services. "The union was important because the City wouldn't give anything voluntarily. That's the way it was. We had to fight for benefits. The

City representative was a tough adversary."

Just before the police strike, some people had already started breaking shop windows.

"It was like they knew about the strike before it happened."

A skeleton force stayed on duty providing a police presence so people would not panic, but there were no patrol officers on the streets. A few police cars had to patrol the whole city. Today fire and police departments are forbidden to strike by a clause in the contract they sign when they join.

Craig grabbed one of the presents from the mantel. I called out, "Hey, grab one for me—the Pez." He and I had already ruptured the wrapping of all the presents to see which ones we wanted to open next. As Craig tossed the present to me, Dad told us about one of his Christmas Days on duty. Firehouses were used as drop-off centers for donated toys during the Christmas season. The Toys for Tots organization would collect them and distribute the gifts to the needy. This Christmas, their driver failed to appear at Dad's firehouse, and the chief wanted the mound of presents removed.

"I piled all of the toys and clothing into the ambulance and transported them to the worst block in the district. My partner and I unloaded the gifts, stacked them in the middle of the street and activated the siren. Dozens of excited children poured out into the street to lay siege to the treasure pile. Everything disappeared in two minutes.

"Having carefully guarded an old black-and-white TV that was in the pile, I asked, 'Who has the most kids and is the poorest?' The crowd directed me to a small home at the end of the block inhabited by a single mother and seven children."

Dad licked his lips, now slightly blackened from the licorice.

"They had absolutely nothing. All they had for seats were orange crates. We carried the TV into the living room and plugged it into the only usable wall socket, hoping that it would operate. Sound resonated throughout the shabby room but the picture was a blurry snowstorm. When nothing else helped, I attached a coat hanger to the TV for an antenna and amid cheers from a grateful family a clear picture suddenly appeared. Overwhelmed with appreciation, the children's mother thanked us again and again.

"We quietly slipped out, leaving the group of eight huddled on the floor with their eyes transfixed by the nineteen-inch screen. The room was totally devoid of furniture, but for a moment, all was well."

Dad shook his head as if he just awoke.

"What's happening, kids?" Dad counted on us to guide him through the board games.

"You're still in jail," Craig said.

"That's all right. At least I'll have three square meals a day and a roof over my head. I might even get some sleep."

He continued, "The police work hard, but some can be cocky. And showing the slightest air of superiority rubs people the wrong way. The cops sometimes step out of their cars acting like John Wayne. They shout things like 'Everybody stand back' and 'I told you not to move,' even when it doesn't make any difference whether the onlookers moved or not. I don't like calling the police out, and I won't—unless I have no choice. Sometimes the cops are like the news media, making a bigger deal of the situation to get the ratings, embellishing the story to make it newsworthy.

"I can't remember his name, but one cop was famous in the west district for stirring up trouble. Everything would be calm; then somehow he would manage to get people worked up. If he arrived on the scene and there wasn't any police work to do, he'd find someone to provide him with an excuse to do something. One time I was bandaging a guy after a domestic quarrel. The couple received vouchers from the government to buy appliances and was able to get a refrigerator from Sears. When it was delivered, the woman ripped the door off of its hinges and hit the man over the head with it. I had just bandaged the guy, and the woman who assaulted him had calmed down. When the police officer arrived this cop tried to stir her up again.

"The conversation went something like this:

"'Monique, why did you hit Darren on the head?'

"'He called me mothereffer.'

"'And you're going to let him get away with that?'

"'No, I'm not going to let him get away with that.'

"Then she hit the guy again. The cop turned to the guy and said, 'Are you going to let her get away with that?' You can imagine what happened next.

"But, as I said, most cops work hard. And in reality, no one else rolls up their sleeves and does much to help people in the ghetto. Politicians use a lot of rhetoric; the government provides handouts; and the majority of the white middle-class just wish the problems would go away. The fire and police personnel deal directly with these folk on a daily basis in the roles of mediator, friend, healer, counselor, motivator and caregiver. We put out the fires, perform dangerous rescues, save property, capture the bad guys and try to keep peace. I don't see anyone else serving the public up close and personal day in and day out. Without all this dedication to duty, there would be no Baltimore City.

"What's going on, kids?" Dad eventually emerged from his monologue. "Is the game over already?"

"Yeah, Craig owns all the railways, both utilities, and the green, magenta and orange streets. I kept ending up in jail. I couldn't build anything and I couldn't afford to pay the rent."

My brother fanned my face with his bills. "Face it, Roach, you just don't have the Midas touch."

I smacked his waving hand away, scattering the play money across the board.

"Stupid. You don't have to act like a baby just because I'm the winner." (Never mind that my brother sulked whenever he lost.)

"I'm not stupid," I shouted. "It's all luck. You got to roll first, and I rolled last. I didn't have a chance to buy anything. And it's not fair." I was on the verge of tears.

"Rachel," Dad said gently, "Life isn't fair."

Inner City Blues (Make Me Wanna Holler)

"Burnout Syndrome, better known as BS, is a malady that affects most dedicated medics," my father often said. Many would quit, leaving a shortage of competent workers. After thirteen years of service as a medic, BS was beginning to wear Bill down. He saw how well-intentioned men were swallowed up by the environment and the demands of the job. Abusive patients could push paramedics to their limits.

One of my father's partners, whom I'll call Max, was a black man who, like Larry, wouldn't tolerate disrespect. One time, when Max was driving, Dad was in the back working on a gunshot victim, trying to stop the bleeding from the entry wound in the arm. From the second the black patient laid eyes on Max, he started calling him "nigger" and "motherfucker." He continued cursing him from the back of the module the whole time they were driving toward Lutheran Hospital.

Max slammed on the brakes and opened the back door.

"You have a choice: shut up or get out."

The bullets were lodged in a bone in his arm, not in an organ or artery.

"If the injury had been life threatening," Dad assured me, "Max would never have done that."

Stunned that Max would give him that ultimatum, the patient fell silent—for a moment. He then started to run his mouth again. "Have it your way motherfucker," he spat at Max as Dad took the IV out and bandaged the puncture wound. They could hear the patient shouting as he staggered down the alley.

Dad said, "We notified the police, and I never heard anything else about it."

Some patients really tested the medics' patience, especially Andy, "Seizure Extraordinaire." Andy had a reputation throughout the city years before my father knew him. Patients experiencing convulsions were not unusual, and, until Dad became a paramedic, he had not known how serious and widespread such cases were in Baltimore. They ranged from grand mal and petit mal epileptic seizures to alcoholic convulsions, and they varied in degree from mild to life-threatening.

Well-meaning friends or relatives administered salt to victims while they were in the midst of a seizure. They liberally sprinkled it on the person's eyes, up their nose, in their mouth, and all over their face and body. Obviously, this added to the patients' discomfort and would present more problems for the attending paramedic. Dad was told that salt warded off the evil spirits which were believed to have initiated the seizure. It was an old-fashioned treatment passed down from one generation to the next.

Heavy drinking and medications can bring on seizures, and both causes were rampant in Dad's part of the city. Prolonged fits would sometimes lead to respiratory arrest. My father and his partners over the years had treated so many of these cases that they had developed the ability to differentiate between legitimate cases and phony ones. Some patients were "regulars" and would feign attacks in an attempt to hustle a trip to the local hospital for a night's lodging.

My father learned to look for indicators. When legitimately convulsing, patients stiffen up, and sweat pours off them. When they wake up, they have difficulty remembering names and numbers. The medics would ask questions. "Where do you live? What's the number of your house? How old are you?" The legitimate patient would be drowsy, partly because they are physically drained. Dad found himself critiquing seizures, as one would judge a contest, considering the best performance.

Andy deserved more than one Academy Award. He was a wiry man, over six and a half feet tall, with a superb ability to outfox even the most experienced paramedic. He would throw himself to the ground, sometimes intentionally striking his head on the side of a car or, worse yet, on the concrete sidewalk. Spectators would gather around Andy to view his well-rehearsed act. Concerned citizens would notify the fire department, and the closest medic unit would respond. Dad and his partner would arrive at the scene to be greeted by a crowd of frantic onlookers demanding that they remove this "poor sick creature" to the nearest hospital. Andy wasn't stiff or shaking, he hadn't bitten his tongue or broken his teeth, and he didn't appear to be disoriented. But they couldn't leave him lying in the street even if he had been faking as usual.

The first time my father encountered Andy, he made "the gross error" of removing him to the hospital. He seemed genuinely sick, writhing around on the litter and frothing at the mouth. Dad dutifully administered treatment, unaware of what was to eventuate when they arrived at the local emergency room. Andy's act lasted until he was in the confines of the emergency treatment area. Then he lashed out.

"If you get close to me I'll smash your mouth in, I'll smash your face in. I'll get you, you sons of bitches. You white motherfuckers."

He growled like an animal. He tried to destroy any supplies and equipment he could reach. Dad and his partner found themselves in the unenviable position of holding him at bay until the arrival of police and security.

All the medics learned their lesson from their first experience of Andy's transformation. After that, before transport, they would always tie him down securely to the litter, tightly strapping his wrists and ankles in leather restraints attached to the bars so he couldn't tear the ambulance apart and attack them. Once Andy succeeded in breaking the restraints. Fortunately, they arrived at the hospital just in time for hospital security to bring him under control. My father would have to warn the hospital staff so they could prepare for a violent patient.

"Just wanted to give you a heads-up. Andy's on his way in."

"Can't you take him somewhere else?"

"No. This is the closest hospital." After a while, whenever picking up Andy, Dad always tried to make the best of it. He'd run into the hospital calling to staff, "Guess who I got?"

"A celebrity?"

"Yeah, in a way. He is an actor." They'd get all excited. He'd keep them guessing for a while, then deflate them with: "Andy."

"We'll get you for this, Bill."

At University Hospital they all knew Andy well. He'd knock nurses down, hit doctors and throw things. They'd cuff him and put him in a padded cell. People looked through the door at him as if he were a caged animal. My father told me, "Andy was always getting stabbed, shot or beat up. One nurse in particular would volunteer to inspect Andy's wounds. 'I can do it,' she'd say, opening the door carefully. It took a lot of guts to do that when he wasn't tied down, but she knew somehow the way to handle him."

The police hated him. So did hospital security. Sarge was a "southern redneck type of security guard" at the Maryland General Hospital. He'd come into the back of the medic unit and whack Andy on the shins with his nightstick. "Now you better behave yourself, you dirty S-O-B." Incredibly enough, hitting Andy that way actually calmed Andy down.

"I was one of the few people who didn't hate Andy. When he was sober, Andy was practically a model citizen. An impeccable dresser, Andy was; he wore well-fitted suits accented with matching derby hats. He had charisma and a hearty laugh. He was well liked by people in the community. I would bump into him at the hospital when he was checking on a bill, or pass him on the street when he was talking with other locals. He seemed perfectly normal. In fact, he knew medical terminology and could talk in depth about medical problems. He seemed to have it all together—until he drank. When he got liquor in him, he was the most obnoxious, destructive person imaginable. Dr. Jekyll and Mr. Hyde. And in his alcoholic state, he would feign seizures in public places."

While my father was aware of postictal states—a condition of aggressiveness following a seizure—he still believed Andy was faking. However, he treated Andy with the same respect he gave all patients.

Andy also infuriated Ed, a paramedic on Medic 1 based at the Steadman Station in downtown Baltimore. He was, according to Dad, "A stocky white guy with a small black moustache." Dad would run across Ed at Maryland General, University Hospital or fire school classes where they went to learn new equipment or techniques.

"Someone would crack a joke or laugh; Ed wouldn't get it. He was always hyper. I privately referred to him as Nutsy because he was fanatical about the job, overzealous, all fired up. He'd get way too involved, sometimes overwrought."

In the early seventies, the medics wore an extra belt around the waist with a two-way radio attached that weighed about two or three pounds. "Ed's radio hung to his knee and would rub against it whenever he took a step. Most radios hung at the waist. He had a pot belly and maybe the belt just didn't stay in place or maybe he just didn't tighten his belt enough. I always asked, in fun, how his knee-chafe was doing. The joke would go over his head and he'd flash me a puzzled look. 'What knee-chafe?' Someone standing near by would get it and laugh."

Over several months, my father began to observe changes in Ed when they crossed paths on the street and in emergency rooms. He still really cared about his patients, working hard, totally committed to his job. However, he was becoming noticeably more short-tempered and less tolerant of unruly patients. He was losing control.

One night, Ed delivered Andy to the emergency room at University Hospital. Andy was being his "usual inebriated self," cursing and writhing on the gurney, trying to loosen the straps that secured him. The hospital staff members placed Andy in a cubicle and pulled the curtains around to give him privacy. He had settled down momentarily. At this point Ed suddenly leaped up on the litter, jumped on top of Andy, straddled his chest, wrapped a roll of gauze tightly around his throat and, pulling tightly, attempted to choke him to death. He kept yelling, "You son of a bitch, I'm going to kill you."

Ed was sweating profusely and his shirt was halfway unbuttoned. Security personnel and my father pulled him off and held him until he calmed down. Soon, probably too soon, Ed was allowed to return to work. This incident displayed a drastic change in Ed's personality and should have been a warning of the tragedy that took place sometime later. The job stresses were beginning to take their toll on a well-intentioned paramedic.

Most of the men, including my father, worked part-time jobs to supplement their incomes. In 1975, when my father was thirty-four years old, he enlisted in the military as a part-time medic. Once a month for five years, he had to attend weekend drill. In addition, the City had to give him two weeks off each year for military training at a summer camp at Kimbrough Army Hospital in Fort Meade. Every few weeks, Dad would leave home at around 3:00 p.m. on Friday afternoon to work a fourteen-hour night shift on the medic unit, with daytime reserve duty taking the place of sleep, arriving home totally exhausted at 8:00 a.m. Monday morning. Dad once said in retrospect, "There had to be a better way to allow more time with family and friends. But I never considered other possibilities."

Ed moonlighted as a cab driver and often had customers in his own medic district. Ed reached the final breaking point when he turned to his passenger in the rear seat, pulled a small-caliber pistol from under his jacket and pointed the weapon at the man's head.

"Please don't shoot me," the passenger begged.

"Well, I've got to shoot somebody." Ed placed the handgun against his chest and pulled the trigger.

His own Medic 1 responded. They rushed their co-worker to the shock trauma unit at University Hospital. He died within the hour at the hospital he had so often frequented. Dad said he felt that the pressures of the relentless medic runs in the ghetto led to Ed's demise.

Andy continued to pose a problem for all the paramedics that he came in contact with, until the day when, at the age of forty-three, he held up a local bank. According to the *Baltimore Sun*, he entered the Maryland National Bank on Light Street and approached the closest female teller. He held up the small bag that he was clenching tightly in his hand. "This is an explosive, like you see in Star Trek. Give me all your money. Don't push the alarm and keep smiling."

The teller had to ask him several times what he was trying to say; Andy was intoxicated and his speech was slurred. He told her that it was a holdup. He demanded all the money in the cash drawer. After the teller placed $1,120 in an envelope and handed it to Andy, he demanded a shoebox in which to place the loot.

When the teller said she didn't have a shoebox, Andy staggered into the G.C. Murphy store, just a few doors away, to search for a suitable container for his ill-gotten gain. The police raced in. Outraged, Andy tackled a nearby female customer, dragged her toward the rear wall and spat, "Get away before I hurt someone." After a few moments his eyes flashed a baffled glance in no direction in particular, as if he had no idea where he was. He softened and released the victim. Officer Kenneth R. Levendoski apprehended him.

Soon the bomb squad showed up, cordoned off the streets and carefully picked the bag apart revealing Snoopy (from the *Peanuts* cartoon) reclining on top of his doghouse. The alleged Star Trek Bomb was, in reality, a deluxe model Snoopy Electric Toothbrush. Andy was sentenced to five years in prison.

From time to time the police would bring Andy in to University Hospital from the penitentiary; occasionally he did have legitimate seizures. He'd be shuffling along wearing leg irons and handcuffs, arm in arm with two guards. He would give Dad a big smile.

"Hey, how you doing?"

"Good to see you, Andy. Keeping busy in the big house?"

"It's great over there. I'm working in the kitchen." He leaned over to my father and whispered, "I got me a good job. I'm making orange wine."

"That's what you don't need, Andy."

When he was released, Andy relocated to the east end of town. My father heard a rumor from a paramedic stationed in that area that he eventually died of AIDS. Dad always said to us, "He needed help, but he wasn't a criminal."

Knowing that he couldn't right the wrongs of others was distressing to my father. Despite my father's faith in God, he could not understand how people could be so heartless. Although he sometimes searched for scriptures to make sense of the evils he witnessed, no verse was strong enough to justify the suffering that some of his patients and colleagues endured. Dad was too humble to profess to know the answers, and he believed that humans have limited comprehension. He would rationalize the tortures that man inflicted against man as a mystery that might someday be explained by God.

My father recalled that the theme from the movie *The Godfather* bellowed throughout the station as Bob Lechner played the tune on the Cordovox. "The song was passionately rendered. Bob brought the instrument to life. I'd always say, 'You really are talented.' He'd just shake his head in denial and dismiss my praise with a wave of his hand."

Once a call interrupted the concert; within minutes they were both stepping from the ambulance and proceeding up the steps of a three-story house. As they entered the front door, a young, well-dressed black man, about twenty years old, came tearing out. He wore an expensive shirt, tie and alligator shoes. Brushing past the medics he called over his shoulder: "Ernie, third floor." My father did not know what to expect as they climbed to the top level. Cautiously, Bob and Dad approached an open doorway leading to a gloomy apartment.

"Hello," Dad shouted. There was no response.

"Ambo, Ambulance."

No response. All was silence as they inched their way into the deplorable surroundings: filthy floors, plaster falling off walls, dirty dishes piled up everywhere. It was as if it had never been cleaned. Again, they announced their presence as they moved halfway through the apartment. A low moan came from the bedroom.

A naked black man lay motionless, face-up on a urine-soaked mattress. Although the victim appeared to be in his sixties, my father later learned later, from the incident report, that his name was Ernie, and he was only thirty-five years old. He had spindly arms and legs, swollen feet and a gaunt face with protruding eyeballs. He was skin and bone. Barely breathing, he stared imploringly at my father as if to say, "Please help me."

He was welded to the mattress, unable to move from a stack of urine- and feces-soaked newspapers. Thousands of wriggling maggots had invaded a one foot long and two inches wide bedsore on his right leg. Morsels of food, obviously days—possibly weeks—old were strewn around his makeshift bed. It was incredible that a man could survive under such conditions. The sight sickened both of the medics. Dad gathered up the intestinal fortitude to check the patient's vital signs. He was barely alive.

In another room a demented old man was wandering around a table picking decaying food from a plate and mumbling, "Either for me or the roaches." He wore an old dirty suit coat, a scarf around his neck and a soiled navy blue beret. Obviously, he wasn't going to be much help to Ernie.

According to my father, "Ernie was so dehydrated and starved that I think he would have been better off under Hitler's care in Dachau or Buchenwald. At least they threw powder on the prisoners to keep down the vermin."

This wreck of a human looked like a corpse that had been dug up after being buried for three months. His wide-open eyes pleaded for mercy. Nearby, my father found a tattered medical card on the floor with the name Ernie Walls printed on it.

Ernie appeared to have been in the same position for weeks, possibly months. His unkempt hair was loaded with roach eggs. Dad applied the beam of the flashlight to reveal roaches, lice, spiders and assorted vermin scattered in all directions.

"Well, Bob, do you want to quit now or later?" He laughed nervously. They both knew that was not an option; they both felt intense compassion for Ernie.

"We have to figure out the best way to get the guy out of here without getting contaminated."

If the victim soiled the first line unit, the medics would have to fumigate the ambulance. At such times, my father would retrieve the second line medic unit and put the patient into the second unit. There was no equipment to clean and scrub down in the empty reserve unit, which made it easier to decontaminate. They would later put a lice bomb in it. When opened, it emitted a poisonous cloud of chemicals similar to those used in household insect spray. This would kill everything

My father always exercised extreme caution so that he wouldn't carry the critters back to our house. Because lice infiltrate everywhere, Dad often washed his head with Quell shampoo, a product specifically designed to kill lice. As for fleas, they were acrobats, able to jump high, up to three, four, even five feet.

The police arrived and kept an eye on Ernie while the medics went back to the firehouse to get the reserve ambulance. On the way, they notified Truck 4 so they could use the Stokes basket, a person-size concave wire scoop. It is easier to use than a stretcher in these situations, because the basket can slide down a ladder. The victim does not have to be carried.

To ward off the appalling stench, Bob used an air mask. Dad chose not to wear one. My father was used to these conditions, and bad sinuses had impaired his sense of smell. He and his partner brought in the backboard to facilitate Ernie's removal from this "living death environment."

As they gingerly peeled Ernie from the newspapers, thousands of roaches darted in all directions from under his body. My father said to me, "The effect of such an encounter lingered with me for days. It keeps coming back in your mind. It replays when you least expect it. It's like a wave that comes over and goes away while you're doing something else. You might be mowing the lawn, washing the car or walking into the store. You can't shake it off."

The stairwells curved too much for Ernie to be taken downstairs in a litter. The truck crew ran their aerial ladder up to the third floor window and provided a Stokes basket to cradle their patient. The medics carefully transferred Ernie from the backboard onto the Stokes basket, hoping desperately that the sheets would not tear. Then Truck 4 lowered him down.

They called the emergency room on the way to the hospital to give them a heads-up. They carried Ernie in the Stokes to a single washroom, which had been made ready. The bugs were crawling in all directions as two orderlies placed him in a bathtub.

When they removed the dry-rotted sheets, a dozen holes of varying sizes in the flesh of his back were revealed. Maggots were pouring from these infected sores. One of the orderlies sat on the edge of the bathtub calmly peeling away bits of sheet with all these creatures scrambling out.

"But when a spider appeared this man freaked out! He took off into the hallway, fluttered his arms around and in a high-pitched voice cried, 'I'm not going in there, I hate spiders. They give me the creeps!'

"Ernie had an Afro full of roach eggs," Dad recalled. "They had made a nest. He had every kind of vermin you can imagine in that 'fro and the orderly was fine. Then one spider threw him! The spider was the least of my worries."

The *Baltimore Sun* later reported that the young man with the alligator shoes and tailored suit was Ernie's caretaker. He had been stealing Ernie's welfare checks intended for food and clothing. The thief was in a hurry, because he suspected Ernie had only a short time to live. It was the worst case of neglect that had ever been seen in the annals of the health department. After hours of cleaning and stabilizing Ernie, they put him in a private room.

"I found it impossible to comprehend the mind of someone who would do such a terrible thing. No human being deserved to exist in such horrific conditions. Ernie died that night, and I would like to think that his last memory was that some of us had compassion."

Throughout his life, my father had frequent nightmares. Occasionally he described them. "Most of the dreams are in subdued lighting and I'm always missing my turnout gear when at the fire ground. I feel panic in many of the dreams where I'm running late for work.

"In other dreams I'm communicating with co-workers who in real life have died. I'm overwhelmed with a feeling of inadequacy. I am not a hero or even a good caregiver, just an outsider looking in with a desperate desire to achieve recognition on some level."

As the years passed the dreams became more frequent and intense, inducing in my father feelings of hopelessness and futility. Sleep deprivation caused him to feel "spaced out" during the night shift. Working four fourteen-hour nights, without a break, made concentration difficult. Proper diagnosis, assessing drug usage, monitoring blood pressure and pulse, and a multitude of other essential procedures were hard to perform.

"As the nights dragged on, I had to stay focused in spite of overwhelming fatigue. Driving home, I'd periodically stop at the red light and then run the light, forgetting that I wasn't in the ambo. When I wasn't working, it was almost impossible to rest, because I still felt hyper and keyed up. It took a while to unwind. Obligations at home would interfere with any chance to obtain much-needed rest. And I never adjusted to the transition from ghetto to home. The lifestyles were just too dramatically different. Long hours at work numbed my senses and left me drained."

As he grew older, my father perpetually berated himself for neglecting his family by his absence, and for trivializing our problems, which, compared to encounters in life in the area he served, seemed unimportant. He realized that he could be impassive, monotonous and indifferent, and he feared he was neglecting to provide us with emotional support and proper involvement. He thought my mother was right: he did live in the ghetto.

Dad was all too aware that, in his absence, my mother had to endure the loneliness, do most of the child rearing and make most of the household decisions. When he was on night shift, he needed to catch up on his sleep during the day. She understood this and would try to keep Craig and me quiet by taking us shopping or sending us outside to play.

"And yet, the connection with my family kept me going many times during difficult nights and days at work. Yes, I felt that I was depriving my family of the better life that they richly deserved. But the pure joy of helping folk in crisis superseded all else. Was it an act of selfishness on my part when I deserted my loved ones even at Christmas? I don't know. I only know that I was driven by an inner force compelling me to try to make a difference."

Don't Fear the Reaper

In the city of Baltimore, villains and heroes collide.

A few days before Easter 1976, a man named Charles A. Hopkins stepped off the elevator in the City of Baltimore's temporary offices in the post office building in search of the mayor. City Hall, located on Holliday Street, was under renovation. But the man seemed to know where he was going as he slipped past the receptionist. With lunchtime bustle all around, he followed a mayoral staff member through a door which closed and locked behind them.

Then Charles Hopkins' pace began to quicken. He jogged down the hallway, turned abruptly into Kathleen Nolan's office, and demanded to see Mayor William Donald Schaefer. The young office manager stood up. She normally greeted visitors with a smile, but not this time. There was something menacing about this stranger.

"Who are you?" Nolan asked Hopkins.

"I'll show you who I am," he growled, exposing a pistol. Unimaginably, he pulled the trigger. A .38 caliber bullet blazed through Nolan's chest, pierced the bookcase behind her, and chipped the wall.

When supervisor Joanne McQuade heard the commotion, she raced over and pushed her way through the crowd gathering outside Nolan's open door. Before her stood Nolan: ashen, wide-eyed, with her legs starting to go out from under her.

"He shot me," said Nolan.

The gunman swung around and now it was Joanne McQuade who stared into at the barrel of the pistol. Hopkins ordered her to take him to the mayor.

McQuade thought, "Oh my God, now I've had it." She took off down the hallway, dashed into an office, and grabbed a phone. As she dialed "0," she felt the gun jabbing into her neck.

"Put down the phone or I'll kill you." Hopkins snatched her by her blouse, bunching her collar in his fist, snarling that he would not be telling her one more time he was here to see the mayor.

McQuade's mind raced. She told the gunman Schaefer had not yet returned from Annapolis, the state capital. But the mayor was just a few yards away, behind his door. She wondered how her baby son would grow up without her when she was dead.

In a fury, Charles Hopkins muscled McQuade out into the corridor in the direction of the city council offices. Meantime, Karen Blair, another assistant to the mayor, had barricaded herself in a nearby office and was seeking frantically to defy strict orders from Mayor Schaefer's top aide, Joan Bereska, whose hand-written sign was taped to the mayor's door: "DO NOT ENTER! Absolutely no one!"

It was the day after the close of the ninety-day General Assembly in Annapolis. Bereska hadn't liked the dark circles under the mayor's eyes. She knew he still had a mound of paperwork to contend with and dangling legislative issues to tie up, so she had turned down the volume on his inner office telephones.

When finally Karen Blair succeeded in getting through on his emergency line, she hysterically told Mayor Schaefer not to open his door, not to come out of his office no matter what: there was a shooter nearby on a rampage, determined to kill him.

With his partner behind the wheel of Medic 4, my father sped to the scene. As they rounded a blind street corner where the handsome old Pratt Library building stood, Medic 4 and another ambulance nearly smashed into each other. Bill, who was thirty-five (about the same age as the gunman, it would later be revealed) ran through the Calvert Street entrance to City Hall and punched "6" in the elevator.

On the seventh floor Charles Hopkins was dragging Joanne McQuade across an enclosed bridge, toward the elevator, so he could get down to the city council offices.

"How about if I help you get out of the building so you can get away?" McQuade's heart pounded.

"Just do what I tell you," said Hopkins. When the elevator didn't come at once, he dragged her down a flight of stairs. As Hopkins prepared to leap over a security gate, McQuade broke free and tore down the stairwell five more floors, escaping to the lobby where she cried out for help. Up on the sixth floor, Hopkins barreled into the office of Councilman Dominic Leone, who was sitting there with William E. Burkman, Clerk of the Elections Board.

The gunman waved his pistol at Burkman and demanded, "Who are you?"

"I ain't nobody," Burkman answered.

"What's the matter, fella?" Councilman Leone asked, rising from behind his desk. On the wall in back of Leone was a picture of the late John F. Kennedy, assassinated in the 1960s. "Why don't you put the gun down?"

Hopkins' bullet struck him in the chest. Leone was dead in the next instant. Hearing the shot, Councilman J. Joseph Curran and other staff members slammed their office doors and locked themselves in as the gunman fired in the direction of Burkman, who was fleeing down the hall. Running into an open office, Hopkins grabbed Councilman Carroll J. Fitzgerald and shoved the pistol into his cheek.

The police had converged, but Fitzgerald called out, "Please back off or he'll shoot me." Hopkins forced Fitzgerald into the council president's vacant office—Walter Orlinsky was in Washington, DC, that day. A shot rang out.

As my father stepped from the elevator into the pandemonium of the sixth floor, employees ran past him screaming. A body against a wall seemed to have been exploded out of its desk chair, which was wheeling around on its own. The brass nameplate on the desk said Dominic Leone. His heart was motionless.

Hearing gunshots on the floor above, Bill ran down the hall and up the staircase. Chaos greeted him on the seventh floor too. He knelt to examine a woman lying on the floor; it was Kathleen Nolan. She gasped out her answers the best she could while slipping into shock. She was pallid and sweating, and her eyelids were closing. Her blood pressure had plummeted, while her heart beat rapidly to compensate for the loss of blood. Bill glanced up at the pop-eyed, perspiring circle of faces above him. These were faces he knew from the news: city councilmen, the Chief of Police, the Mayor of Baltimore City. They were all in shock.

Just after 12:30 p.m., police charged into the office.

"I've been shot," Fitzgerald said.

At that moment, Officer Robert C. Smith shot the gunman twice. Police fired three more times. The gunman stumbled toward the wall and fell to the floor. Hopkins had taken two bullets in the abdomen, one in his left arm and finger, and one in his backside. During the scuffle, Officer Thomas Gaither had been shot in the knee.

Meanwhile, one floor below, my father attended to the wounded secretary. Pale and dripping with sweat, Nolan stared at Dad, her gaze distant beneath heavy eyelids. She was losing consciousness. He wrapped his fingers around her wrist and felt her clammy skin. Her weak pulse beat rapidly.

"What's your name?"

"Kathleen," she groaned. The fact that she was speaking at all was a good sign.

Dad wrapped the gray blood-pressure cuff around her arm between the elbow and the shoulder and quickly squeezed the bulb, pumping air until the cuff expanded. The needle on the gauge dropped steadily down. As he heard the rapid thumping through his stethoscope, he knew every second counted. He needed to get her to the hospital as soon as possible. Because Kathleen was still conscious, he did not think a major artery had been hit, but he couldn't be sure. After all, he wasn't a doctor. In a hospital, physicians work in a controlled setting; all around my father was chaos. Dad heard Kathleen's co-workers and well-meaning strangers yelling but he stayed focused on her.

He looked up for a split second and saw the faces looking down—Schaefer, council members, co-workers and dignitaries. And there my father was, on his knees at their feet. He hovered over Kathleen Nolan trying desperately to keep her lifeblood pumping, while the politicians, still in shock, towered above him powerless. Dad's every move was being watched.

There was no room for error.

He traced Nolan's arm to the elbow to get a good vein, shoved in the needle, and pulled back on the casing until the tube and needle were deep in her flesh. After a trauma, the vein can close; he had to be sure to keep the vein open. Nolan needed the intravenous fluids right away. While keeping pressure on the arm, he used his thumb to hook up the 1000-cc bag of lactate fluid to keep her alive until he could get her to the hospital.

Amazingly, she was soon stable enough to move.

"You okay?" Dad asked.

"Mmm," she replied.

He raised her shirt and spotted a small hole about the size of a nail head in the upper part of her chest. Dad gently lifted her and quickly looked at her back but no exit wound was apparent. He had seen enough gunshot wounds to know that the bullet could have ricocheted inside her body and damaged the organs. He put a compress over the entrance wound. He and his partner put her on the litter. Someone cleared a path for them. They wheeled her away. Once inside the medic unit, Dad gave her oxygen, hooked her up to the cardiac monitor, sent the EKG to the hospital and radioed the doctor at Mercy Hospital with the readout. "ETA (estimated time of arrival) four minutes."

The next day Councilman J. Joseph Curran Sr., who was seventy-one, was treated for heart problems attributed to witnessing the events. He died the following year.

Medic 1 delivered the gunman to University Hospital where he recovered after five hours of surgical care. Hopkins had been the owner-operator of a small carryout business on Baltimore's Rutland Avenue. He testified that he wanted to kill the mayor because the city health department had closed his establishment. He was found not guilty by reason of insanity and has spent his life in mental health facilities where he has been treated for schizophrenia.

Kathleen Nolan survived.

Even now, whenever another government-office massacre occurs in the United States, the shootout at Baltimore's City Hall in 1976, America's Bicentennial, inevitably resurfaces in local newspapers. People old enough to remember it often contribute yet another forgotten tidbit about the day Mayor Schaefer was almost assassinated. Medic Bill Hennick's name is never mentioned.

I will always think of that day as the time when, for a few minutes, the mayor of Baltimore looked to my father for guidance.

Hard Times (No One Knows Better Than I)

I cherished Saturday mornings. Because of his irregular sleeping patterns, my father could not always sleep in. Sometimes I would arise early and, through the heating vent at the foot of my bed, I could hear him humming downstairs. I would slip into the kitchen to join him for a cup of coffee. Dad made it just the way I liked it—loads of milk and sugar with about a teaspoon of coffee. Sometimes he made me eggs just the way I like them too—beaten, then fried. Mom said he cooked them until they were like slabs of leather.

My father loved to read the newspaper aloud to me. Sometimes he would cut out a cartoon or a photo of Sean Cassidy (on whom I had a ridiculous crush), blacken the singer's teeth and write some silly caption on it. Then he would sneak it in the lunch my mother packed for me and I would be mortified to discover it in the presence of my friends in the school cafeteria.

After we settled down with our coffees and fried eggs, he would spread the paper out on the kitchen table. The simplest newspaper headline or photo could prompt him to recount a story about his work. If I saw a photo or an article on Martin Luther King, I knew I was going to miss a few Saturday morning cartoons. "I'm telling you," he'd say, "when he got shot it was a mess down there. I'm telling you, Rachel. People were stealing anything they could get their hands on. I've never seen anything like it. Those were some horrible times. Stinking slumlords. The blasted Vietnam War. No-good politicians . . ."

When Dad applied adjectives like "stinking," "blasted" and "no-good," I knew he was furious. As a grade school student, I found his morning editorializing difficult to comprehend. "What are you talking about, Dad?"

"President Johnson was a bum. Blah, blah, blah. That had to be the worst decade. And the city hasn't been the same since . . ." He began raving about the "stinking medic equipment" and the "blasted shortage of supplies."

My mother would slip into the kitchen, pour herself a cup of black coffee and take a seat. "This has been some week, Bill." She regularly reported to my father the tribulations of life in the suburbs. Mom wore one of my father's t-shirts and a pair of sweatpants. Her hair was pulled back. She would never let anyone outside of the immediate family see her in casual attire, and she wouldn't leave the house unless she was dressed to the nines.

"The same stinkin' bullcrap is going on down there night after blasted night and nobody cares." Dad shook the paper to get out the creases.

"The dog's been vomiting."

"I know, Eunice."

My father took a sip of coffee and turned the page.

"All over the living room floor. I gave her some leftover goulash the other night. She didn't even touch it. She loves goulash. I think we need to take her to the vet. Rachel and Jessica aren't friends anymore. Jessica teased her in front of the other girls. Craig lost his soccer game. He was excellent. Some boys on the team looked tired. They were playing slow. Mom threw her back out, and the doctors are deciding whether to operate. She wants your opinion. And Dad's having ulcers again. His color doesn't look good."

"Mmm." My father flipped another page.

"Bill?"

"What, Eunice?"

"You haven't heard a word I've said."

"I have, Eunice. I'm just trying to wake up."

Even as a child, I couldn't understand how the government and especially the bosses of the fire department could have so little regard for my father. Sometimes he looked utterly exhausted. Once in a while he didn't talk: that was scary. My brother and I would try to make him laugh, and he would just grunt. "He had a rough night," is all my mother would say. I would wonder which one of his friends might have died or if he had had yet another close call.

"What are we going to do about the dog?" Mom persisted.

"Snuggles isn't a puppy anymore. You have to expect these things to happen."

"So we just let her vomit to death?"

"I didn't say that, Eunice. I just said that you need to be prepared for the fact that Snuggles isn't going to be around forever."

"Great. So I'll just tell the kids we've decided to let her die."

"I didn't say that. What I am trying to say is that the kids need to realize that death is part of life."

"Thank you, Professor Medic. I think you've already drilled that into their heads." Mom stood up from the kitchen table, marched over to the cabinet and retrieved the big orange Betty Crocker cookbook. She plopped it on the counter and flipped it open to one of the sticky pages.

In a tone nearing desperation, Dad said, "The young ones, I'm talking as young as eight, are dealing drugs down there. People shoot each other for a few bucks, and the only one making money is the man at the top. Shootings happen all the time, but they escalate from June to August. When they clean house, when they get rid of the old regime of gangsters: it's like a political election. Statistics downplay the injuries and headline homicides. Hit men shoot people in front of security guards; criminals don't care.

"The other night I walk into the lobby of one of the Murphy Homes. The security guard is staring at me wide-eyed with his teeth clenched in an eerie grin. Sweat is pouring down his face and arms. He's unable to speak, obviously in shock. A dead man is sprawled across his feet. Twenty feet away, another victim is lying face down in an elevator with his body partially extended into the lobby. The black security guard was probably a would-be cop, only earning minimum wages, trying to support himself. Two stinking drug addicts had shot the victims in the head."

Dad pulled the handkerchief from the left breast pocket of his pajamas and blew his nose. The old stress-congestion again. "Ugh, I couldn't wait to get off the meat wagon that night."

His doleful aria continued. "Almost every night a group of big men wearing skirts and stilettos walk past the firehouse and call out, "How you doin' boys? Where you going tonight? We're looking for some action.' It's like the 'Twilight Zone.'" Dad gazed into space.

"Bill?"

"What, Eunice?"

"Get out of the kitchen."

"Why?"

"Because I don't want to hear it."

"Nobody wants to hear it, but it's the truth. You don't see people down there blubbering about a sick dog or crying when they lose a game, Eunice. Now, how would I react if one of those scenarios invaded my own home, my own neighborhood?"

My father frequently asked this question.

He often referred to the lessons he kept learning about the strength of the people he served.

"There was that time when—"

"Bill, I've just gotten out of bed. I don't want to listen to this now." Mom turned on the electric mixer, Dad raised his voice and took a deep breath.

"To some ghetto dwellers, material life is what it's about—getting the Cadillac, the lambskin coats, the jewelry. But scattered gems live down there too; people in the middle of all that mess who still survive in spite of it. You can go into a block of row homes where the houses on both sides are total wrecks, drug houses where they shoot up, houses with burnt-out interiors, and then this one house gives you hope and makes you think that things might change for the better.

"These human gems seem to be much more content than affluent people even though they don't have anything. They can't even step outside without risking getting knocked over the head, and drug deals are taking place on their front steps. Yet they found the secret to what's needed in life. They keep their houses neat, try to make a go of life, exercise patience—even though they don't have anything. In most cases, these gems have a spiritual connection that keeps them strong. These are people with character and values. They're forced to live in a cesspool, but somehow they are able to maintain an upright life despite the daily heartaches."

Teresa was one such person. Her grandchild "ripped her off," took her television, even took her rugs. Three or four times, she spent every penny she had to send him to rehab.

"She gave everything she had, even though she didn't *have* anything. The block she lived on was bad, but she kept her place tidy and tried to deal with the surroundings. She was always sewing dolls and make stuffed toy animals for the children. Even though she was fighting cancer, she smiled. She was one of those gems."

"Come back down from the ambulance, Bill," Mom said as she put the electric beaters aside on a plate so Craig and I could lick the batter from them later. "You're home, you're in the kitchen with a sick dog and a washing machine that needs to be fixed. Earth to Bill. Can you hear me, Bill?"

"Huh, Eunice?"

"Bill, are you death?" A Freudian slip; Mom corrected herself. "Deaf?"

"Eh?" putting his hand behind one ear, Dad would persist. He hated to see honest, hardworking people struggle.

"I'll never forget that time when this stringy-haired, raggedy girl about nineteen years old greeted us in broken sentences at the door of a roach-infested, dimly lit row home. I couldn't understand her phrasing. I quickly figured out that she was mentally handicapped, so I relied on her gestures.

"She leads us down the hallway. We find ourselves in a small, dark room. The stench of urine and feces assaults our nostrils to the point where it was almost intolerable. I can hear faint breathing on the far side of the room but can't see past an arm's length. The only light is coming from a single, weak bulb in the hallway. My partner retrieves a flashlight from the medic unit and uses it to illuminate the room.

"An emaciated man dressed in rags lay on the floor, obviously dying of starvation. I figured out gradually that he got no real meals, just got tossed scraps, like he was an animal. How could he have survived under those conditions? He was barely alive. The girl was doing the best she could do. It was pitiful. How could you call it abuse? She was doing everything she could. I don't know whether she was the one who called or if someone else did. That kind of situation should have never existed in the first place. Why didn't anyone do anything about this? How could it be that nobody checked up to see what was going on? She tried to take care of him; she wasn't capable. She needed to be taken care of herself.

"Poverty and ignorance go together, and that's the way it is. You wish you could do more but you can't do anything. She is handicapped, he is starving and it's too late to do anything for them."

"Bi . . . ii . . . iill," Mom chanted, "I'm talking to you . . ."

Dad cleared his throat, looked at her squarely and said, "Many families tried to create stability in the midst of the chaos, but they were stymied. Take that time I went into a house a young black woman had rented from a slumlord. It looked like it had survived a war. She was newly married, and the couple seemed hardworking, decent, like they were trying to create a good life. Remember that couple in the movie *It's a Wonderful Life*, turning a dilapidated house into a home?

"Anyway, the floor around the radiator had rotted away, and their slumlord, who in this case was black, had laid down corrugated cardboard and painted it to match the floor. The wife was trying to hang curtains. She had put a wooden chair next to the radiator, stood on the radiator, and then, as she stepped onto the chair, its legs went straight through the cardboard. She fell down and hit her back on the sharp edge of the radiator, damaging her spine. It left her permanently paralyzed from the waist down. She was just trying to improve her home. Why did it have to happen to them?"

"Speaking of the kitchen floor, Bill, when are we going to replace the tiles?" Before Dad could reply with another story, Mom asked another question. "Bill, do you think we can afford to get the kids a Carvel ice cream cake for their birthday party?"

"Eunice, I'm working around the clock. If the money's not there, it's not there. And when it's gone, it's gone."

"Bill, it's Craig and Rachel's birthday party. We have thirty-five kids coming. We have to give them something."

My father leaned against the counter and casually took a cookie from the tray Mom had pulled from the oven a few minutes prior. He spoke between bites.

"On one hand, because the only jobs available to black people, even a hundred years after the Civil War, are meager and low-paying, they retaliate by bleeding the system. Some are gems but others take advantage of the welfare programs as a protest. Doing that only ends up hurting them. I believe that black people should have the same rights as anyone else. I'll believe that until the day I die. These citizens have fought in all of America's wars for over two hundred years. Rosa Parks was right; it was ridiculous that any person couldn't take any seat on the bus. Reverend Martin Luther King Jr. was an outstanding hero for Americans, black and white. There was no rhyme or reason for him being shot.

"But I can't understand why some folk on food stamps are eating better than us. I'll never forget the Pantry Pride store at Mondawmin Mall, seeing the carts being pushed past me by some of the local shoppers. They were loaded to the hilt with prime cuts of meat—New York Strip Steaks, center cut pork chops, brand-name bread.

"Fire department pay provides the basics. I'm relegated to the world of gristly ground beef, end cuts of pork, off-brand bread and canned goods. I clip coupons. My motto is 'NPR (Never Pay Retail),' and I follow it religiously."

"There's my answer. We'll buy generic from Pantry Pride." Mom could be as much a comedian as my father.

He picked up another cookie.

"Leave some for the kids, Bill."

Dad shook his head and said, "I'll tell you, people don't have it easy down there. Every once in a while when you've seen man's inhumanity to man sink to the lowest depths you thought possible, something even more despicable happens on the street . . ."

"Well, thank you for answering my question about the party dessert, Bill." Mom picked up the newspaper and cut out two coupons for Breyers ice cream.

Dad brushed the cookie crumbs from his t-shirt and kept on,

regardless. "I know how resilient the people in the ghetto have to be and that's a lesson for me. Because no matter how bad it gets in my life, it can't get as bad as it gets for the people down there."

Right Place, Wrong Time

My father says he lost count of the number of times his life was threatened while trying to deliver care. The firefighters still tormented him with comments like, "I'd rather have my sister in a whorehouse than ride on a medic unit."

"How can you stand it on there?" The white firefighters often suggested he transfer to a white area.

"Not because they were all bigots," Dad added, "but because they know that being a medic in that area is tough."

Harry Dennis, from Truck 4, was a forty-three-year-old black man with a hearty laugh and personality plus. He looked after my father the way Larry Burch had done earlier. He always arrived at his day shift early to prepare his breakfast of pancakes, sausage and bacon on his own hotplate.

Dad admired Harry's realistic assessment of people. Harry didn't have any patience with folk who used drugs, abused alcohol or blamed others for their misfortunes. Harry wanted his black brothers and sisters to be responsible and self-disciplined. He spoke freely about how people needed to resist temptations and maintain their pride.

"He was always optimistic on the job. We needed someone like him around. Harry lit up the room every time he walked in," Dad said.

One night, several of the men crowded into a decrepit, slow-moving elevator headed for the tenth floor of one of the Murphys. Harry and Dad were joking about the stench of urine and the general condition of the elevator car when the elevator lurched to an abrupt stop between floors.

A hand appeared brandishing a pistol through the two-by-two-foot opening in the ceiling where the escape hatch had been removed. The hand was attached to a very young man.

"Gimme your wallets," the gunman demanded.

"You little motherfucker!" Harry shouted. He swung his axe at the intruder and just missed slicing his arm off. The youth leapt across the abyss to the next elevator, escaping Harry's wrath.

A happy Thanksgiving celebration in the Murphys turned sour when a father and his son began arguing over the remnants of the holiday turkey. Both wanted the few scraps of white meat that remained. The argument escalated until the son shot his father in the chest with a 22 gauge pistol, killing him instantly.

In another incident, an impatient young man shot his cousin because he was making an excessively long phone call. The cousin died. The perpetrator of the crime was quickly apprehended. "Ironically, under the law he was allowed one phone call," Dad said.

In these precarious situations, my father sometimes found that playing along with the killers or the mentally disturbed was necessary for survival.

One day they got a call to attend to an injured man over at the cut-rate liquor store on Fulton Avenue. My father charged through the entrance. A man was standing there still holding a pistol. A dead man was lying in the corner with his head tilted upward. The assailant had fired five or six shots into him. The police hadn't yet arrived. Dad was stuck. He didn't know whether there were any bullets left in the gun. So he struck up a conversation with the killer. He talked with him about sports, the weather, "real matter-of-fact as though nothing out of the ordinary had happened. Then I casually asked, 'Any reason why you shot this guy?'

"The killer paused a moment then shook his gun at me. 'That man, that man owed me a quarter.'

" 'Well it doesn't look like you'll it get it back now. Guess you showed him. I might be a little upset myself if somebody borrowed twenty-five cents from me and didn't pay it back.' " My father just kept on talking until the police arrived.

Another time, Dad had just stepped through the front door and was about to attend to a man sprawled out on the floor when a guy put a knife to his throat. Dad said. "Look, I haven't slept for four days. If you want to kill me go ahead, at least then I might be able to get some rest. But I'm trying to help out your brother here. So you need to decide whether you want him to live or you want him to die."

He released my father. The man on the floor survived.

One day, Chief McMahon phoned my father from his office. "I have a good opening at Medic 11 on Roland Avenue in Hampden." He seemed to think he was doing my father a big favor.

But Dad didn't want to be transferred to that "white, low-income, redneck area." He told the Chief, "I'd rather stay here. I like this house. I like my co-workers. It's closer to the action." He hung up the phone and went back to work.

A Change Is Gonna Come

My father's appearance didn't change much throughout his career. In the late seventies he still had a full head of hair, neatly parted on the right side. It had only just begun to turn gray in the front and at the temples. We could tell if the shift had been a rough one because his eyes bulged out and the pitch of his voice rose when he recounted the day's events.

My brother and I did not recall him yelling at us any more, or any less, during times of great stress. Certainly Dad would scold us if we fought or if we were being noisy when he was trying to nap, but it usually took a lot to make him lose his temper. Whatever had happened at work, he did not vent any anger or frustration on us.

If Craig and I misbehaved, Mom would give Dad the full report when he came home. He would sit us down and ask us to explain why we did or did not do something. Sometimes his voice would be slurred or hoarse from sheer exhaustion.

Even after nearly fifteen years with the Baltimore City Fire Department, Dad still usually appeared jovial and easygoing to his family. Was it because he was emotionally reticent? Or was it because we children were oblivious to his inner struggles? I don't know. For whatever reason, we were unaware of the battle he was fighting within, and we would not learn of his declining enthusiasm until much later.

I once asked him how he coped. Dad said, "My desire was to do the best job possible with no regrets. I kept from dwelling on tragedies by being completely absorbed in the business at hand. Seconds made all the difference in saving lives and property. There was no time to lament."

That's why my father hated to cover the watch desk. As a paramedic, he was exempt from watch duty except when companies were out on runs. Although they were allowed to read on duty, he dreaded the moments when he'd finished skimming the newspaper and had time to think. He preferred to be busy, to lack a moment to dwell on the squalor of the neighborhood. In many situations, he felt powerless and could not help wondering why so many terrible things kept happening. "At times, it would seem as though every member of society was pitted one against the other, with no hope of a better day to come."

So when he sat at the watch desk Dad would analyze his life too much and begin to feel depressed. On one particular day he settled down to wait for the calls. The pace of the day had been slow, allowing time to clean and check the ambulance's equipment. The other companies and the Chief were out on a run; only Dad and his partner Dave Quigley were at the station.

Firefighters Quigley (white) and Chaney (black) often kept up comic, highly non-politically-correct repartee. Quigley might strut into the house and say, "Hey, Chaney, you're invited to our next cookout. You've been appointed Imperial Wizard of a K.K.K. klavern in my neighborhood."

"Whatsa matter, don't you hillbilly honkies believe in ropes and trees anymore?" Chaney's replies were cool and mellow, like those of a southern gentleman.

Quigley might say, "I'm beating my dog with a black baby doll."

"You rednecks sure got some kinky ways. What's wrong with you? Can't you get a date with a real sista?" Chaney always had a biting retort. Those two loved ribbing each other, yet they genuinely cared for each other. They both got a kick out of ridiculing society. My father told me that a reporter once happened to hear these two going at it: "His jaw dropped."

But that day, Chaney had off. Dad and Quigley were bored and waiting for something to happen. It would have been great to be outside on such a fresh, sunny day in February, especially after the recent blizzard followed by two weeks of rain and snow. The afternoon dragged on. It was 2:00 p.m.: only three hours left until the change of shift. Dad turned up the volume on the watch desk radio, got up, stretched and headed for the door just a few feet away. As he reached the ramp, he took a deep breath of the crisp air, noticing, at the same time, a thick black column of smoke penetrating the unbroken blue of the sky in the vicinity of the Beethoven Apartments. It appeared to be the kind of cloud emitted from a high-rise incinerator, but the smoke had some force behind it.

He found himself hoping against hope that his "beloved landmark," this newly renovated nineteenth-century wonder, remained unscarred by fire, but his thoughts were interrupted by communications. A fire had broken out at Park Avenue and McMechen Street. Indeed the smoke was coming from the Beethoven. My father and his partner took off in the medic unit and parked on McMechen Street.

Dad would later learn in the *Baltimore Sun* what had happened. A boy, aged ten, living in a second floor apartment, was playing with a tennis ball. When it rolled out of sight, he used a candle to look for it under his bed. Fire caught hold and ravaged the second floor. The apartment building's young maintenance man, Jerry Brown, heard the bewildered little boy shouting, "Our apartment's on fire!" and other residents crying, "Fire." Jerry ran to the nearest firebox, pulled the switch and triggered the first fire alarm at 2:01 p.m.

Police Officer Edgar J. Rumpf was nearby and arrived first. He and Mr. George Augins Jr., a mailman visiting his father, dashed into the entrance of the main building in search of people in danger. They helped two children escape. Rumpf ran in again and did not come out.

"The last time I saw him was on the second floor and he was going up," Augins said.

Dad and his partner were the first men from the fire department to arrive. Engine 13 and Truck 4 from their station, together with other area companies, were delayed at a dwelling fire on Druid Hill Avenue only three blocks away from the station and didn't arrive until a bit later. It was bad timing that could not have been prevented.

The Beethoven was ablaze. Smoke and flames poured from the two windows above the main entrance. Just as Dad and his partner pulled up, a man came out of a side door leading an elderly lady and two small children. It was Slats, well-known as the "skinny guy from Engine 25 who could smoke a cigarette up to the filter without flicking or dropping the ash." Dad took the three victims into the module of the ambulance to give them care. All four had escaped uninjured. Slats, who was off duty, happened to be just around the corner when he saw the smoke and went in looking for occupants.

"He loved firefighting, Slats did. As far as I know, he never received any credit for saving that lady and children. Never wanted any."

My father turned his attention toward the flames leaping more forcibly than ever from the two second-story windows. A cop came up to Dad and asked if he had seen his partner, Edgar Rumpf.

"No."

"I think he went into the building."

"Well, he made a mistake doing that," Dad said.

Rumpf desired a career in firefighting and used to hang around at my father's firehouse. While he was on his beat, he used to come into Engine 13, sit in the chair, lean against the wall and ask Dad to wake him up in fifteen minutes. He would doze off.

"He probably dreamed about working with the fire department, Anyway, I could see why he chose to go in. At first it didn't look out of control. Rumpf probably thought it was contained in the one apartment; that's how it appeared from the outside. Instead, the blaze was spreading, but it was hidden in the walls and ceilings. It suddenly erupted and spread throughout the entire interior of the building."

Other companies began to arrive. Cops and firefighters banged on the doors, alerting occupants who fled down the stairs and scurried outside to escape the burning building. Together, they all gazed in disbelief as the flames destroyed their apartments.

"Help, I'm trapped on the third floor," the police heard Rumpf's voice shout on the radio. Firefighters desperately searched for him until the surging blaze prevented further efforts.

Eight other alarms summoned fifty pieces of fire apparatus and 175 men. Nancy Bethke, a resident who had just returned from checking in on her ill grandmother, told firemen that her dog and cat were in danger. They found the dog, a stray she had taken in. Some pets did not survive.

A charred V branded the building, its point beginning at the second-story window and widening at the roof. Chief Schneider could read the building. To him, it looked like more than just an apartment fire. He ordered the men to evacuate. They scurried single file down the aerial ladder raised from the top floor on the McMechen Street side. The last man had just stepped onto the ladder when the whole building mushroomed into a huge inferno. If it wasn't for the chief's ability to read what was happening they probably would all have been killed.

The fire gained in fury and momentum. The gallant efforts of the firefighters were hampered by the intensity of the roaring flames. To my father, this was an especially terrible sight to behold; he had loved those apartments for their beautifully restored architecture. In less than two hours, the roof had caved in. The interior was completely burned out, except for the lower floors, which were flooded with water and filled with rubble. Rumpf's co-workers, those who had started work at 7:00 that morning, finished their shift at 3:00 p.m. and rushed to the scene. They congregated at a command post established by police hoping against hope that Rumpf had escaped and survived. At 4:25 p.m. some of the men thought they caught a glimpse of a cop's uniform in the wreckage and called in the Chaplain of the Fire Department, Reverend Joseph Martel. But they were mistaken.

The fire ruled supreme all afternoon and into the evening. My father's shift ended at 5:00 p.m. and, as he and his partner departed, they saw the crowds growing. Workers returning home from their offices stopped to watch the battle. The following morning Dad read in the papers what had transpired after he and his partner left.

The weary police officers eventually joined the seventy-two displaced residents being sheltered at nearby Brown Memorial Church. All the occupants had survived uninjured; another five were away at the time. Three policemen and seven firefighters were taken to medical facilities to be treated for smoke inhalation and minor injuries. The stubborn blaze was declared under control at 6:27 p.m.

After the sun had set, trucks carrying portable generators and floodlights arrived to illuminate the scene. A crane plowed down sections of the building, which was in danger of collapsing, and bulldozers shoveled away the debris. As the air grew colder, men scoured the whole building without success and could only conclude that Rumpf lay buried beneath tons of debris.

A firewall prevented the full force of the nine-alarm fire from consuming most of next-door Beethoven South, since only the roof of the adjoining building had been infiltrated. Snorkels (hydraulically elevated platforms) were raised, and men standing in the baskets extinguished the blaze in the roof one section at a time. Even with multiple streams of water pouring onto it, the roof fire took an hour to extinguish. Its flames engulfed the southeast corner of the building, and, just as it seemed to subside and firefighters prepared to work in other areas, the flames leapt out again, repeatedly challenging the men to a rematch. Debris cascading from the roof and increasing water levels in the basement made searching the building impossible until later that night.

All night the men labored, pumping water from the basement and clearing rubble in the smoldering remains, until at last they gained access to the elevator. There they found Rumpf's body. In his late thirties, a war veteran, he had only recently married and had a nine-month-old baby.

The front of the Beethoven, on Park Avenue, had been bulldozed to get to the elevator shaft to gain access to Rumpf. Except for this area, most of the exterior of the building's south end remained intact, but the north end was destroyed. The McMechen side still stood, but the interior had been totally gutted by the fire. Firefighters kept the inferno contained, but a strong wind could have spread this disastrous conflagration through Bolton Hill. Still, the fact that the walls of the old building remained standing instilled hope that this old representative of the past would live once more. But its interior was gutted so completely that the place would never be the same again.

"Two familiar faces gone," Dad murmured sadly.

The Thrill Is Gone

It was time for a change. At the beginning of the decade, in 1981, Mayor William Donald Schaefer donned a 1920s bathing suit, complete with a straw hat. Posing for photographers he tucked a large inflatable duck under his arm and leapt into the pool at the grand opening of Baltimore's National Aquarium located at the newly developed tourist site on Baltimore's waterfront. This picture hit the front page of many national publications. My father often said, "Schaefer was the right mayor for Baltimore at a time when we needed to enhance our image. He was enthusiastic. He sang the praises of his beloved city."

A year earlier, under Schaefer's leadership, the inner harbor complex, Harborplace, opened, transforming old coal piers and derelict buildings into a bustling tourist mecca of specialty shops, restaurants and promenades. Later the city opened the Maryland Science Center and the Pier Six Concert Pavilion in that area.

Unarguably, development of the Inner Harbor boosted Baltimore's economy and image; tourism quickly became the city's second-biggest source of revenue. However, poverty still swarmed around the glittering attraction.

Many firefighters felt that Schaefer worked against their department, offering meager raises and little support. Some men wore t-shirts emblazoned on the front with a cartoon firefighter penetrated by a big screw through his chest. When Schaefer stopped off at a deli on Eutaw Street, a firefighter from the Steadman House put a sticker on his car and the mayor drove off with the caption "Baltimore's Worst Mayor" on the rear bumper. Schaefer later went into the firehouse where the captain lined up the whole shift. No one confessed.

"He was probably Baltimore's best mayor, but he had some serious conflicts with the Local 734 Union," Dad told me. Giff, whose story Dad proceeded to tell me, was one of the men my father worked with in the early eighties. Intelligent and a good writer, Giff wrote frequent letters to the editor of the *Baltimore Sun*, many of which appeared in print. Sometimes when the medics received a call, Giff broadcast a recording of "Another One Bites the Dust" (a song by the band Queen) over the firehouse intercom, cueing the medics to respond. Dad would sing the tune to himself on his way out. But there were moments when neither music nor laughter could give my father respite from the job at hand.

For forty-eight hours, a large black man had been seen roaming the neighborhood naked as the day he was born. His wife had not been seen at work for that same amount of time. After he entered a small row house on Sinclair Lane on the East Side, neighbors notified the authorities.

Along with the police, medics received a call to attend to an injured person. My father and his partner had been nearby and were the first to arrive. Dad dashed from the parked ambulance to the house. Neighbors standing outside expressed concern about what had been happening. Although my father wondered why it took them two days to call, he realized that perhaps this kind of behavior on the man's part was not out of the ordinary.

The door was ajar. My father could see a huge unclothed man seated on the living room floor, leaning against the far wall next to a stairway in the middle of the house. He was sweating profusely and staring wild-eyed at nothing in particular.

"What seems to be the problem?" Dad asked, "Where are you hurt?" The man just sat there, breathing heavily, with sweat pouring off him. Something was not right. At this point, a muffled cry came from somewhere on the second floor. As Dad was deciding his next move, the cops arrived—a most welcome sight.

The police questioned the man for a few minutes but he didn't move or reply, just kept gazing into space. Not feeling threatened, one cop leaned his shotgun against the wall. Instantly the nude man lunged for the gun. Half a dozen cops, my father and his partner tackled him. The man didn't say a word as they shackled him and was still in a trance when they dragged him out.

A young black girl of sixteen appeared at the top of the stairway and stood peering at the cops and medics. She was hysterical, screaming, shoving her fists in the air. She appeared to be afraid to come down. The police escorted her out of the house.

My father decided to search for possible victims. As he went into the kitchen, he slipped on a clear substance covering the entire tile floor and momentarily lost his balance. He figured there was a plumbing problem, a water leak. A hacksaw was lying on the kitchen table, and an open wooden barrel stood in the corner, its lid lying on the floor. Dad peered in and saw hams and ham hocks.

"But wait, at second glance, the hams were gams!" Dad was unable to resist a pun, even when he was describing something this horrific: a woman had been dismembered. It took a few moments for my father to focus on the reality of the situation. Then he wondered what was on the soles of his shoes. The killer had probably tried to wash down the floor with cleaning solutions. A door in the kitchen led to the basement, and Dad stopped just as he was about to descend the stairs, realizing that the murderer could have had an accomplice.

Later investigation revealed that the naked man, acting alone, had shot his wife in the basement, then dragged her body up to the kitchen where he had carved her up with a hacksaw and shoved her assorted parts in a wooden barrel.

After that incident, my father's zest for his job had run its course. He was in his mid-forties, and the stress was taking a toll.

Dad reflected that, among the firemen, infidelity ran rampant, and divorces were common. "It's too difficult for some spouses, because nobody understands what our work entails."

When local units in another district were out on calls, it would sometimes take the medics fifteen minutes to travel to a scene. This time lapse got the medics a lot of bad press.

"Reporters wouldn't mention that people were abusing the service," Dad said.

He and his partner might be attending to someone with a stubbed toe, while elsewhere the victim of a massive heart attack could die waiting for them to arrive.

"That stuff plays with your mind too."

And then there was the risk of catching AIDS. One day the medics were called to a young pregnant woman who had been shot with a bow and arrow. She was hemorrhaging profusely. In their vain attempt to save the mother and unborn child, the team was splattered with blood. Afterwards, they were tested for the HIV virus. They waited anxiously for months: negative this time, but what about the next?

In the late eighties, when women were being hired for the first time as firefighters and, more frequently, as EMTs in Baltimore, they confronted the same challenges as their male counterparts yet endured additional pressures of discriminatory practices in the fire department. Many of them were experiencing sexual harassment, excessive scrutiny of their work performance, and lack of support from family and colleagues.

Fourteen-hour night shifts became exhausting, as the run count each shift steadily increased. Homicidal attacks occurred practically every night. One time, five people leaving a party on Linden Avenue were stabbed and lay sprawled on the street. Dad called for police assistance; meanwhile, he and his partner established IVs, for the victims were bleeding to death. No other units were nearby. There was no time to waste. Immediate transport was essential. Dad had to put two victims in the patrol car and drive the other three in the medic unit. As far as he knew, they all survived.

Not long after that incident, Bill and his partner—whom I'll call Viola—in the early evening of a hot summer night were called to a shooting on 20th Street off Greenmount Avenue. My father had no problem working with a female medic as long as she did her job. He'd worked previously with a female medic at Medic 6—a disheveled blond, who was perpetually sad. He said she was a skilled medic but no fun to work with.

Viola bathed in cheap perfume and wore "glow-in-the-dark red lipstick." Several detailed firefighters who had allergies could not work with her. My father said, "I have to admit she could deal better with imminent childbirths than any male medic and she kept her calm in difficult situations."

Within three minutes, they pulled up alongside the curb behind half a dozen other ambulances and Dad could see this was a difficult situation. Additional medic units had been requested by the initial attendees. About twenty injured people were stretched out on the ground all over the block. The medics attended to a young guy wearing a baseball cap cocked to one side. He did not know what had happened. Out of the blue he had been shot in the arm and leg. A craps game on the corner had turned nasty, and an angry player had cut loose with an automatic weapon, indiscriminately spraying the entire block. Paramedics set up triage—working on people in order of priority and urgency, depending on the severity of their wounds. They transported the victims to four or five different hospitals.

This shooting spree involved the greatest number of people injured in a single incident during my father's time in the ambulance service. "The amazing thing is that no one died," he said. However, soon after that, a dozen people were shot—most were killed—in a drive-by shooting outside a nightclub at the nearby intersection of North Avenue and Charles Street.

As the eighties continued, my father started to lose his patience. The comments that he had once tolerated—"That man can't walk," "If he was white you would work faster," "What took you so long"—began irritating him. Dad was always under pressure to hurry up and transport the patient. He could no longer endure people screaming and cursing at his partner and himself. Realizing that most residents knew he was there to help, he tried to ignore the gestures and remarks made by others and continue about his job. But they were wearing him down.

And then there were individuals like Charlie, the boy who suffered from seizures, the boy my father met when he first started on the medic unit. He was one of those people who—like my dad, in a way—started out with enthusiasm, courage and self-determination but eventually are overcome by the ghetto. One day word about Charlie finally came to my father. Firefighters from Engine 13 responded to a vacant-dwelling fire in their district and found a lifeless twenty-year-old black man on the first floor of an empty trash-strewn house. Charlie had become a street person. My father never got over the tragic ending to a life with so many possibilities. He vainly tried to make sense of this experience.

Having a good partner is a key factor in making the job bearable. Alcohol and drug abuse among medics were increasing, and, although the city performed random drug checks, offenders were merely enrolled in thirty-day drug treatment programs, which often resulted in no change in their behavior. Second or even third chances were given before the offenders were dismissed. My father wanted to work with clean and sober partners, but this was rapidly becoming next to impossible.

"There was this one medic who made stupid mistakes and was totally absentminded. He seemed upset when he approached me one night during change of shift.

" 'I can't believe what I did. I put the IV in the wrong way.'

" 'You what?' I couldn't believe it either.

" 'I put it in pointing toward the hand.' The IV catheter should have pointed toward the shoulder.

" 'That's unusual. How did you manage to do that?'

" 'I don't know what I was thinking. I feel terrible.' "

Not long after that incident, the man was fired for heroin use. He had spent twenty years in the department but lost his job and his pension. This strong disciplinary action, however, was unusual.

Another medic would doze off while Dad was speaking to him about an important line-of-work matter. The medic would murmur, "Uh huh, uh huh, uh huh." Then his head would slump, and his eyelids would drop. My father just thought the medic had a low energy level.

He was dismissed for using cocaine. Even Viola was eventually fired: for cocaine use.

Now measures and consequences are more stringent to prevent medics from working under the influence of narcotics, but back then the behavior of some of them was putting my father and patients in jeopardy.

More than a few firefighters had major alcohol problems. They would keep a bottle in the back of their car, or even in the unit, taking a swig during the shift. Two of my father's partners smoked pot in the medic unit. One guy was driving. Dad was in the back and could smell it. He thought of turning them in, but it would have been his word against theirs.

Dad thought he wanted to treat patients occasionally who were not victims of senseless shootings, stabbings and drug overdoses. At Medic 4, he made roughly twenty runs per twenty-four-hour day. He tried switching medic units and went to work on Medic 6 on Harford Road below Cold Spring Lane, where medics most often were called for cardiac cases and strokes. Medic 6 served older homeowners and low-to-middle-income working men and women who typically called only if the situation was a matter of life or death, whereas Medic 4 served the poorest of the poor who sometimes only needed a friend. But, although Medic 6 had fewer calls, once Dad got away from Medic 4, away from the ghetto, he missed it.

Dad was working on Medic 6 one Valentine's Day when a severe ice storm blanketed the area. Citywide, multiple accidents were occurring. In one instance, two cars collided head-on while negotiating the Hanover Street Bridge, and other cars plowed into them. One of the drivers was a woman taking her eight-year-old daughter to a Valentine's Day party. The bitter wind was blowing the snow and sleet horizontally, making extrication of the injured difficult. My father said, "I'll never forget her little white dress with tiny red hearts all over it spattered with blood." He and his partner transported them to the ER, where both survived.

Dad was certain he would wreck the ambulance in the icy conditions. "The sheer number of accidents was overwhelming and maneuvering the medic unit was next to impossible." Near the end of the night, after thirteen hours of work, he and his partner Dave were on their way to attend to victims of a car accident on Erdman Avenue and Sinclair Lane when their unit broke down. They had to sit there, helpless, freezing in the wicked subzero chill. There was no way to reach the accident scene up ahead. They were lucky to survive the night themselves.

Although he had learned over the years to shut many horrific sights out of his mind and go on with the business of public service, some incidents left an indelible and overwhelming impression. He told me about this incident as a case in point. At 4:00 a.m., he ascended the well-worn marble steps to the front door of a brick three-story row home on Argyle Avenue. He always feared the unknown but tried to remain focused on doing his job. All was quiet, except for the sound of the boards creaking beneath his feet as he navigated the darkened hallway. The door was cracked open at the end of the corridor and, as he entered, the light of a TV screen permeated the darkness of the sparsely furnished room.

"Ambo," he called out.

Two tattered easy chairs were occupied by a man and a woman. Both were seated, with legs crossed and hands folded in their laps. There was no response. Each had been blasted once in the head with a shotgun. Their positions indicated that at least their deaths had been instantaneous and without suffering. Both heads had been blown into pulp. Police surmised that a desperate drug user invaded the premises to search for cash or items that could be sold to support his addiction. The victims were well regarded on Argyle Avenue; the brutality of the crime was beyond comprehension.

My father readily admitted this experience shattered him, nearly sent him over the edge. He told this story without humor, without a hint of understanding or faith, without even a trace of objectivity. Whenever he recalled that evening, he sat very still, and all inflection drained from his voice. I do not remember where any of us were or what we possibly could have been doing when first he told it. I just remember being stunned, as if I had stumbled upon the abyss of depression that my father usually kept well hidden. I became acutely aware that my seemingly invincible father had a breaking point.

He once said, "The memory of that night is not unlike a great wave increasing in intensity, washing over my body and then subsiding. Thinking about it leaves me teary-eyed, mentally exhausted. It plagues me with a sense of helplessness."

My father was at Medic 6 for only a brief time before he realized that he wanted to quit being a paramedic altogether. His enthusiasm had plummeted to rock bottom.

"It's hopeless, the same stuff going on all the time. You wonder if you are making a dent. I'm not the type to blubber. Being detached is not a bad thing in this line of work. If I was going to do an effective job, I had no choice but to distance myself. That's how you can cope. I was determined not to cave in. I realized that, in order to provide people with the best possible service, I could not fall apart. It's ironic, but you can't get emotionally entangled when conducting a mission of mercy." But now he was becoming increasingly aware of his inability to deal with such tragedies.

It was mid-morning and my father felt like a runner after eighteen to twenty miles in a marathon. He described the feeling this way: "They hit the wall and the next five to six miles are tough. Beyond the wall looms the real challenge. They have to push; they stagger, crawl, struggle to make it. I began to hate what I was doing. I was rapidly becoming insensitive and disinterested, even worse, callous and indifferent. I didn't like it. I was losing my compassion. That's when I knew I'd hit the wall, and I wasn't going to get beyond it. I was finished. I knew if I didn't get out of the medic service I would resign from the fire department altogether."

The only way to save others was to rescue himself. He picked up the phone.

"I guess you've got your mind made up," John Johnson, Chief of the Medical Bureau, said after giving Dad a sales pitch, trying to convince him to stay.

"Grant me a reduction in rank and place me back in a fire company. I want to get off this meat wagon as soon as possible. Get me off quick, or I'm going to walk out the door." A week later Dad was readjusting to his career in an engine company.

He later told me, "I was in shock and didn't care where they put me. I threw my CRT [cardiac rescue technician] collar pins in a drawer. I was trying to get myself together mentally. But I don't think I ever did."

Roll With It

On a spring day in 1985, Dad dashed across the parking lots toward the front entrance of the Mondawmin branch of the Motor Vehicle Administration and stopped short. He couldn't believe his eyes. His old pal Larry Burch was standing on the sidewalk outside giving out Bible tracts. He handed one to Dad as he shook his hand and gave him a playful punch on the shoulder. Other than his salt-and-pepper hair, Larry looked about the same.

"What are you doing here? You're the biggest con man on the West Side." Dad smiled from ear to ear.

"I think I found what I was looking for."

Dad and Mom visited the church where Larry was an assistant to the bishop. It was a little storefront place on Reisterstown Road. They sat on metal chairs with about twenty other people and listened to the message given by the fiery preacher. Everybody was shouting, "Amen." Mom said that she never forgot the power of the sermon that night. There was a huge drum set and loudspeakers fit to blow your ears out. The parishioners sang a hymn, something about how Jesus put on his walking shoes and walked all over heaven. That hymn played over and over at pounding volume to fill them with the Holy Spirit and sustain them through the week.

"Does anyone want to pray?" One woman knelt down on the floor. Although she may have had next to nothing in the way of material goods, she cried, "Thank you for the utensils in my home. I've got a knife and fork. Thank you for the metal chairs in the church, thank you for protecting me on my way here tonight, thank you for the coat on my back . . ."

Before Dad and Mom left, my father walked toward the back of the church to say goodbye to Larry. A door was partly open. "He and the preacher were huddled in a little room counting up receipts. It's a mystery. He seemed like he changed—handing out gospel tracts and talking with people. I'd like to believe that he changed—not losing his spirit, but quitting his incessant con games—but who knows?"

Dad was a ghetto medic. He never stopped thinking of himself that way. When he left the ambulance and returned to firefighting, the transition was difficult. By that time, the late eighties, my brother and I were teenagers and spending more time with our friends. And probably, like typical teenagers, we were not attentive to changes going on in our parents' lives. Although he said he was numb when he took that reduction in rank, I noticed only subtle changes in my father. For example, he started wearing eyeglasses—after all, he had reached the age of fifty—but he still parted his hair on the right. And he still hunted down immediate and distant relatives to share his war stories. And he still made us laugh until we cried.

I remember him pulling into the driveway after work. Even from the kitchen I could smell the smoke on his uniform, which he hung on the back porch before stepping inside.

"Had a good day, huh?" I asked him in jest. From the spot of pink blemishing his forehead, I knew he had had a rough afternoon. I looked for that blemish the way someone might look for the capital "S" on Superman's chest. Though doctors might view the rash as evidence of stress, I always saw it as an emblem of strength and victory.

"I'm getting too old for this," was the reply. But then he smiled. "It's still a challenge."

Kneading the muscle on his left shoulder, he continued, "We had a big fire today. The family survived, and we were able to protect most of the house. Had an attempted suicide. An elderly man slit his wrists. He'll be all right though."

My father gazed away and furrowed his brow. "A disc jockey accidentally shot himself with a handgun. A young guy. It's a shame. He wanted to live, but he died. The other man wanted to die, but he lived." I remember times when he was too upset to speak at all. But he still said "I love you" to his family every day. We would still go to the movies or watch a classic on television. Whenever *Blazing Saddles*, *Young Frankenstein*, or *The Producers* was on TV he'd call me. I'd come running. "You gotta see this." Mel Brooks could always make him release a good old hearty laugh, ending with a loud exhale and an, "Oh, man, that was funny."

As I grew older I listened to my father's stories more closely and interrupted him less.

After Medic 6, he ended up at Engine 3. "But looking back on it later, I would have preferred a different engine company." E-3 on Pulaski Highway was in a drab area near run-down commercial properties: paint shops, hazardous material dumps, manufacturing plants, a matchbox company, chemical storage facilities, prefabricated housing. There were white "redneck hillbillies" (I quote Dad on that) housed at one end of the district and impoverished blacks at the other. Looming in the distance were neighborhoods including Hollander Ridge, a predominantly black government high-rise apartment development ("riddled with trouble") and Armistead Gardens, inhabited mostly by whites who had moved up from Appalachia.

This development, cheap dwellings built for factory workers during the World War II, was supposed to be temporary housing, but it was still in use forty years later. Both sections had their share of crime and fire calls. Prostitutes loitered in the street and drug addicts walked along the highway. The area was so drab it made sunny days look cloudy and gray. E-3 adjoined the fire academy and serviced the school when needed.

My father put in for a transfer from Engine 3 in the late eighties. He told me, "E-56 was in a residential district closer to home. With Steve Barnaba, Al Cook and Captain Carlisle, it was a good group. I was glad to be out of E-3 even though, as the new guy at E-56, I was at the bottom of the roster and still got detailed to work on medic units all over the city."

Later, when another mayor led a campaign to improve the city's illiteracy rate, bus stop benches throughout town were painted with the slogan "The City that Reads." The words were altered in no time by graffiti artists to "The City that Bleeds," or "The City that Breeds," depending on the Baltimoreans' concerns with the homicide rate or the number of unwanted children in the city.

"All of the guys at E-56 were friendly, seasoned, had worked in the ghetto at some point. Most of them had transferred to other houses after many years in the fire service. We called it 'The Last Outpost' because it was on the fringe of the city just before the county line and we wore patches on our jacket bearing the nickname. My own name for it was 'The Last Resort' because most of us were aging and ready to get out.

"The atmosphere was relaxed. Regis Smith, our lieutenant, deserved all the credit for transforming E-56 into a museum with memorabilia, helmets, tools, pictures and other artifacts. He spent months gathering items from all over the city and country.

"One co-worker, Jerry Rigby, would sit in an unused area on the second floor of the firehouse and play smooth jazz selections on his saxophone. He was a private person and did not want to disturb anyone. An experienced firefighter, Jerry had worked as a paramedic for a brief time before he too took a reduction in rank and went to E-56. He always considered getting off the medic unit as the best decision he ever made. He had liked the idea that medics could stop on the street for lunch or breakfast. That's how he got sucked into that job.

"Before becoming a firefighter, Steve Barnaba was rumored to have been the best bartender ever at Gianerini's, an Italian restaurant and bar on Harford Road. With his energy and laughter he was a natural at that job. He was a hard worker. He painted houses on the side so he could give his three daughters a top-notch private education. Steve reflected on his bartending days and, because he is Italian, I'd say things like 'Steve, why don't you open your own restaurant and call it the Wop Stop?'

"'Sure and then you can open the Kraut House next door.'

"The district we served consisted of white middle-class homeowners. Most of the residents actually expressed appreciation for our work. On the other hand, I missed the continuous action in the ghetto."

My father did not know that for him the action had not yet ceased.

Ring of Fire

Baltimore, Wednesday, February 5, 1992. The day had been dim for hours. Furnaces were pumping out warmth for the evening, and smokestacks exhaled apathetic clouds into the black face of the winter sky. Most small children were fast asleep, but the night was not still. In Govans, on Baltimore's northern side, a fury of flames kicked and roared, consuming the interior of a two-story storefront that held three-story apartments in the rear. In minutes, the sirens wailed. Battalion Four, comprising half a dozen firehouses, more or less, pulled onto Winston Avenue where they saw smoke billowing from the wooden frame structure. Chief Ray Lehr knew from the pulsing of the black smoke that the fire was spreading, but the dense clouds concealed the flames, so he couldn't determine where it was concentrated. He would have to send his men in to investigate.

Sizing up the scene, Chief Lehr spoke into his hand radio: "They're taking a one-and-a-half-inch line into the front. The building is being ventilated. Have the air cascade unit respond to this location."

"Okay, Battalion Chief Four, message received. We're dispatching the air cascade unit. The air cascade unit is en route to your location, ten minutes ETA."

"Grab the plug," the Captain commanded.

The leadoff man attached the main line to the fireplug and signaled to the pump operator that it was ready to go. When the pump operator rotated his arm signaling his men to charge the line, the leadoff man activated the hydrants and then raced to help the other men. The pump operator adjusted the water pressure, flooding the one-and-a-half-inch hoses. The engine moved to the front of the building, trailing the main line in the street.

The fire broke through the roof. On Chief Lehr's orders, two men dashed into the burning building with handheld lines. Tightly gripping the nozzles, they advanced up the wobbly stairway to move on the fire. The lieutenant sprinted into the building to assist the other men. Inside, flames accelerated through the partitions and sprawled over the second floor. The men were battling an obstinate demon.

Weighed down by air packs on their backs, they crawled across the floor under the smoke layer to avoid the lashing flames and reduce exposure to the merciless heat. Straining to find their way in the darkness, the men dodged planks falling in a soot shower, struggling to find the heart of the blaze. First the biting winter night, then the heat of the fire, then the hard-fought battle drained their energy. Chief Lehr needed more firefighters if the savage inferno was to be conquered.

Meanwhile, three miles away, the fire crew of Engine 56 had already responded to three calls. They were dog-tired. Two men had already headed to their bunks, but Steve and Dad stayed in the kitchen joking over the 1965 Department yearbook. They were laughing at a black-and-white picture of Dad in his rookie year. Steve said something like, "You could've hosted for American Bandstand."

"You're right. I do bear a striking resemblance to Dick Clark, now that you mention it."

Steve looked at the photo again. "Bill, you haven't changed a bit. How old are you anyway, fifty-one, fifty-two?"

"Fifty-one. It's a miracle that I'm still alive." As my dad spoke, Steve had a fleeting vision of my father's death. The glimpse slipped away so fast that, as soon as he tried to make out the details, he realized that his mind had formed an image not from the past but from the future.

They continued bantering until Communications alerted them: "Battalion Chief Eight on the scene. We have a three-story building fully involved. Heavy smoke. Grab the fire plug on the corner of Winston and Govans and bring water." The voice on the radio was panicked, hoarse and fatigued. "Engine 56 respond second alarm Winston Avenue and York Road."

Dad sounded the gong to alert the other men. They jumped into their boots, pulled up their turnout pants and slipped their arms through the suspenders. They clipped their yellow coats. The engine was moving in seconds.

Seven miles away, on South Eutaw Street next to the "Bromo Seltzer

Tower" (an early nineteenth-century replica of a famous Italian tower, but sporting an enormous, lit-up, true-to-life replica of the bright blue bottle in which a popular stomach remedy was sold), sits the "Superhouse," the John F. Steadman Fire Station named after a "fireman's fireman" for his loyalty. Second Deputy Chief Steadman died of a heart attack in 1940 shortly after fighting a blaze at the Baltimore Lumber Company.

Captain Joe Brocato, an officer of Rescue 1, was reclining on his bunk watching television before trying to get a little shut-eye, when, during the evening news, he heard incessant chatter from the six-channel radio. A fire in the Govans area was burgeoning out of control. Captain Brocato jumped up, and, as he was turning up the radio volume, the other firefighters entered. All five men of Rescue 1 stood waiting, prepared to take action if required.

Then a voice cut through the radio chatter: "This is Chief Lehr. The fire is gaining strength. We need a second alarm."

The crew tore through the office door and slid down the thirty-foot brass poles to the first floor. As the engine roared, they suited up in the back of the squad unit. Captain Brocato pushed the button marked "en route" to notify Communications and sounded the air horn to clear the intersection. Sirens screaming, the apparatus sped through the open bay doors into the chilling night.

The rescue squad was on its way from the other side of town as Chief Lehr called his men out of the burning building. Using three hose lines, the men shot huge streams of water from the ground outside of the building but still couldn't hit the third-floor heart of the fire. The cascading water ricocheted from the walls and failed to extinguish the flames, so they would have to go inside.

The second alarm units arrived: four engine and two truck companies, a Battalion Chief, and a Deputy Chief of Operations. When Engine 56 pulled up on York Road north of the fire ground, the building appeared to be smoldering. The Lieutenant sat in front with the driver while Steve and Bill were in the rear of the cab. Dad sized up the situation. The smoke was dissipating. He was sure that the black smoke would soon turn white, indicating that the fire was under control. The air began to clear. Steve and Dad kidded around.

"They called us in for this?"

"Yeah, seems to be contained," Dad replied. "If we'd had it on the first alarm we would have finished it off." He slipped his arms through the shoulder straps attached to his mask and buckled his waist belt. When he leaned forward to step out of the engine, the air cylinder popped out of the metal bracket in the cab and was secured on his back.

"Come on, Hennick," Steve said, "The sooner we knock it out, the sooner we can get the hell outta here."

At the time, they had no way of knowing the fire was regaining strength. The flames gnawed an opening in the roof, accessed oxygen, and flared up again to begin ravaging the second floor.

Dad stepped off the pumper. The cold air seeped into his skin and hovered between flesh and bones. He blew hot breath into his palms and rubbed them together, thawing them for a moment, then pulled a pair of fire retardant gloves from his pocket and slipped them on.

Lieutenant Chuck Johnson instructed Dad and Steve to cover the rear of the building. They were met by Chief Bob Williams who told them to enter the stairwell and advance the line into the upper floors. Obeying his orders, Dad and his crew stretched a one-and-a-half-inch hose line to the rear exit. Johnson left the scene to get an air pack (self-contained breathing apparatus) while Steve, Dad and two men from Old Town Station advanced the line up the deteriorating stairway to the second floor. Visibility was zero. It was a slow struggle as they fought their way through the dense smoke and heat, plowing down the corridor twenty feet.

Inside, they continued forging blindly ahead, trying to make progress in the blackness. In such circumstances, more dangerous than flames is the absence of fire. The enemy cloaks itself in darkness, lurking within the walls and beneath floorboards. Sly and ruthless, the villain might suddenly sneak up by leaping across the ceiling, then vanish and reappear behind.

The two men nearest the nozzle led the way, with Steve and Dad protecting the rear. Knowing that a direct stream can cause a flare-up, one of them opened the nozzle wide, spraying a pattern of gentle mist in the direction of the heat. The searing heat battled them all the way as they progressed down the hall, tar and debris falling onto their helmets. Smoke tumbled over them like a hot rolling fog.

If the hidden fire did emerge, they would need to be prepared for combat. They knew that hitting a fire in a confined area could instantly create steam which would attack them, scalding them, cooking them like lobsters. If they stayed close to the floor, the steam would escape over their heads. They stayed low.

Dad felt a tap on his shoulder and heard Steve's muffled voice behind him. He strained to hear him speaking through his mask, but found it difficult, with the crackling of the fire, the building remnants crashing and men shouting in the distance. He turned around but, in the blackness, any attempt to see a facial expression or a hand gesture was futile.

"We've been ordered to evacuate." Dad heard Steve's faint voice. "The building's going to collapse."

Instinctively, Dad reached forward in the black heat, feeling for the firefighter just in front of him to relay the message. Under his feet, he felt a startling jolt from the floor, which then began to sink. It was as if he were standing in quicksand. He was initially puzzled. Then there was a resounding crash. The second floor collapsed, along with the third floor and the roof. As my father dropped downward, the contents of the room, sofas, chairs, lamps, tables, floorboards and china fell with and onto him.

He fell halfway through the first floor and came to an abrupt stop when the air pack on his back prevented him from dropping all the way through the hole. Dad dangled in midair between the first floor and the basement in an upright position as though the spot had been made for him. He was pinned at the waist between a sofa bed, flooring and mounds of debris. The roof, third floor and second floor had crashed onto the first. Would there be a secondary collapse? He pictured more debris falling from above, covering him over. He saw himself left to burn to death. He imagined that the two firefighters just ahead of him were buried under the rubble. There is no way they could have escaped the collapse.

Wedged, Dad found it difficult to move. Stiff and aching all over, he somehow managed to reach his right arm over and trigger the alarm attached to his belt stuck above the floorboard. As the alarm sounded, Dad's thoughts alternated between panic for his own seemingly hopeless situation and fear for the other men.

Other than distant voices outside, he did not hear any of the others. Steve must have escaped in time, but Dad could not be sure. He was sure of two things: one, there would be a secondary collapse, and two, both of the men who were in front of him must have been crushed to death.

Listening to the movement of debris in the crackling of the fire, Dad clenched his teeth in fury, frustrated because he was powerless. He wanted to break free, but the slightest motion could have sent his body crashing to the basement floor. He was convinced the standing remains of the three floors and roof were going to come down, taking him to an inevitable death.

At first he was angry, because he could not do anything to escape. Then, trying to make the best of the situation, Dad began looking forward to his funeral.

Dad told me later that, while he hung there trapped, he figured he was a shoo-in for this year's Fallen Firefighter's Memorial Service held at Dulaney Valley Memorial Gardens. "I'll have my casket carried on top of a pumper followed by a big procession of firefighters from all over the world throwing hand salutes, while bagpipes play 'Amazing Grace' and tears stream down the faces of my beloved wife and children. As long as Eunice doesn't remarry, she'll get the full tax-free pension and grants from the federal and state government for emergency workers killed in the line of duty. I can hear the men talking about me after the funeral over drinks.

" 'You know I never heard him curse and he didn't drink.'

" 'Yeah, he was a strange fellow.'

" 'I'll drink to that; I'll drink to anything.'

"And I'll get buried for no cost; it's all on the house, but if I live through it, I won't get anything. The more I think about it, if I miraculously survive and they try to carry me out of here I'll beg 'em to carry me back in and collapse the rest of the building." The heat enveloped my father's body and he began to suffocate as his air pack was depleted. He tilted his head back and peered through his face piece. There was a circular opening in the roof, a hoop of fire that framed the sky. The smoke began to clear. Dad removed his face piece. Stars twinkled in the midnight-blue canvas.

To comfort himself, Dad began softly to sing that old tune by Johnny Cash. "I fell for you like a little child, oh and the flames got wild. I fell into that burnin' ring of fire I went down, down, down, and the flames they got higher and it burns, burns, burns, that ring of fire, that ring of fire. I'm burnin' in a ring of fire and the flames get higher and the flames get higher . . ."

At about 6:00 a.m., news stations throughout Maryland broadcast the story that firefighter Bill Hennick had been trapped. My mother, Eunice, was in the kitchen of our Towson home. She was quietly going about the business of starting the day for her family. She plugged in the coffee pot for Craig who would soon awake for work. She heard on WRBS Radio, a Christian station, that a terrible fire had occurred in the Govans area. Just at that moment she received a phone call from a childhood friend who was crying hysterically. "I'm so sorry about your husband."

"My husband's not dead. I know he's not. The Lord would have told me," my mother said.

During the course of their almost thirty-year marriage, my mother had become a fervent intercessor, praying ceaselessly for her husband and the strength to raise their two children. After thanking the woman for her concern, she gently hung up the phone, confident that my father was still alive. She puttered around in the kitchen and entered deep meditation with God.

Bill should have been home at 8:00 a.m. Four hours later, Pastor Blight, my father's minister, called to express his condolences. My mother and the pastor prayed together before she politely thanked him and hung up the phone.

My mother waited for a call from my father to say that he was all right.

Before the collapse that had trapped my father, when Rescue 1 arrived, Captain Brocato met with Chief Lehr to strategize their attack. The Chief told the Captain that the structure was weak from the weight of the water the fighters had been bailing in. Because he did not want to put the men at risk by sending them inside, he ordered Brocato to ventilate the building at the roof level and to see from there if the fire was spreading.

Captain Brocato and his crew raised Truck 25's one-hundred-foot aerial ladder. Two men at the turntable were prepared to rotate the ladder while two more ascended. They knocked out the windows and cut holes in the roof with axes, Halligan tools (bars used for forcible entry) and power saws. Lines were ready to extinguish the fire that was expected to explode when the building was vented.

Outside, Chief Lehr realized it was hopeless. He ordered everyone to evacuate. The building was deteriorating and would soon collapse.

As Steve received the order, he started to warn Bill about the evacuation and the collapse. Then he heard a boom ahead of him and felt the hose line bend directly downward. However, he could not see what had happened due to the thick smoke.

"Bill! Bill!" he called several times but received no answer. He remembered his premonition, not even an hour before, of my father's death. Steve reached out to feel for somebody, anybody; then the horror of what had happened struck him. There was no more floor. Following the hose line, Steve quickly traced his way to the exit. He tore outside to inform Chief Williams and found the firefighters already scrambling to assist.

Chief Lehr and the Deputy Chief of Operations quickly changed their strategy from attacking the fire to rescuing the men trapped inside of the collapsed building. They requested a third alarm.

On the first floor several firefighters climbed through a window. As Hartsock, Brocato and Williams ascended the aerial ladder, the Rescue 1 team heard the flooring crash inside. Brocato peered into a filmy window and prepared himself for the worst, when, in the smoke and embers, he made out the yellow sleeve of a turnout coat extending from the rubble. It covered an unmoving arm.

"Go back down!" Captain Brocato ordered his men. "Grab the airbags, cribbing and lights."

Taking a closer look, he saw that my father was dangling, pinned at the waist by the debris. Another man stood trapped in the basement, up to his neck in water. Several firefighters lifted that man up out of the water and assisted him out of the first-floor window and down the ladder to waiting medics.

Meanwhile, on Brocato's orders, Kisser and Townsend remained prepared at the window with the airbag system, which consisted of sturdy, neoprene bags that are slipped into tight spaces and inflated like pillows, along with wooden supports in various sizes to prevent weak areas from caving in. In the event of a secondary collapse, Townsend and Kisser would act as the back-up team to lead the others out.

Men from several companies, including Brocato, Hartsock and Williams of Rescue 1, crawled inch by inch over the rubble in the soot and smoke, gently pressing each step to test the stability of the surface. They worked up a sweat, pausing at each shudder and creak of the rapidly disintegrating building, until at last they reached Bill, who was now semi-conscious. He had fallen two stories and was buried in debris from his waist to his neck while his legs hung free in midair.

The men delicately removed the rubble, one piece at a time, pausing after each step; any hasty move could have resulted in Bill falling into the basement. The fire stormed above them.

"Get me the large airbag!" Brocato called. Williams reached through the window, grabbed the bag from Kisser and Townsend, and handed it to Hartsock, who passed it in turn to Captain Brocato. The latter inserted the deflated airbag in a crack between the two timber floorboards wedging my father.

"Hand me the dead man," Hartsock called, referring to the controller used to inflate the airbags. Hearing Hartsock, some spectators outside cried, "Who's dead?"

"No one, I was referring to the regulator." He quickly inflated the bag.

The pillow expanded, breaking the hold of the planks, while, in the same moment, Brocato and another firefighter lifted my father from the hole. They were exhausted and the combined weight of his body, his soaked attire and his equipment required enormous effort by the men struggling to pull him onto stable ground. As they lifted him, fiery debris went crashing down into the water below, producing steam when it landed in the basement pool. The exhausted Rescue Team mustered up enough strength to carry my father, secure him onto a stretcher and guide him to the waiting paramedics at the back of the building.

Reports later stated that a child playing with matches had caused the fire.

When Dad walked into our home and saw my mother, their eyes locked. He could see that she was livid by the way she stared at him, as if she was both relieved to see him alive but also prepared to kill him. My father was totally unaware that this incident led off the news and had spread across the State of Maryland. My mother was quiet for a long while and then said, "Why didn't you call?"

"I didn't feel it was necessary, because I didn't think it was a big deal. I've been in worse situations," he said.

Blushing, he told her that, as the medics wheeled him toward the ambulance Barnaba rushed over, leaned down and kissed him on the cheek. "Though I was flattered, I found that more upsetting than being trapped in the rubble."

At Mercy Hospital, he recounted, he had been examined and treated for bumps, bruises, and a couple of scratches on his back and shoulders. When he returned to Engine 56 at 4:30 a.m. to complete his shift, my father said that Battalion Chief Wayne Burgess could not believe it.

"I could have milked several days off, or even weeks."

Dad told me later, "I was grateful to the Lord for sparing me. But even though it was a precarious situation, all of the debris falling on me, I didn't think much of that incident. It's just part of the job. Many of us have experienced close calls. I didn't call your mother because I didn't want to wake her up. And I just wanted a few hours of sleep myself."

He added in retrospect, "Even though this was part of our job, I felt terrible that the men endangered their lives to rescue me." He maintained steadfastly that this incident was "no big deal" and often expressed his relief that no one had died trying to rescue him.

He'd always add: "Fire didn't win."

The Song is Ended (But the Melody Lingers On)

"Welcome to Baltimore—HON."

Nearly every morning in the 1990s, the anonymous "Hon Man" would hang the letters H-O-N on a wooden sign posted next to the standard, city-issued welcome sign on the Baltimore-Washington Parkway. The authorities kept ripping the homemade sign down, and this phantom put it right back up again. These days, sign sightings are rare. While the greeting is a bit deceptive—there are not many apple pies cooling on the windowsills of the row homes, and residents check their deadbolts twice—the words are not just a veneer of hospitality.

"Thanks, Hon." The term of endearment is expressed by waitresses, mechanics and bartenders alike. The feeling is genuine, deep from the heart of Baltimore's working-class immigrant past and reflective of its village-like atmosphere.

It's a cool and breezy Sunday afternoon in August, which is, in itself, unusual for Baltimore's dog days. Dad sits behind the wheel of his green Mazda; I'm in the passenger seat. We whiz past the welcome sign. Today, there is no "Hon." My father is taking me on yet another tour of his Charm City. I'm in my early thirties, but I still cherish these father-daughter days. Sometimes, Mom will join us, but more often than not, she'll stay behind to prepare dinner. My brother Craig is at his children's soccer game. He's the spitting image of my father, semi-smirk and all, with the same sense of loyalty and faithfulness, but he doesn't share our fascination with the ghetto, or, rather, the various ghettoes within this city of neighborhoods with names. He lives out in the country and won't enter the city unless he must.

My father still has a full head of hair, still neatly combed, still parted on the right side. He has serious leg problems, possibly dating back to the fire that changed his life, but, stoic as ever, he refuses to use a cane and instead slowly pushes one leg in front of the other with the broken stride of a wounded soldier. He retired from his career as a firefighter at about the time the "Hon Man" emerged.

In the late part of 1993, as he headed toward the pumper for a run, a co-worker said "You look like you're limping a bit."

"I didn't even know I was," Dad told me.

It kept getting worse. The doctor thought B12 injections might help. They didn't. A neurologist found a protein in a spinal tap and thought the limp could be a symptom of multiple sclerosis. The trouble started out in my father's right leg. The right foot would catch behind the left leg, making him trip and fall. Soon both legs became weak. He underwent numerous tests: MRIs, injections, CT scans, brain scans and X-rays, with varying opinions from physicians. Whatever the cause, the condition persisted.

Three months after the limp became noticeable, my father was again temporarily detailed on a medic unit. Together with his partner, Laura Shiloh, now EMS Battalion Chief, my father attended to a stroke victim in Hamilton, a neighborhood just off Harford Road. When they tried to lift the patient on the litter, Dad struggled. Try as he might, he no longer had the strength. He felt humiliated. Hoping the weakness was momentary, he tried again after a short pause, but to no avail. "I looked into my partner's questioning eyes and sensed the inevitable. It was over."

He was offered a desk job at headquarters, but he didn't want to shuffle papers. After nearly thirty years of service to the city, he opted for a regular pension, rather than disability pension.

"You don't want to go down there, do you?" Dad taunts, and, before I can answer, the parkway becomes Russell Street. The Mazda is ambling over potholes, past gas stations and old motels. Dad says, "Ah, nothing like a Grand Entrance."

Dad likes to vary the tour. Sometimes we begin on the north side, in Hampden. Baltimoreans are proud of their working-class heritage. I am. After all, where else will you find a Hubcap Christmas Tree? In Hampden on West 34th Street, during the holiday season, every house on the block is covered in lights; the neighbors work for months ahead of time to create the most elaborate, most unique and brightest décor. One pair of neighbors who live across the street from each other actually string a brilliantly lit toy train track between the houses, high above the cars and tour buses in which, each year, people from all over the U.S. travel to behold Baltimore's "Miracle on 34th Street."

Today, we're approaching the city from the south. As Dad and I continue our drive, we hear the faint cheers of fans at the Orioles' baseball game being played a few blocks away at Oriole Park. The air has a pungent scent of fish that wafts in through my open window. In moments, my father stops at a red light on Pratt Street, and in the distance we can see tourists paddle-boating on the waters of the city's harbor.

"The Inner Harbor draws tourists like a magnet. Bodies float in the water once in a while, but that's part of the ambience. They usually surface every spring, come up like flowers." He feigns hatred for the city, but deep down he's never left it.

He collects newspaper clippings and reminds me daily of the city's dangers. From time to time, statistics dub it the The Murder Capital of the World, he points out. Baltimore consistently rivals Detroit as the deadliest city in the United States—in a population of approximately 642,000, nearly 300 murders occur each year. The homicide rate has remained virtually unchanged for well over a decade. Thanks to their HBO-generated fame, Baltimore's crime statistics are no secret. And while the local daily paper, the *Baltimore Sun*, tallies violent deaths, the fatal stabbings and shootings, it seldom cites the nonfatal injuries.

We drive past people dining al fresco at seafood restaurants. Seated at tables covered in brown paper, they're hammering away at hard-shell crabs and sipping cold pale ales.

"The crabs feast on the bodies and the people eat the crabs. It's all part of the food chain." Dad smiles when I grimace.

Maybe it is no coincidence then that Maryland's State Crustacean is the blue crab, an opportunistic predator that feeds on the dead and decaying, though its grace and surprisingly romantic "love life" have been chronicled in William Warner's now-classic book, *Beautiful Swimmers*. Baltimoreans have created some of the most delectable dishes from this scavenger: crab soup, crab dip, crab potato chips, crab cakes, soft-shell crabs, crab marinara sauce, shrimp stuffed with crab, crab-stuffed mushrooms, California crab wraps, crabmeat quesadillas, crab omelets, crab imperial, crab salad and crab panini. Sushi made with "real crab" (not crab sticks, a horrid imitation) is known as a Baltimore Roll.

Young women walk along the promenade trying to lock eyes with European sailors as they disembark from visiting naval ships. Packs of children carry balloons and lap ice cream while watching a busker on stilts. The light changes. My father steps on the accelerator.

About a thousand people have fled the city each month since 1991. Occasionally, however, after a long sojourn elsewhere, some people are mysteriously lured back. As if under a spell, they reach for words but often cannot explain why they chose to return. In the Gram Parsons song, "Streets of Baltimore," the singer loses his lover to Baltimore as if she has been swallowed up by a cult. Baltimore, for some people, is infectious:

Well I did my best to bring her back to what she used to be
Then I soon learned she loved those bright lights more than she loved me
Now I'm a going back on that same train that brought me here before
While my baby walks the streets of Baltimore

My father wrote a song about our hometown too. He is now pounding the steering wheel with the palms of his hands and rocking back and forth as we ease along Pratt Street. He becomes a human beat box whenever he bellows "The Cracker Rapper." Dad is convinced that it will someday become a classic hit in a Broadway musical.

Cruisin' through the hood in the middle of the night,
Fearin' repercussions 'cause my clammy skin was white.
In the distance I'd hear the unmistakable sounds,
Of a gun firin' off semi-automatic rounds.
The dude with the piece done took it on the lam,
And the crowd at the scene, 'don't know nothin' man.'
The victim on the ground was wounded in the chest,
A young, black dude maybe twenty-five at best.

Everything was done to keep the man alive,

But this was not enough as he took a breath and died.

So keep in mind this story as you step into the night,

Reconsider your decision and wait until it's light.

I roll my eyes and he catches me. "What's the matter? Don't you like it?"

Illusionless as he was or became, my father never completely lost his sense of humor. While he might have momentarily misplaced it now and again it always returned with a wry vengeance. He repeats the song line by line, just in case I missed something, as we head east.

I love joking about Baltimore with my father, but I resent it when the uninitiated poke fun at our hometown and its socioeconomic challenges. "Smalltimore," as locals call it, indicates Baltimore's pride in everybody-knowing-everybody-else combined with its inferiority complex when this very old U.S. city is compared to New York, Boston or Washington, DC. The dual attitude shows in the fact that Baltimore is often called upon to play the part of Manhattan or Washington of the 1800s in movies. The nationally lauded TV dramas "Homicide" and "The Wire" feature the city's seamiest side. Although the meteorologists on the national news provide the forecast for Washington, Philadelphia and New York, they skip Baltimore—or if they do mention it, they often stammer as if it were a mistake.

I'll be the first to say that Baltimore is the "big city" of Maryland, America's east coast state positioned most literally in the mid-Atlantic region. Maryland is an enchanting little chunk of multiple topographies: ocean beaches, rolling hills, fertile valleys, lush forests. Divided by the Chesapeake Bay, beaches, marinas and quaint boating towns dapple the bay's shorelines, offering residents solace from work after only a short drive. Mountainous ski slopes and deeply rural mountain areas lie in the westernmost part of the state.

When speaking to "foreigners," I'll tout the convenience of the city. From Baltimore, a two-hour train ride delivers people to be razzle-dazzled in New York. In a little over an hour by car they can retreat to the Blue Ridge

Mountains of Virginia, visit the Smithsonian Institution in Washington, DC, or shop at the Amish markets of Pennsylvania.

Dad often likes to begin his tour at the Johns Hopkins Hospital, saving the city's West Side for dessert. The world's leading medical facility hasn't developed a cure for the city's ills. Hopkins continues to expand, dominating much of the city's East Side. It is Maryland's largest employer, but residents do not appear to be getting healthier. As "The Heroin Capital" of the USA, Baltimore has the highest rate of heroin use in the United States, with 10 percent of its population addicted—over sixty thousand people. The city's drug epidemic has a domino effect—burglaries, assaults, rape, prostitution, sexually transmitted diseases, crowded prisons, murder—creating an atmosphere of hopelessness, despair and fear.

We roll through Greektown where locals dash out of storefronts with bags of cheeses and pastries. We wind around the Belgian block cobbled streets of Fell's Point filled with popular restaurants, bars and shops now, many of them in buildings that are unchanged structurally from when they were erected in the early 1700s. We pass the Cat's Eye Pub on Thames Street, where, more than a hundred years ago, tugboat captains sat at the mullioned windows watching for vessels coming into the harbor. Legend has it that many a knifing occurred as the tug operators raced to get to the vessel first—murder has been part of the city's story for centuries, it seems.

Dad's bottle of iced tea shakes in the cup holder beneath the dashboard.

"Why do they have these blasted cobblestone streets? These roads go back to the day of horse and buggies. Now I gotta go two miles an hour or the front end of the car will be trashed."

Baltimore was once an economically booming city and since its inception nearly three hundred years earlier, it had been able to reshape itself to meet the world's changing demands. It emerged as a commercial port in 1729, demonstrating courage and innovation in the shipping industry. For example, Baltimore Clippers, two-masted schooners, were designed and built at Fells Point. These vessels were ahead of their time, with limited cargo space and plenty of sail, giving the privateers the speed to break the English blockade during the War of 1812, a major contribution to the ultimate victory. With the ambience of a slightly down-at-the-heels gentlemen's club, Baltimore is still tinged with the scent of old money made by railroad barons, brewmeisters and business tycoons from the sweat and back-breaking toil of their laborers. Many men, including black free men and slaves, took jobs as ship caulkers. Abolitionist and orator Frederick Douglass labored as such until he escaped to freedom in the north.

As we slow, a thin black man wearing a shower cap flags us and points at an open parking space. If we park, he will hit us up for spare change. Dad waves to indicate we're not stopping.

It is hard to imagine shackled slaves being bought and sold here in the Broadway Market square where there is now a snowball stand, park benches and pigeons. Dad and I are conversing just inches away from where parts of the film *Sleepless in Seattle* were filmed.

Through its military, industrial and maritime contributions—along with its strategic location allowing access to the south and west via its harbor and railroad—Baltimore became the third-largest city in the United States. Necessity impelled Baltimore's focus toward textile production and canneries for packaging fishery products from its then healthy Chesapeake Bay.

With job opportunities abundant, Baltimore became the gateway to America for tens of thousands of people seeking a new life. Tides of Europeans flowed in to work in the canneries, on the docks or in the steel mills. Baltimore was a leading port of immigration, second only to Ellis Island in New York. Its unique inner harbor—the harbor is enclosed by the city, not, like most harbors, on the outskirts of town—is now too shallow for the huge "container" ships laden with multiple boxcars of goods which do most of the nation's commercial shipping; in Baltimore, such shipping has now moved mostly to the Dundalk Marina, near the home of the city's once monumental industrial plant.

Bethlehem Steel Corporation, established in 1890—headquartered in Pennsylvania but with its major plant located at Sparrows Point on

Baltimore's outer harbor—was once the world's largest steelmaker. The company somehow survived the Great Depression, with production booming again as the demand for steel soared during World War II. In the 1950s, the company continued to thrive as it made parts for automobiles, appliances, buildings and bridges, and multitudes of other goods. At the time, securing employment with Bethlehem Steel practically guaranteed a middle-class income. In 1960, the company employed thirty thousand people. Subsequently, it failed to cope with international competition. With the 1982 recession Bethlehem Steel lost nearly one-and-a-half billion dollars. Massive layoffs occurred, leaving thousands unemployed and devastating Baltimore's working-class neighborhoods. In the mid-1990s, after a brief recovery, bankruptcy followed in 2001. Many of Bethlehem Steel's last workers were left in service sector jobs on minimum wages with paltry benefits and virtually no security. They fled in huge numbers.

Baltimore once had the third-highest population in America. In the 1990s, population decline resulted in a housing surplus and nearly sixty thousand jobs disappeared in that decade alone. The scarcity of unskilled jobs and lack of training for technical roles is a common complaint, as is the fact that Baltimore has the highest property taxes in Maryland. Stories of corruption still abound as Maryland's politicians have been accused of nepotism, embezzlement and extortion.

"Nowadays, Baltimore manages to stay afloat with state and federal government funds," my dad points out sadly. He has made sure I've practically memorized the history that has made it come to this.

We cut down "Corned Beef Row" near Atmann's Deli and glide past spectators hanging out in Little Italy watching bocce games as they eat gelati. We near the prison, its central building a Dickensian nineteenth-century structure whose crenellated towers make it look like a dark stone castle despite the much larger modern additions hooked on it. Dad and I both say in unison, "Never Again," the words of a sign he used to see hanging over the exit. "Yeah, most of 'em ended back in there the next week."

A stone's throw away is the Reginald F. Lewis Museum of Maryland

African American History and Culture. Over 65 percent of the city's people are African-American. Although Baltimore's African-American history is honored in its many museums, including The National Great Blacks in Wax Museum, the Cab Calloway Jazz Institute, the Eubie Blake National Jazz Institute, and the Lillie Mae Carroll Jackson House and Museum, many of its inner-city residents, most of them black, are still living in Third World conditions.

Baltimoreans are always paying homage to the city's greats, both past and present. Home of the late, great baseball legend, Babe Ruth, first African-American Supreme Court Justice Thurgood Marshall, and journalist H. L. Mencken. It is the former dwelling place of Gertrude Stein and the Baltimore Museum of Art houses The Cone Collection, one of the world's finest collections of impressionist art. Hometown of filmmaker Barry Levinson and singer/songwriter Frank Zappa. One of my all-time favorite musicians, David Byrne (founding member of the critically acclaimed band Talking Heads) grew up in Baltimore. It is the birthplace of actor David Hasselhoff. Elizabeth Patterson Bonaparte—first wife of Napoleon I's brother, Jerome Bonaparte—is buried in Baltimore. She is the lady for whom My Lady's Manor, site of one of Maryland's three famous steeple chases, is named; it was her property. The ashes of literary figure Dorothy Parker are embedded in the soil of a memorial garden at the site of the National Association for the Advancement of Colored People's (NAACP) headquarters in "The City of Firsts." While he was not born in Baltimore, it's where Edgar Allan Poe began writing his short stories and where he returned to die. It's where novelist Anne Tyler, who has lived all over the world, has settled for decades. It was the home for even more decades of poet and fiction writer Josephine Jacobsen, the first female Poet Laureate of the United States. It is part of filmmaker John Waters' lifeblood. My father is glad that I know those facts as well as the crime stats.

Dad takes so many shortcuts and back roads that I lose my bearings. I only know we're now on the West Side, his old stamping ground, because he pushes a button and I hear all the car doors lock. "All right, let's hope we don't break down." Dad grins. "Our hubcaps would disappear in thirty seconds flat."

Since the '68 riots, much of Baltimore has undergone restoration to preserve its rich heritage; West Baltimore remains the final frontier. Today it consists of nearly three hundred blocks including the neighborhoods Penn-North, Upton, Harlem Park, Druid Heights and Sandtown-Winchester.

"Nothing's changed," Dad says, as we meander around a trash-strewn schoolyard. Numerous houses have burnt to charcoal frames, others are tattooed with graffiti. "Private Property, No Trespassing, No Loitering" read the black stenciled words on the doors of boarded-up row homes. Iron grates cover shop windows. An emaciated woman in a denim coat and blue jeans is swaying at a bus stop. Her eyes are closed. She looks as if she's going to topple into the street. No one seems to notice, not the youths sauntering by, the residents sitting on the marble steps of their row homes socializing with neighbors or the children playing on the sidewalks.

Nestled among liquor stores, bail bondsmen's offices and a string of vacant buildings is a storefront church with a handmade sign: "Come to Jesus While You Still Have Time."

Sirens begin to wail. "Ah, now we know we're in Charm City," Dad grins. He zips down an alley which suddenly dead-ends. "Oh nuts. This is confusing. This road is completely different."

Not everything remains the same. When the Murphy Homes were razed in 1999, only thirty-six years after they were built, deadly asbestos, rats and lead paint had to be removed lest they escape into the surrounding area during the demolition. During the razing, dust storms blew through the surrounding neighborhood, blanketing cars and furniture, and the seventy-five thousand cubic yards of rubble is said to have reeked of rodent waste. The Murphys were replaced with Heritage Crossing, a group of townhomes owned or rented by people of mixed incomes.

We edge along Pennsylvania Avenue. Club Tijuana is now a vacant lot. The Regent Theatre once stood where the Shake and Bake Family Fun Center is today. In place of the Frolic Club is a church.

"You lose some, you win some," Dad muses.

Despite the open-air drug markets on playgrounds, street corners and porches, Penn-North and Upton are still home to some middle-class folk. Caring residents try to hold their community together by teaching people how to read, providing food for the hungry and painting murals over graffiti.

We pass Engine 13, home to Medic 4. At the beginning of the twenty-first century, under the leadership of Mayor Martin O'Malley, Baltimore's slogan became "Believe." Locals amended the slogan to read "B'lieve, Hon." A large black banner with this mantra emblazoned in white print stretches across the front of the firehouse. Inevitably, Dad launches into stories of the Old Mack, the race riots and especially Larry Burch.

Two teenage boys without helmets on brand-new, street-illegal dirt bikes overtake us, do a few wheelies, spin, speed out of sight.

"There's no way the police can catch 'em," Dad interrupts his reverie. "They get away with it—unless they crash."

When we drive by the Orchard Street Church, founded in 1825, I remember hearing that it was part of the Underground Railroad and still has an escape tunnel. Though I've never been inside, I can't help but wonder where the tunnel led. Not everyone escaped: some of their descendants are still here in this city.

We park on the roadside on a tidy block near the home of Guy Cephas, curator of the Arthur Smokestack Hardy Fire Museum, and step cautiously out of the car. My dad points in the direction of Harlem Park, where Jungle Man was discovered grazing. A well-dressed black man walks past us carrying a few wooden planks and a toolkit. He pauses. "How you all doing?" he greets us.

My father and I are lost in time, but I realize to this man we must look plain lost. We smile, and Dad says, "Hello there, looks like you've got your hands full."

"Just bought a home, renovating the kitchen." He shifts the belongings to get a more comfortable hold. "Can I help you?"

I tell him that my father knows the district well and that we are just reminiscing. He's a few decades younger than my father, but he too knows all the old West Baltimore haunts and has even heard of Andy, the man who held up the bank with the Snoopy electric toothbrush. Dad jokes about the crime and the Thunderbird. The man chuckles.

"We gotta keep the faith." He calls back over his shoulder as he starts to cross the street.

Dad and I hit the road. When we near the intersection of Mount Royal and North Avenues, he says, "I often saw a skinny white guy standing right here at the fringe of the ghetto holding a sign. Normally it's 'Will work for food.' Not this guy. He looked like a nutcase, a displaced mountaineer, gaunt and wild-eyed. He had a long pointed beard and a knit cap. This guy would be standing there holding a sign that said, 'Please Help Me I'm Losing It.' The words were made up of raggedy letters that he had been scribbled on the sign. He didn't have quite enough room to write the whole statement the same size and direction, so the words 'I'm Losing It' ran steadily downward on the cardboard. Uh, hee, hee hee, I know the feeling, I thought."

As we head north toward the county and its suburbs, the sun begins to set over west Baltimore. My father adds with a smile, "But I don't look back. I never look back."

Acknowledgments

Although writing often demands isolation, the genre of creative nonfiction requires empathy, sharing and communication. Over several years, I nurtured this work with the encouragement of teachers, friends and even strangers. I therefore thank the following people.

I worship my editor, Clarinda Harriss, Dad's childhood friend. As fated, through a series of events, which can only be described as serendipitous, Clarinda would ironically and magically be "The One" to apply her extraordinary enthusiasm and immense experience in helping me cross the finish line.

My gorgeous husband Dr. Andrew Bashford provided tremendous insight and support. He's my rock and his belief in me sustained me through difficult moments.

My brother Craig reenacted family scenarios, making me roar with laughter. He still insists that he is the sanest member of our family, but I have my doubts.

Dr. Thomas Shapcott gave me the courage to embark on this journey.

In the early stages, Judith Burgemeister's astute analysis and editorial skills helped to achieve the authenticity of my father's voice.

Dr. Susan Hosking and Dr. Jan Harrow, my talented supervisors at The University of Adelaide, offered valuable observations on early drafts when I was struggling to find the most appropriate perspective for this story. They inspired me to persevere.

I am honored to have been mentored by Professor Lee Gutkind. His guidance helped me to capture my father's essence.

All of my instructors from Stevenson University (then Villa Julie College) have my heartfelt gratitude for giving me a strong foundation. They taught me critical research skills and identified my potential as a writer: Kent Sutorious, Gary Pedroni, Dr. Edward Sparrow, Pat Ellis.

In addition, the following friends gave me steadfast love and support during this often painstaking, yet ultimately rewarding, process. Some of them fed me, others made me take breaks and several of them paid me visits when I was lonely: Gary Alexander, Melissa Arnoff, Amanda Bridge, Katya Chilingiri, Joe Compton, Fawzy Eldeeb, Fouad Eldeeb, Tony and Ketut Elliott, Dr. Nelson Hendler, Rachel Hennessy, Caroline Hoare, Joyce and Phil Pfanschmidt, Andy Kaslow, Stuart Lewis, Adrienne Scally, Philip Walkley, and Roberta Zapf.

The children I raised, Justin Beckenheimer and Kaila Beckenheimer, were an impetus behind this book. Conversations with Justin, filmmaker and co-owner Stratatek Studios, inspired me to resolve structural issues and complete the work for publication.

The work was also made possible with help from the following people and organizations: Arts SA, The Baltimore City Fire Department, *The Baltimore Sun*, Justine Bashford, Jean Bayne, Nancy Bennett, Cathryn Charnock, Guy Cephas, curator of the Arthur "Smokestack" Hardy Fire Museum, Michael Cora, Dan Davis, Division Chief 4, Joseph Brocato, Dr. Phillip Edmonds, The Enoch Pratt Free Library, the firefighters at Engine 25, Bill Hall, Baltimore City Fire Marshal's Office, Fire Museum of Maryland in Lutherville, Professor Nicholas Jose, Sarah Lord, Lieutenant Malary, Maryland Institute for Emergency Medical Services Systems, Education, Licensing and Certification, Captain Kenneth E. Morris, Dr. Carl Nightingale, paramedics Dale Blackwell and Patty Smith from Medic 4, Retired Firefighters' Association, Deborah Stein (BrickHouse Books' associate editor), Unions 734 and 964, The University of Adelaide Library.

I thank the University of Baltimore for their timeline on the race riots which assisted me in the final fact checking.

Mr. Paul Reidl of Ernest and Gallo Winery in Modesto, California, stated that permission is not required for my use of the wording in the Thunderbird jingle.

Several attempts have been made to contact the copyright owner of the Mondawmin Mall jingle but, according to the corporation, the author is unknown. Every attempt has been made to contact the copyright owners for the lyrics to "Streets of Baltimore," but as yet I have been unable to get a response.

If I forgot someone please accept my apologies. Like my father, I shared his stories with anyone who would listen. And so many people cheered me on: cab drivers, waiters, flight attendants, street people, the medics from SA Ambulance who picked me up after a car accident . . . They are too numerous to mention; however, their suggestions and well-wishes are not forgotten.

About the Author

Rachel Hennick holds a PhD in English (Creative Writing) from the University of Adelaide, South Australia (2009), where she completed her dissertation on "The Responsibilities, Roles, and Rights of the Creative Nonfiction Writer." She earned an Interdisciplinary BS degree in Business and Writing from Stevenson University (2002) and an AA Degree in Communication Arts: Television and Theatre from Stevenson University (1990). In 2004, she was awarded the Arts South Australia prize for creative writing and an International Scholarship from the University of Adelaide. Her short stories have appeared in the literary journal *Island* and *The Australian Women's Book Review*, and on Radio Adelaide's *Arts Breakfast*. In addition to *Ghetto Medic*, Rachel is also the author of *Ketut's Kitchen: With Love From Bali*, a soon-to-be released biographical cookbook about a Balinese chef. Rachel lives in South Australia with her husband, and vacations in Baltimore where she devours crab cakes for breakfast.